RULE OF LAW, LEGITIMATE GOVERNANCE & DEVELOPMENT IN THE PACIFIC

RULE OF LAW, LEGITIMATE GOVERNANCE & DEVELOPMENT IN THE PACIFIC

Iutisone
SALEVAO

ANU
E PRESS

Asia Pacific Press at
The Australian National University

If angels were to govern men, neither external nor internal controls on government would be necessary. In framing a government which is to be administered by men over men, the great difficulty lies in this: you must first enable the government to control the governed, and in the next place oblige it to control itself.

James Madison

The better the society, the less law there will be. In Heaven there will be no law, and the lion will lie down with the lamb. In Hell there will be nothing but law, and due process will be meticulously observed.

Grant Gilmore

ANU

E PRESS

Co-published by ANU E Press and Asia Pacific Press
Asia Pacific School of Economics and Government
The Australian National Unversity
Canberra ACT 0200
Ph: 61-2-6125 4700
Email: books@asiapacificpress.com
Website: http://www.asiapacificpress.com

National Library of Australia Cataloguing-in-Publication entry

Salevao, Iutisone.

Rule of law, legitimate governance and development in the Pacific.

Bibliography.
ISBN 0 7315 3721 1.

1. Rule of law - Oceania. 2. Constitutions - Oceania. 3. Constitutional law - Oceania. I. Title.

340.11

Editor: Bridget Maidment and Matthew May
Publisher: Asia Pacific Press and ANU E-press
Design: Annie di Nallo

Contents

Abbreviations

APSEG	Asia Pacific School of Economics and Government
AusAID	Australian Agency for International Development
CJ	Chief Justice
CSCE	Commission for Security and Cooperation in Europe
PNG	Papua New Guinea
UNDP	United Nations Development Programme
US	United States

Acknowledgments

I owe a special debt of gratitude to a number of individuals and institutions for making this work possible. The Asia Pacific School of Economics and Government (APSEG) of the Australian National University in Canberra, kindly offered a Research Fellowship which made possible my work on Law and Justice in the Pacific. This book is the result of that undertaking. Professor Andrew Macintyre, Director of APSEG, and my other workmates at APSEG were very positive and supportive. I wish them success in all their academic endeavours.

I wish to thank Ms Maree Tait, the production staff, and editors of the Asia Pacific Press for publishing my work.

Professor Richard Mulgan, Director of the Governance Program at APSEG, deserves a special word of thanks for reading and commenting on the entire manuscript, and for his intellectual and moral support. Your informed analysis, from a public policy perspective, was positively profound.

Professor Anthony Angelo of the Faculty of Law, Victoria University of Wellington, New Zealand, greatly stimulated my thinking on Western and Pacific legal issues. Your critical analysis of the entire manuscript, from the internal perspective of law, kept my (sometimes strange) legal mind within the bounds of reason.

Needless to state the obvious, I claim sole responsibility for any errors in the book.

Finally, I owe a huge debt of gratitude to my dear wife, Falanika, my beloved children (Siava, Eline, Ennoia, and Berakah), and my source-of-joy grandchildren (Tyler, Ezra-Lee, and Maea) for their love, support and patience. For almost the entire duration of the fellowship, I was physically absent from home in New Zealand because of my work commitments in Canberra.

I dedicate this book to my wife, children and grandchildren.

Introduction

The focus of this study is the idea and social practice of law in the Pacific. The notion that the rule of law embodies or guarantees all the essential requirements for a perfectly just society is, unfortunately, extravagant and naïve. That said, it is certainly the case that the rule of law remains an essential human good whose usefulness the world has yet to outgrow.

Promulgating the rule of law as mobilising theme, this study emphasises that the demands of the rule of law—the equality of all citizens, fairness in the way government treats its citizens, the absence of arbitrary rule, responsibility and accountability of government to the governed, equity, respect for human dignity, the protection of rights and liberties—provide some guarantee that government will be conducted justly, fairly, honestly, and openly for the benefit of all citizens of the state.

While the main interest of the study is in Polynesian nations (especially Samoa and Tonga), I will attempt, as far as possible, to draw comparisons with other Pacific jurisdictions, teasing out both common modalities and differences among the diverse legal, socio-political contexts of the Pacific. Similarities provide a legal and political unity for the different jurisdictions, thus enabling us to draw parallels and identify common characteristics at a fundamental level, while guarding against ignoring distinctions and disparities produced by the divergent legal and political histories of the different Pacific nations.

In terms of methodology, even though this study is primarily a legal analysis, important factors demand the utilisation of a multidisciplinary perspective. One such factor is the essential interface between the rule of law, on the one hand, and the good governance and development agendas, on the other, which this study seeks to explore. The latter inevitably move this discourse into areas such as political science, development economics, and public ethics. The multifaceted nature of the societies under examination likewise necessitates taking into account the cultural, postcolonial, and postmodern understanding of Pacific peoples. Critical theory informs my analysis of these legitimate interests and extends its parameters beyond the confines of syllogistic legal reasoning.

The extensive scope and complex nature of the subject-matter demand the adoption of a topical approach. And while the issues chosen for analysis cannot conceivably capture the topic in its entirety, the chosen issues will, hopefully, shed some light on what has been happening and why, and how they could be addressed and resolved.

Ultimately, my objectives are to inform, resolve ideological conflicts, facilitate development and change, and provoke informed critique— always the warp and woof of progress. Abjuring brutal force as a source of change, we are thrown back to honest and frank criticism as a way of fomenting positive change. After all, the major advances in civilisation have been events, processes, and movements which transformed—in a peaceful manner—the societies in which they occurred.

Where and when this study is critical of Western theories of law, good governance, and development, my aims are, first, to expose how Western theories, institutions and structures themselves are, to some extent, the cause of our Pacific problems; and, second, to problematise established assumptions, structures and institutions from the perspective of the Pacific peoples' own values, ideologies, social structures, and forms of practice. The challenge is making Western theories relevant to the concrete and normative contexts of the Pacific peoples, and to accommodate Pacific values, ideologies, structures, and practices within modern discourses on law, good governance, and development.

To my Pacific colleagues, I cannot emphasise enough that change is inevitable. Our Pacific conservatives need to accept this simple fact. We have to retain what should not be changed; we need to change what needs to be changed. Prostrating without reserve before the tribal deities of nationalism and conservatism is to court the sin of neurotic narcissism, and to allow ourselves to become trapped in our own parochialism. In the long run, such mental myopia will result in the loss of much more than a place in the global socioeconomic village of modernity. We need, therefore, to transcend our own prejudices and self-imposed limitations.

This study is, more fundamentally, a call for justice, admittedly a term with multiple meanings and nuances. For present purposes, justice is examined in the context of good (read legitimate) governance, and is accordingly defined in terms of government's just and fair treatment of its citizens, the exercise of government powers in ways that are just and are seen to be just, honest fulfilment of the functions which government was instituted to perform, reasonable gratification of citizens' legitimate expectations, equitable allocation of government resources, and protection of rights and liberties. Justice, on this broad reading, means equality, fairness, and equity in the relationship between government and governed.

Finally, should this study contribute in some significant way to the ongoing struggle for justice in the Pacific, it will have served its purpose. But, first, injustices must be studied, remembered, lamented, condemned, and then redressed.

1

The rule of law: principles, issues and challenges

In this chapter, I set out the analytic frameworks and theoretical positions that inform and govern this study, and introduce the issues that I will focus on in the remaining chapters. The rule of law, both as theory and as praxis, occupies the centre and the circumference of the entire edifice. And justice, broadly defined in procedural and substantive terms, constitutes the overriding test of both legal theorisation and the social practice of law.

The paradigmatic significance of the rule of law

The rule of law is a site of multiple meanings and nuances—a contested site. There is a broad consensus, however, concerning the paradigmatic significance of the rule of law: it is 'an unqualified human good' that should never be belittled through intellectual abstraction or by giving up 'the struggle against bad laws and class-bound procedures, and to disarm ourselves before power', thereby exposing citizens of the body politic to 'immediate danger' (Thompson 1975:266).

Subject to qualifications and caveats set out below, this text accentuates the value of the rule of law as the legal and moral warrant of government rule, and, equally importantly, as a bridle on government powers. This is a basic dogma in Western jurisprudence, from Aristotle's idealisation of law as reason without passion to St Thomas Aquinas' natural law theory and Vincent Albert Dicey's strictures of positive law. Take away the rule of law and government becomes a euphemistic government of men—naturally vulnerable to extravagant notions of power—and citizens surrender themselves to the discretion of political rulers. History has shown (sadly, I might add) that even the best rulers have fallen prey to the cruel desires of naked power, and that reliance on the goodwill of politicians is often a risky act of good faith.

A critical issue is the actual application of this 'unqualified human good' in Pacific societies. This is the ultimate test of the significance of the rule of law—whether or not it has practical effect in the life of a given community, and the nature—good or bad—of that effect. In order to adequately appraise this, the rule of law must be approached as both legal theorisation and as praxis framed in jurisprudential terms. By following the complex operation of the rule of law, we endeavour to evaluate its worth—whether it has procured justice and curbed injustice, where it has failed when its principles are bent and twisted to suit the whims of rulers, how its noble values are falsified in practice when it becomes an instrument of arbitrary rule, or when it is violated to serve the interests of sections of the community. To do this, investigative analysis must enter into the fray of the communities in which the rule of law is supposed to operate. My interest in the broader jurisprudential debate about the nature, meaning and function of the rule of law is, therefore, more specifically circumscribed by how Western conceptions translate into Pacific theory and praxis. In pursuing this focus, the rule of law must be treated as more than a theoretical construction or an abstract model of some utopian praxis divorced from practical reality.

The rule of law, in other words, cannot be sensibly detached from the wider normative context of a community's history, politics, morality, ethics and culture. The grounding of the rule of law in concrete existential contexts thus broaches the following caveat of caution: for the rule of law to have any force or value at all, there must be a shared commitment from both government and governed to uphold the dictates of the law; such a commitment is based on common respect for the foundational values deemed essential to a just society, and in the absence of which the rule of law is not likely to command a powerful following.

The practical implication is clear: in order for the rule of law to compel fundamental change in society and to cause a public stir when it is violated or even abandoned, it must first win the minds and hearts of the people, command their respect and satisfy their acquiescence therein. Adopting a postmodern perspective, '[w]e start from where we are', (Rorty 1989:198) with our moralities and notions of justice that are always embedded in our different cultures. As Alasdair MacIntyre (1984:265–6) puts it, '[m]orality which is no particular society's morality is to be found nowhere'. Put simply, the rule of law must be firmly grounded in the existential reality of a given community's political morality, ethical judgment and cultural underpinnings. Failing that, we run the risk of reducing the rule of law to just an abstract model of rules without any practical relevance.

The significance of the rule of law also lies in its ambivalent intersection with democracy: it both confirms and limits democracy by curbing the excesses of majority rule. Accordingly, democracy is conceived, not as the simplistic notion of majority rule, rather, as majority rule subject to constitutional limits and controls. The underlying logic for this is simple—the will of the majority is important in that it provides the mechanism for making decisions for the body politic. But there is always the danger that majority rule may degenerate into the tyrannical rule of despots who ruthlessly destroy rights, enact oppressive laws and casually manipulate the rule of law to suit their whims.

The rule of law, therefore, mandates that even democratic majority rule is limited by law: '[t]he first requirement for a liberal democratic society…is the rule of law' (Walker 1995:187). Majority rule is important; but, as T.R.S. Allan (2001:25) has pointed out, it deserves 'no special political or constitutional reverence except in so far as it is truly consistent with the values of equal human dignity and individual autonomy: politics, in its ordinary institutional forms, should be the servant of justice rather than its master'.

The limitation of government rule by law is the essence of constitutionalism, privileging the rule of law and setting out the rules that define government powers and their limits in advance of government action. Though engendered by the emergence of Leviathan states in the past, this constitutional wisdom is equally relevant today given the inherent proclivity of modern states (including Pacific nations) to enlarge their orbit and increase their power. Constitutionalism thus appropriately seeks to pre-empt the emergence of more political monsters through the practice of limited and enumerated government powers.

It may be noted that Samoa (like most Pacific nations) lies squarely on this trajectory of constitutional thinking. The fact that Samoa has a written constitution is important.[1] As a written text, the *Constitution of Samoa 1960* is a positive, bold and highly evocative legal metaphor expressing optimistic faith in the power of the written word to construct reality and impose order on the potentially disordered. Even more critical is the constitutional mandate that the Constitution is supreme law (article 2) and that the Samoan judiciary has power to declare invalid laws that are inconsistent with constitutional provisions (that is, to the extent of the inconsistency) pursuant to article 2(2).[2] The supremacy provision, fortified by the inconsistency clause, is not about the supremacy of a written document; rather, it means that law is not, and should not be, the arbitrary will of the lawmakers, usually grounded in caprice and self-interest; that state laws bind both government and governed; and that the Constitution creates the institutions of government, defines their powers and functions, and imposes limits on those powers. That is, parliament, the executive and the judiciary in Samoa are creatures of the Constitution—created, governed, limited and controlled by the Constitution. The rule of law takes priority over every institution of the state.

The precedence of the rule of law is important for the citizens of the state. Confronted with a political construct that is always predisposed to extend its reach and increase its power, citizens cannot help feeling overwhelmed by the machinery of government. Given also that the state is involved in virtually all areas of life, citizens are constantly threatened by the arbitrary use of government powers. This highlights the need for better protection of citizens' rights and liberties. The written Constitution, given in the name of the people as supreme law and one that embodies an entrenched bill of rights, goes a long way towards meeting that need through the Constitution's control of the powers and reach of government.

But herein lies a familiar contradiction—a Constitution that, as supreme law, overrides the representative will of the people appears to undermine democracy in a mighty act of anti-majoritarianism and renders the term constitutional democracy almost oxymoronic.[3] To elucidate this matter, it can be purported that the threat of a despotic government with unlimited powers is always real and immediate. Shielding citizens against that threat, constitutional democracy presents a bulwark against despotism. That bulwark is the rule of law. Ultimately, constitutionalism is about keeping government under control; it is 'the name given to the trust which men repose in the power of words engrossed on parchment to keep a government in order' (Hamilton 1931:255). This order is achieved by limiting the reach of government and setting out fixed, *a priori* ground rules for the exercise of public power.

Finally, the intersection between the rule of law and good governance, deemed to be a precondition to development, is now a common motif in reform discourse. Good governance apparently means different things to different people.[4] A recommendation of the authors of the *Eminent Persons' Group Review of the Pacific Islands Forum* regarding good governance in the Pacific is noteworthy.

> Good governance inspires confidence among citizens and partners, both regional and international. In fact, we would argue that observation of the principles of good governance is vital to the future development of the Pacific. The promotion of good governance must be carried out in ways that are meaningful to Pacific societies and people. Often in the Pacific there is tension between inherited political and legal structures and pre-existing cultural traditions. There is a need to work towards achieving a better 'fit' between the two in order to achieve more relevant, responsive and accountable patterns of governance (Eminent Persons' Group 2004:n.p.).

Within the diversity of meanings and interests that now inform the good governance agenda, the centrality of the rule of law is a constant and resounding theme. This seems reasonable since public and private sector reforms, protecting rights and liberties, reforming property rights and reducing poverty—all presuppose the operation of a strong rule of law. There is, in fact, a growing conviction that all aspects of good governance and development hinge on the rule of law, and that promoting the rule of law is a way of advancing both principles (human rights, accountability, democratic forms of government) and profits (by establishing free, unregulated markets). Now offered as a panacea for the social, political, legal and economic ills of developing economies, the rule of law has become a battle cry of the reform movement. Accordingly, improving and strengthening the rule of law is a major objective of many aid projects in developing economies, including those of the Pacific. Beyond the outcomes of those projects and the reasons for their success or failure, the broad issue for present purposes is the ambiguous meaning of the term rule of law and its problematic use as an engine of socioeconomic development.

Rule of law: the problem of definition

It is difficult to ascribe a precise meaning to the term rule of law as it is a contested concept with an 'unstable meaning' (Dallmayr 1990:1451). Is it a mere Aristotelian ideal to which every just state should aspire? Or perhaps it is nothing more than a refrain of the politico-economic jargon that drives reform, one that conflates the different goods of 'democracy promotion' (Alford 2000:1678). Is it nothing more than a facade masking the rule of a class for the protection of property interests as classical Marxists would have it,[5] or a means of facilitating 'exploitation and discrimination' (Adelman and Foster 1992:39), masquerading as political democracy? To what extent has it become a reified concept itself justifying the reification of other concepts such as property rights, contract, trusts and wills? And if so, the possibility exists that such reification is not only a distortion but also 'a form of coercion in the guise of passive acceptance of the existing world within the framework of capitalism' (Russell 1986:19).

Given the 'unstable meaning' of the term rule of law, the issue is the ideological abuse of the concept. Beyond its usual rhetorical significance, the rule of law rather unfortunately betrays an ambivalent character as both a blessing and a threat—

> an object of understandable suspicion as much as one of reverence: its uncertain and contested content allows it to be readily invoked in support of positions whose cogency might not withstand careful scrutiny (Allan 2001:1).

Part of the problem is that the rule of law is a complex phenomenon combining different legal, moral and ethical, political and democratic principles. In addition, every proposed definition faces a number of issues—the formal/normative (substantive) distinction, the internal/external perspective dichotomy, the legitimate functions of the law, and so forth. The rule of law, however, can and must be understood as the guiding 'principle of legitimate governance' and which, as a basic component of liberal constitutionalism, forms 'an integrated theory of constitutional government' (Allan 2001:4, 31). This is a principal tenet of the guiding theory for this study.

Rule of law as the governance of rules

Whatever else the rule of law is, it is fundamentally a form of social control—'the enterprise of subjecting human conduct to the governance of rules' (Fuller 1969:124). There seems to be an implicit assumption that people will follow the rules set down by their institutions (including the state, social clubs, churches, schools and other forms of human association) because human beings are 'rule-following animal[s] as much as purpose-seeking one[s]' (Hayek 1973:11).[6] For the rules to have maximum effect they must be widely known, concretely rooted in the community's political culture, and actually command the citizens' assent.

This optimistic faith in the governance of rules,[7] and the alleged human predisposition to follow legal rules aside, rule-following is a complex phenomenon. A common explanation is the fear of punishment when rules are not obeyed (Bentham 1970), but such negative rationales are not complete. In more prosaic circumstances, people obey the law for reasons other than the fear of sanctions, which suggests that more positive dynamics are at play. The predisposition to adhere to society's underlying political morality is one important consideration. Invested with pre-emptive authority, political morality demands obedience to institutional rules, perhaps as a moral duty or simply as a matter of ordinary prudence.

In some contexts, rule-following is also a function of custom. Max Weber described this as 'a result of unreflective habituation to a regularity of life that has engraved itself as a custom' (Weber 1966:12). Custom, broadly defined, includes mores, institutions, traditions, protocols, practices and processes that together make up the sum total of a people's way of life. Embedded in custom are the community's normative rules and the entrenched reasons for rule-following. The proposition that custom is a legitimate source of law, legal validity, authority and normativity (subject, for example, to the requirements of justice, such as respect for individual liberties) is a major refrain running through this text.

In summary, the different explanations show that rule-following is a complex phenomenon that resists reductive description.[8] The varying explanations are nevertheless based on the common presumption that rule-following results in the attainment of some common good—social equilibrium, public order, security and justice. The extent to which rules and behaviour correspond is another matter.

Beyond legal rules: procedure and substantive evaluation

Beyond the general (though not universal) recognition of the rule of law as the governance of rules, there is no agreement regarding the nature of those rules. Is the law only rules of evidence and formal procedure, or more? This is the focal point of the debate between proponents of a formal definition of the rule of law and those who argue for a normative or substantive meaning.

The main difference between the two positions is that formal theories generally posit 'an important distinction between law and justice' (Allan 2001:23), a distinction wherein justice is construed as an external criterion of evaluation. Eschewing (subjective) external evaluations (moral, ethical, political, etc), a characteristic feature of formal theories is their professed moral neutrality and the exclusion of value judgments. The rule of law, according to a formalist reading, is strictly defined by formal characteristics: it is prospective, open and clear, and is relatively stable; the lawmaking procedure is governed by stable, open and clear general rules, and an independent judiciary. This distinction is predicated on the concern that by extending the meaning of the rule of law beyond procedural justice, as defined by the rules of evidence and formal procedure, procedural justice will be confused with some other theory of justice (for example, religious or racial). Understandably, in a society like Fiji, with its ethnic and religious pluralism, such a theory is not likely to command universal assent. The issue is the potential divisiveness of competing or conflicting versions of justice, once we leave the certainty and formalism of the terrain of procedural justice. Furthermore, formal theorists argue, it is naïve to hold that the rule of law means the rule of the good law, one predicated on some moral ideal of justice. 'We have no need to be converted to the rule of law', Joseph Raz (1979:211) argues, 'just in order to discover that to believe in it is to believe that good should triumph'.

I take the position that the rule of law consists not only of rules of evidence and formal procedure, but also standards and principles. As the authors of the *Document of the Copenhagen Meeting of the Conference on Human Dimension of the CSCE* put it,

> [t]he rule of law does not merely mean formal legality which assures regularity and consistency in the achievement and enforcement of democratic order, but justice based on the recognition and full acceptance of the supreme value of the human personality providing a framework for its fullest expression (Commission for Security and Cooperation in Europe 1990:3).

Justice as an external criterion of evaluation, rooted either in some divine command (as in Samoa with its privileging of God's commandments and Christian principles),[9] or in human nature (conscience and/or reason), is indeed an essential variable of jurisprudential analysis. Completely eliminating justice and other substantive values from the jurisprudential equation impoverishes legal theorisation. It also renders unjustifiable the claim to substantive legitimacy that formal theorisation is at pains to sustain. The impropriety of an *a priori* out of court rejection of substantive principles thus warrants an inclusive jurisprudence that does not screen out substantive considerations like justice and equity, but instead makes them the criteria and goal of the rule of law.

My point is that, as the guiding principle of good (that is, legitimate) governance, the rule of law cannot afford to exclude or ignore matters such as the monopolisation of political power by the élite few; inequities in the treatment of rich and poor, the influential and the impotent; and economic injustices—unremedied by the courts owing to institutional overpoliteness, lack of jurisdiction, or sheer weakness. Excluding or ignoring such matters destroys the moral fabric of the community we are trying to aid, creates a new set of socioeconomic problems without solving old ones, and constructs new forms of exploitation and alienation, and/or reinforces existing ones. In light of those potential problems, good governance and development agendas, and the rule of law that legitimises them, cannot afford to shut up normative principles. These, too, are legitimate parties to a negotiated solution, one that respects the social and moral conscience of the community. Sometimes this requires us to move beyond a one-dimensional view of the world, and demands a better understanding of the morality (MacIntyre 1984), the ethics, and the notions of justice that regulate the lives of our intended beneficiaries in the Pacific and elsewhere.

The following definition accordingly risks the combination of procedure and substance. For the purpose of legitimate governance, a rigid distinction between the two is 'artificial and unworkable' since they are 'closely linked in ways that a satisfactory theory of the rule of law must accommodate' (Allan 2001:1, 26). This has important implications for legislators whose constitutional duty is to enact laws that not merely authorise the delivery of public goods but are consistent with 'an acceptable order of justice' (Allan 2001:41) achieved through public debate. Implications for the judiciary are also significant. In undertaking its constitutional role of checking the abuse of power by both the legislature and the executive, the courts should ensure that the state adheres to 'a general scheme of just governance' (Allan 2001:41). In a sense, this requires the courts to move beyond their preoccupation with procedural matters. Private citizens, while submitting to the promulgated laws of the state as demanded by their right of citizenship, nevertheless reserve the right to judge whether or not those laws are just, fair and equitable. They should never abdicate their moral judgment to the state.

Within this broad framework of legitimate governance, the rule of law is critical. The principle of the supremacy of law is central to this connection. In Dicey's conception of jurisprudence, the rule of law means 'the absolute supremacy or predominance of regular law as opposed to the influence of arbitrary power, and excludes the existence of arbitrariness, of prerogative, or even of wide discretionary authority on the part of the government' (Dicey 1959:202). Although the rule of law 'has diverse manifestations', Keith Mason explains 'each has one thing in common: the supremacy of law over naked power and unbridled discretion' (Mason 1995:114). Hayek similarly opposed government's exercise of discretionary powers as inherently arbitrary (Hayek 1960).[10] Pushing back the increasingly interventionist state, Hayek (1960:107) stated that

> [l]aw, liberty, and property are an inseparable trinity. There can be no law in the sense of universal rules of conduct which does not determine boundaries of the domains of freedom by laying down rules that enable each to ascertain where he is free to act.

The pertinent issue here is the proper extent of government discretion—when does lawful discretion become arbitrary rule? Completely eliminating government's powers of discretion (following Hayek's model of the rule of law) would effectively strangle government and render it powerless to undertake important functions, for example, the redistribution of wealth and the management of the national economy. Joseph Raz (1979:211) makes this point in his critique of the privileging of the rule of law: 'Sacrificing too many social goals on the altar of the rule of law may make the law barren and empty'. Analysis suggests, however, that instead of diluting the requirement for total government compliance with the rule of law as Raz proposes, the Madisonian solution would be most appropriate. First, empower the government to govern on behalf of citizens and, next, oblige it to control itself. On this reading, the rule of law is the antithesis of arbitrary rule and unbridled power; the rule of law constitutes a fetter on the powers of government. This is important given the increasing proclivity of modern governments (including Pacific ones) to increase their power and extend their orbit.

Pre-empting the abuse of the state's powers of coercion, the rule of law mandates punishment of a citizen only for a proven breach of a distinct legal rule. Thus, enjoined Dicey (1959:183–4), no one 'can be lawfully made to suffer in body or goods except for a distinct breach of the law established in the ordinary legal manner before ordinary courts of the land'. This ensures that citizens are not punished merely for criticising or disagreeing with the government, and that government itself remains a government of laws. Government 'must act in accordance with the law…in everything it does' (Palmer 1987:13). The law ought to bind both the governed and the government. Put bluntly, 'no man is above the law' (Marshall 1971:138). Unless the law also binds the rulers, the rule of law has no binding moral or legal force; the law becomes a sham. This is the problem with some Pacific states: lawmakers are not bound by their own laws, the law loses its legal and moral force, and the rule of law becomes a mask for the unbridled power of those in government.

Notably, according to a strictly formalist reading, the principles referred to above are encapsulated in the procedural criterion of equality under the law and related formal criteria, like certainty in the law when the laws are clear, specific about what they prohibit, understandable, relatively stable, not retrospective, and universal in their application. This is true to a large extent. Nevertheless, compliance with procedure may not provide sufficient protection against tyranny. When governments duly enact laws that rob citizens and the media of their freedoms (as recent events in the Pacific have shown), or take citizens' property without adequate compensation or with no compensation at all (as my discussion in the following chapters will show), obstruct the administration of justice (as the proposed bill on unity and reconciliation in Fiji is likely to do), and fundamentally change the nature of government from a government of, by, and for the people into some kind of business corporation (the end-result of public sector reforms now being undertaken in the Pacific), procedure does not save people from tyranny, injustice and unfairness. It is oppression, injustice and unfairness sanctioned by law.

In addition, theoretically, the formal understanding of the rule of law has its own blindspots. The discrepancy between the rules of evidence and formal procedure and the actual application of those rules is an issue, especially when there is a marked departure from the stated rules.[11] The selected formal characteristics also betray subjective preferences. Formal theories, in fact, proceed on the implicit presumption that compliance with the selected rules will result in a particular substantively-defined functional outcome, thus blurring the rigid distinction between substance and procedure which formal theorists are wont to maintain. Sometimes the proclaimed objectivity of formal theories is either misleading—a pretentious disengagement from the real world—or just a way of tranquilising the human senses through indifference. The proclaimed rationality of law as a predicate of formal theories similarly ignores the possibility that reason is sometimes a function of the status quo, a servant of power politics or some other ideology, one that offers its services to the highest bidder.

But even if these issues were successfully resolved, there still remains the gnawing doubt that procedural justice will save citizens from tyranny at all. As Raz (notwithstanding his formalist inclinations) has had to admit, '[a] non-democratic legal system, based on the denial of human rights, on extensive poverty, on racial segregation, sexual inequalities, and religious persecution may, in principle, conform to the requirements of the rule of law better than any of the legal systems of the more enlightened Western democracies' (Raz 1979:211). Procedure, in other words, is blind to the wider implications of either the whole legal system or specific laws, and their application to the practice of government. As a consequence, while not discounting the importance of procedural justice as a barrier against arbitrary power, we need to extend the formal conception of the rule of law to embrace 'more demanding constitutional conditions and constraints, once it is applied to the practice of law and government, while leaving ample scope for political choice according to the theories of justice that citizens and their representatives espouse' (Allan 2001:23). In the final analysis, the proper test of a theory of law is 'its capacity to illuminate the questions of legitimate constitutional governance…and here the connection between law and justice is intrinsic rather than contingent' (Allan 2001:28).

Pursuing legitimate governance, predicated on that intrinsic connection between law and justice, this study defines justice in broad terms: government's just treatment of its citizens; just and fair promulgated laws; proper exercise of government powers within prescribed limits and controls; honest performance of the functions for which government was instituted; reasonable gratification of citizens' legitimate expectations; equitable allocation of public resources; and secure protection of citizens' rights and liberties. This definition presupposes certain minimum conditions, such as a broad conception of the common good that is at once congruent with diverse systems of interests in society and transcendent of those interests vying for control of the social order. This, in turn, presupposes a shared social conscience regarding the common good.

For good governance and development propagandists, this demands getting into the mind, heart and soul of our communities of Pacific beneficiaries, and feeling the pulse of those communities (Ray 2003).

Rule of law as guiding principle of legitimate governance: exit legal positivism; enter reciprocity, integrity and (quasi)naturalism

The theory of law herein promoted has important implications. One is the rejection of a crude legal positivism that has nothing to do with morals or ethics (Allan 2001:6).[12] Although legal positivists do not strictly deny the importance of the moral, ethical and political dimensions of the law, most either push these matters to the periphery or ignore them altogether, thus effectively excluding them from serious consideration in jurisprudential analysis. I take the view that moral judgment and public ethics should occupy the centre of jurisprudential discourse, especially in this age of unbridled government powers. Thus, legal formalism, as the 'bastardisation of legal positivism' (McCoubrey and White 1993:187), should be seen to be of limited application for the purpose of legitimate governance. As Lon Fuller has noted, positive law serves 'only to fill that comparatively narrow area of possible dispute where conflicts are not automatically resolved by a reference to tacitly accepted conceptions of rightness', and outside that limited area there can be 'no sharp division between the rule that is and the rule that ought to be' (Fuller 1969:111).

For the purpose of legitimate governance, therefore, positive law and substantive principles should be treated as mutually reinforcing. In an attempt to mitigate crude legal positivism, we could adopt H.L.A. Hart's 'minimum content of natural law' (in keeping with his modified positivism) on the ground that, without such a content, 'laws and morals could not forward the minimum purpose of survival which men have in associating with each other' (Hart 1961:189). Fuller's 'internal morality of the law', as a measure of proper lawmaking, can further elucidate this position. This notion comprises eight negative criteria described as 'eight ways to fail to make law', including the use of legal rules to 'express blind hatreds' (Fuller 1969:33,168) as in the totalitarian abuses of law in Nazi Germany.

It may be noted that, whereas no elected Pacific government has yet expressly enacted into law the systematic extermination of people based on 'blind hatreds', the violations of rights and liberties that frequently erupt in some quarters of the region (for example, the coups in Fiji and the recent situation in the Solomon Islands) are no less serious. The German experiment and Pacific tentative experimentation with legal oppression constitute a resounding reminder that the positivist notion that law is whatever a sovereign lawmaking power deems to be so (regardless of moral imperatives), while important for descriptive analysis, is of limited use for the purpose of legitimate governance. It is therefore imperative to extend the definition of the rule of law beyond an exclusively descriptive frame of reference.

In extending our conception of the rule of law as the guiding and unifying principle of legitimate governance, Fuller's notion of reciprocity is of relevance.[13] Legitimate governance on the basis of this notion places mutual responsibility on both the citizens and the state: citizens comply with state laws, subject to moral scrutiny; the state, for its part, fulfils its obligations in keeping with citizens' legitimate expectations. This requires the maintenance of 'channels of communication' (Fuller 1969:186) between the citizens and their state through public debate and negotiation, and dismantles the crude positivist view of the law as a 'one-way projection of authority' which short-circuits the operation of the law as a process involving the 'discharge of interlocking responsibilities—of government toward the citizen and of the citizen toward government' (Fuller 1969:33). Law, in light of this reciprocal gratification of mutual obligations, is therefore a cooperative venture between the government and the governed.

Also of relevance to the practice of legitimate governance is Ronald Dworkin's notion of law as integrity.[14] Rejecting exclusive legal positivism as a rigid regime of legal rules, Dworkin argues that in cases where the law is unclear, the judiciary (the main focus of his analysis) must rely on principles such as individual and minority rights. This privileging of principles as opposed to policies (for example, a government policy in favour of a subsidy for the manufacture of aircrafts justified on the ground of improving national defence) informs his opposition to legal pragmatism.

> Pragmatism does not rule out any theory about what makes a community better. But it does not take legal rights seriously. It rejects what other conceptions of law accept: that people can have distinctly legal rights as trumps over what would otherwise be the best future properly understood. According to pragmatism what we call legal rights are only the servants of the best future: they are instruments we construct for that purpose and have no independent force or ground (Dworkin 1977:22).

While permitting the pursuit of diverse interests in the community, law as integrity requires state action to be undertaken pursuant to 'a single, coherent set of principles even when its citizens are divided about [what] the right principles of justice and fairness really are' (Dworkin 1986:166).

In summary, a substantive theory of the rule of law is essential to legitimate governance. That is to say, 'we should not need wait for the concentration camps' (Foucault 1982:210) to realise all over again the evils of unbridled power. Moral indifference—in the guise of moral neutrality—gives rise to gross irresponsibility. Leslie Stephen (1907:142) illustrates the sort of acquiescence cognate to moral indifference, arguing

> [i]f a legislature decided that all blue-eyed babies should be murdered, the preservation of all blue-eyed babies would be illegal; but legislators must go mad before they could pass such a law, and subjects be idiotic before they could submit to it.

Refusing to resist such a law is to 'empty the idea of the rule of law of all meaning' (Dyzenhaus 2000:172). This example reveals normative evaluation to be an essential component of the rule of law, construed and applied as the guiding and unifying principle of legitimate governance. Of course, one cannot govern the state with the Sermon on the Mount as Chancellor Bismark once retorted. But neither should citizens surrender their conscience to the state; nor should they acquiesce to a popular morality that institutionalises racism and blind hatred, oppression and exploitation for whatever reason.

I must note that deference to such substantive principles as external criteria of evaluation is in keeping with the jurisprudential theory that guides the government of Samoa and most Pacific nations.[15] The introduction of the preamble to the Constitution of Samoa 1960 thus declares governance '[i]n the holy name of God, the Almighty, the Ever Loving'. This is underscored by the first recital of the preamble, which affirms that 'sovereignty over the Universe belongs to the Omnipresent God alone, and the authority to be exercised by the people of Samoa within the limits prescribed by His commandments is a sacred heritage'. Extending the requirement for governance within the parameters of substantive principles, the second recital of the preamble declares that the State of Samoa is to be 'based on Christian principles and Samoan custom'. Given that, it is difficult to avoid defining the term 'religion' and its cognate 'morality' as instituting reasonable restrictions on the exercise of rights and liberties guaranteed under part II of the Constitution.

From a formal legal positivist perspective, these recitals would seem to be nothing more than a declaration of the religious faith of the people, bereft of legal force. This was, in fact, the explanation given by one of the constitutional law advisers in the Constitutional Convention 1960 (Constitutional Convention of Western Samoa 1960:Vol.1, 886). Whereas Davidson's explanation might be correct in a strictly positivist sense, it is not so for the majority of the Samoan people, for whom the most important and authoritative part of the national Constitution are the recitals cited above, construed as legal and moral prescriptions (Meleisea 1987:212). These contradictory views inevitably throw into sharp focus the discrepant views of the nature and function of the law in Samoa. The result is legal and moral confusion.

Offering a reappraisal, I note two possibilities here. One is that Samoa has adopted a species of natural law, skewed in favour of divine commands and Christian principles. Enshrined in the national Constitution and adopted as part of Samoa's political morality, these normative principles are essential variables of Samoa's jurisprudence. Law, on this naturalist reading, must conform to the standards of justice, morality and reason. Contrary to the legal positivist claim that the empirical existence of a legal rule is something independent from its merits or demerits, law means just, fair and reasonable promulgated laws that are compatible with moral principles. There can be no separation of law and morals here. Reconciling that divorce, Deryck Beyleveld and Roger Brownsword (1986:4) charge that 'our target…is the thesis that the concept of law is morally neutral, which involves *inter alia* the claim that the *de facto* [formal] criteria of legality are decisive…The central contention…is that this thesis is wrong'. Law, in other words, is a moral phenomenon, and the obligation to obey the law directly relates to the moral quality of the law.

> Laws, for us, are morally legitimate prescriptions under the [principle of generic consistency], and they straightforwardly generate legal-moral obligations' (Beyleveld and Brownsword 1986:325).

State lawmakers, on this view, do not have legal or moral authority to authorise the murder of political opponents, violation of rights, misappropriation of public funds or property, or any such unlawful act. For the purpose of legitimate governance, natural law precepts like justice and equity constitute fetters on the exercise of government powers by requiring Samoan lawmakers to conform to and promote moral standards. In the extreme, the 'indisputable truth that the command of an earthly superior which violated the law of God or Natural Reason', enjoined Lord Radcliffe (1961:6) 'not only owned title to no obedience but might even involve the positive duty of resistance'.

Alternatively, the constitutional framers might have defined law in inclusive legal positivist terms. Inclusive legal positivism, as Jules L. Coleman (2001:108) defines it, 'is the claim that positivism *allows* or *permits* substantive or moral tests of legality; it is not the view that positivism *requires* such tests'. Inclusive legal positivism does not necessarily posit any inconsistency between the core commitments of positivism and the existence of moral criteria of legality. As a theory of possible grounds of legality, legal authority and legal normativity, inclusive legal positivism

> says, in effect, that a positivist can accept not just that moral principles can sometimes figure in legal argument; not just that such principles can be binding on officials; but that sometimes they can be binding on officials because they are legally valid or part of the community's law, and—most significantly—that they may even be part of the community's law in virtue of their merits—provided the rule of recognition has such provisions (Coleman 2001:108).

Evaluating it either as a species of full-blown natural law theory or as a case of inclusive legal positivism, we find that the fundamental law of Samoa expressly recognises moral tests of legality. The essential difference is that inclusive legal positivism merely allows or permits moral considerations as tests of legal validity; mainstream natural law requires moral principles as tests of legal validity. Be that as it may, the recitals and moral thrust of the Constitution of Samoa force a recognition of the moral component of the Constitution and the importance of both government and governed acting in accordance with morality; that morality is part of the chosen conceptual lens through which Samoans view reality, define what law is and what its legitimate functions are, and how they prefer to be governed.

This has important implications. First, it is incompatible with an exclusive legal positivist perspective. There is no separation between law and morality in Samoa's legal universe. For the purpose of legitimate governance, substantive principles must play a critical and decisive role. Second, Samoa's present lawmakers and government officials are responsible for giving effect to the constitutional framers' clear intentions, notwithstanding exclusive legal positivism's domination of the contemporary legal world. Against pretensions to universality, it must be said that

> there is clearly strong reason to favour the view of one's jurisdiction that best serves the requirements of justice and the common good, as one understands them. It is foolish—an unfortunate by-product of legal positivism—to believe that even descriptive analysis, where it has practical consequences, can detach itself from normative judgment and evaluation (Allan 2001:5).

This connection requires a caveat. In a negative sense, religious bigotry—to some extent engendered by a conservative law/religion/politics alliance has the negative effect of undermining legitimate governance in Samoa and other Pacific nations.[16] The problem is the violation of rights either in the name of religion or in the worship of some religious denomination's idiosyncratic sectional morality. Whenever that happens, morality is hijacked, owned and exploited in the service of narrow sectional interests, thereby reducing it to some kind of tribal harlot that offers its services to the highest bidder and thus undermining the significance, value and force of morality itself as a legitimate factor in the construction and maintenance of the community's legal universe. Problems like this make doubtful the propriety of haphazardly mixing positive law and morality, for example, in the Devlin sense of popular morality (Devlin 1965:13–4).[17] At stake is the protection of the unpopular religious minority from the popular religious majority.

While these problems do not signal a final victory for exclusive legal positivism, they do raise important issues. One is the essential need to protect freedom of conscience within reasonable limits. The other is that community morality does not necessarily mean the institutionalisation of immoral practices such as racial hatred, religious intolerance and interpersonal enmity. There is also the important reminder that one should not coercively impose one's religious beliefs on others through mad acts of violence, and that the violation of rights is as much a moral issue as it is a legal one. I will return to these issues below.

The internal/external perspective dichotomy: an integrated viewpoint

In addition to the rejection of legal positivism, another implication of the theory of law promoted here relates to the dichotomy between the internal perspective of officials (judges, lawyers and lawmakers), on the one hand, and the external, third-person perspective of outsiders, on the other.[18] I adopt a broad perspective combining the internal and external perspectives, because this allows a more comprehensive assessment of the justice of particular laws and indeed the entire legal system and their application to the practice of government—jurisprudence requires this.

Even dogmatic proponents of the internal perspective concede this much, albeit half-heartedly. Arguing against the external slant in John Austin's theory of law (that is, law as a system of commands backed by sanctions imposed from above), Hart postulated law as a system of rules that enables members of a given society to behave in an orderly manner. This insight led Hart to hold that laws have both an external perspective and an internal one, and that jurisprudence must take into consideration both perspectives 'and not to define one of them out of existence' (Hart 1961:88,55). Similarly, Dworkin, though intent on critiquing Hart's conception of law, emphasises the need for both perspectives and that 'each must take account of the other' (Dworkin 1986a:13).

This challenges the one-sided promulgation of the internal point of view, sometimes advanced with a non-negotiable dogmatism, that forecloses conversation with external critics as if the terms, procedures and objectives internal to the social practice of the legal system need neither explanation nor justification. Such dogmatism unfortunately entails the exclusion of the external perspective of anthropologists, sociologists, economists, development agencies, cultural theorists, postmodernists, postcolonial theorists, feminists and others less inclined to adopt the perspective of law officials. But, as Alan Hunt (1987:12) correctly notes, '[i]nternal theory is simply too close to its subject matter'. While not hopelessly mired in the internal perspective all the time, the internalist retreat behind 'Chinese walls' and exclusive focus on internal matters such as *ratio decidendi* and *stare decisis* often preclude serious questioning of the legal system as a whole and the justice of particular statutes and regulations. This often stifles development of the law in keeping with the needs, expectations and distinctive nature of a given society. The external perspective, because it is really critical of the law as praxis, is therefore necessary to balance the somewhat static focus of strict legal analysis and account for diversity in the social practice of law.

We find a compelling interest in law as praxis in the US version of legal realism. Legal realism, reacting against the black-letter approach to law, shifts the focus of legal analysis away from law in the books to law in action. It asserts both the influence of extra-legal, external factors (for example, class, race, gender and morality) in judicial decision-making and also the significance of the law as a vehicle of change. Oliver Wendell Holmes contention is intructive on this matter,

> [t]he life of the law has not been logic, it has been experience. The felt necessities of the time, the prevalent moral and political theories, intuitions of public policy, avowed or unconscious, even the prejudices which judges share with their fellow men, have had a good deal more to do than the syllogism in determining the rules by which men should be governed (Holmes, in Lerner 1943:51)

A similar focus on law as praxis is central to the critical legal studies genre, which is characterised by a distrust of traditional legal reasoning as in legal positivism, and a strong preference for the external perspective on the social practice of law. The critical legal studies view, like legal realism, problematises the internal/external distinction, asserting the influence of extra-legal, external factors in judicial decision-making and rejecting a value-free conception of the law. It posits that legal theory must take into account the wider implications and consequences of the social practice of law, and affirms the law as an essential 'aspect of the social totality, not just the tail of the dog' (Kennedy 1990:47).

But both legal realism and critical legal studies could ultimately be crippling for the traditional ideal of the rule of law. While scepticism is warranted, absolute scepticism is self-defeating. The claim that the legal system is ultimately flawed, biased and arbitrary could throw the entire legal order into chaos. At worst, it would result in a kind of legal nihilism whereby the entire legal system is utterly and perilously distrusted. Further, the unlimited incursion of the law into the extra-legal arena seemingly advocated by legal realism and critical legal studies risks reducing law to politics or collapsing it into economics. The positive contribution to jurisprudence of these critical legal genres is the recognition that the law is infected with ideologies, power relations and power structures that need to be exposed and redressed, and that the law has a legitimate role to play in the other dimensions of the social order.

For the purpose of legitimate governance—the specific focus of this study—one needs to look not only at the internal working of the law (the internal perspective) but also at the functional significance of the legal system as a whole for other dimensions of the social order (the external perspective). This emphasises the need for both perspectives. Abjuring a one-sided focus on either, a more reasonable approach admits the legal system as a coherent decision-making process while, at the same time, subjecting that process to the scrupulous analysis of critical external perspectives.

Postmodernism, postcolonialism, and Pacific customary laws

I note in this context the postmodern sensibilities of Pacific peoples as a species of the external perspective. In addition to problematising the internal/external distinction, postmodernism is generally critical of the law, its nature and function. For Michel Foucault, law includes codified laws and a system of disciplines (that is, institutions like prisons, courts, and so forth) that supplement the law, creating a new, repressive model of the legal system in which '[l]aw is neither the truth of power nor its alibi. It is an instrument of power which is at once complex and partial' (Foucault 1980:141). This conception of the law directly impacts on governance or the problem of 'governmentality', as Foucault (1991) describes it. It challenges the political strategy of decentralising public power, and calls into question the traditional view of lawmaking as a function of sovereign power.

Foucault, adopting an external perspective, deconstructs established legal concepts by showing that their accepted usage masks hidden ideological interests. For example, from a postmodern Papua New Guinean perspective, the institution of individual property rights brings a particular history with its own contradictions and vested interests. In line with the Foucauldian perspective, for a Papua New Guinean living on customary land that is owned by his family subject to the control of his tribe, individual property is not a neutral medium for the negotiation of legal entitlements as it comes loaded with its own arrangement of power relations (that is, in favour of the propertied and the powerful), and that the incorporation of this institution into legal discourse (as in the proposed change of communal ownership of customary land into estates in fee simple that some donor agencies and uninformed cosmopolitan academics are advocating) actually masks its constructed nature and glorifies it as a natural element of the universe. The postmodern perspective, as the example above shows, thus urges and advances a genealogical questioning of how the legal order is constructed, legitimated and maintained; it seeks to expose established institutions and practices as sites of violent power struggles.

But, whereas the significance of the postmodern perspective as a stimulus for change is notable, its anti-foundational orientation is highly questionable (Mootz 1993; Hunt 1992). Taken to the extreme, postmodernism is liable to land law, politics, ethics, governance and other dimensions of the social order in chaos. And while the postmodernist attempt to free the law from its ideological baggage is commendable, its rejection of foundational notions like due process must be resisted on the ground that it unnecessarily deprives us of a normative vision of the law. Subject to that caveat of caution, postmodernism, properly appreciated and adopted within reasonable limits, remains an important stimulus for social change and is also valued for its contextual orientation.

The prevailing Pacific people's resistance to totalising systems of thought, values, procedures and processes suggests postmodern sensibilities. Privileging difference, heterogeneity and the particularity of contexts and perspectives, postmodern metaphysics reject the notion of universal systems, ideologies and standards that are applicable at all times, at all places, for all peoples. Instead, systems, ideologies, and standards are seen as contingent, constructed and pluralistic. This makes tenuous, and in some cases subverts, the Western view of law, lawmaking authority, mechanisms of dispute resolution, and so on. For Pacific people the questions have always been: What is law? Which law? Whose law? This is not a naïve compulsion to be simplistically tribalistic. Rather, the issue goes to the heart of a jurisprudence that is relevant to the diverse situations of the Pacific peoples themselves. It is also, fundamentally, about the legal, moral and practical justification for the peoples' acquiescence in the law (as a manifestation of the state) as a fundamental question in jurisprudence.

Here the people's postmodern sensibilities overlap with their postcolonial sensitivities, questioning the credibility of the Western law now adopted as their own. The reason for this consternation is clear. Western law was often used in the former colonies as the fist of the colonial powers. Not surprisingly, Western law has been denounced as 'the cutting edge of colonialism' (Chanock 1985:4) and 'a sharp sword [used] by the powerful to conquer, and hold subject, the powerless' (Narokobi 1982:13). So, while the rule of law has been praised as the bedrock of Western civilisation, some former colonies see it quite differently, and not without good reason. Seen from their perspective and historical experience, Western law has been an oppressive force used by the colonial powers 'to destroy cultures, civilisations, religions and the entire moral fabric of a people' (Narokobi 1982:13). For example, Samoa was made a protectorate of the German government in February 1900 and Dr Wilhelm Solf of Germany became the governor of Samoa. The problem was that Solf's political aim was essentially paternalistic: to enhance his own political power and to abolish Samoan custom and cultural institutions, including part of the chiefly (*matai*) system (Davidson 1967). Similarly, New Zealander George Richardson (1923–28) undertook the administration of Samoa in the manner of a military chief, using the Samoan Offenders Ordinance 1922 to order the banishment of the natives and deprive chiefs (*matais*) of their customary titles.

These historical facts inevitably bring to the fore the issue of why former colonies should continue to use Western law as part of their own postcolonial independent states. If modern Samoan/Pacific jurisprudence is to be able to transform postcolonial scepticism of Western law into a more positive and trusting embrace of the rule of law as an essential human good, this issue must be faced honestly. To ignore it is to screen out history and its continuing effects, thereby risking the people's opposition to, or even outright rejection of, the rule of law, with dangerous ramifications for legitimate governance, law and order.

The recognition of Samoan custom as a source of law is therefore significant and necessary for a number of reasons.[19] The sovereignty of the people demands that their values and practices be reflected in state laws and the way the state of Samoa operates. From a postcolonial perspective, recognition of Samoan custom moderates the hegemony of the Western system of law and provides part of the legal, moral and practical justification for the people's acquiescence in the law.[20]

There are important implications of the recognition of custom as a source of law.

First, custom is a legitimate way of achieving legal validity, authority and normativity. Whereas legal positivism posits that the authority of the law derives from the authority of the lawmaker, customary law shows that there are other equally valid ways of establishing legal authority. Furthermore, developing Pacific laws in keeping with historical experience, social necessity and cultural contingency is not entirely revolutionary. After all, English common law and equity jurisdictions are themselves products of the history and development of England. Seen in this light, Pacific customary laws are not some deviant Pacific attempt to be tribalistic but are products of particular histories, expressions of community interests and reflections of the social conscience of the Pacific peoples themselves.

Second, Pacific customary laws contradict, to a significant degree, the structuralist legal anthropological thought that underlies most Western theories of law. For instance, whereas Western law is a command of a sovereign, imposed from above and backed by threats as in Austin's theory of law, customary law is a negotiated solution, achieved through the processes of consultation, negotiation and mediation amongst all members of the group. Customary lawmaking is not the sole prerogative of an armchair sovereign but a community enterprise; everyone's consent is essential and sought. This raises the issue that, oftentimes, the presupposition that non-Western societies do not have laws is, without reflection, converted into a conclusion and propagated as an absolute truth (see Salmond 1957; Hart 1961).

Even legal anthropologists of so-called primitive societies (including some with the best of intentions) do not escape the appeal of this one-dimensional view of the law. For instance, invoking Pound's definition of law as 'social control through the systematic application of force of a politically organised society', A.R. Radcliffe-Brown (1952:212) concluded that non-Western societies that do not satisfy the criterion of his study (that is, law presupposes political structures, specifically Western political structures) could only be classified as cultures without law.[21] Against such arbitrary judgment regarding what is and is not law, it is argued that custom should be a defining variable of a Samoan/Pacific theory of the rule of law. Proper recognition of this social fact has resulted (correctly, I might add) in a significant paradigm shift in Pacific legal systems—giving indigenous laws the status of valid conceptions of law, albeit in different voices and faces. There is also a need, first, not to impose Western definitions of law on non-Western societies since in doing so one 'is bound to overlook essential elements which only become apparent when the culture is considered as a whole' (Hogbin 1972:290) and, second, to take each non-Western culture as an independent phenomenon in its own right. To do this requires viewing customary law as the aggregate of rules, norms, institutions and so forth, which not only grow out of the life of a community but also govern the life of that community. Law, in other words, springs from the land and is rooted in the ways of life of the people. Its generation and maintenance occur in a cycle of consensus; it is not a top-down kind of thing.

Third, law in Samoa's traditional jurisprudence is not the command of a King Rex, an absolute monarch sitting on a majestic throne, dishing out non-negotiable demands and wishes. Rather, it is the collective wisdom of the people (often embodied in the elderly) achieved through regular practice and defined through the social processes of consultation, negotiation, and mediation. Moreover, traditional law rather is the collective will of a people who approach and treat each other as equals, that is, over and above the façade of ceremonial postures and structures. In substance, customary law encompasses both the people's habits of the heart, their intellectual predispositions, and mundane rules which govern their everday pre-theoretical lives. It is not atomistic; it does not treat reality as discrete segments. Rather, it deals with reality as a totality. The transcendent and the mundane, the spiritual and the physical and the psychosocial have equal value.

Traditional law is therefore holistic in approach and reach; its function is primarily restorative. Maintaining social harmony is everybody's imperative.

Fourth, the recognition of customary laws has given rise to legal pluralism, encapsulating a complex combination of different legal traditions. Negatively, this new legal creature may seem to be nothing more than a confusing aggregate of legal strands haphazardly thrown together. Or, positively, it could be seen as an amalgam of traditions that are congruent with the people's values, norms and expectations. Unique though it may be, this legal pluralism has created problems such as uncertainty in the law, instability of the legal order, and the pressing need for a more definitive legal and moral justification for the people's acquiescence in the law as force. These issues are particularly pertinent to Pacific jurisdictions. When clashes of different legal mindsets occur, questions of authority and legitimacy arise. When someone is murdered pursuant to an (alleged) customary duty to avenge the death of a family member (as in the Solomon Islands case of *Loumia* v *Director of Public Prosecutions* [1986] SBCA 1; [1985-1986] SLR 158, 24 February 1986), or, an (alleged) adulteress is murdered in line with native custom (as in the PNG case of *Public Prosecutor* v *Kerua* [1985] PNGLR 85), the disparity between the different legal mindsets becomes apparent and demands reconciliation. I will return to these issues in chapter five.

Finally, reconciling competing substantive principles and values is also necessary for a number of reasons. For instance, in recognising indigenous custom (with its own ideologies, procedures, processes and objectives), a dichotomy is revealed between liberal-individualism—a hallmark of Western law—and the conservative collectivism of Pacific societies. I will deal with the individual/collective dichotomy in chapter four. Suffice, at this juncture, to note the following.

In keeping with the ethos of libertarian rights and freedoms, part II of Samoa's Constitution appropriately guarantees fundamental rights and freedoms through an entrenched bill of rights (for example, life, liberty, religion, speech, assembly, association and property).[22] The Constitution as a bill of rights compels the state to protect the rights and freedoms of Samoan individuals and, at the same time, withholds from all state institutions the power to take these freedoms away. At a fundamental level, the Constitution is an expression of the natural right of every Samoan citizen to govern himself or herself, and to specify the terms according to which he or she agrees to give up that right upon submitting to the rules of the state. The Constitution thus emphasises the fundamental importance of the Samoan individual in the creation and the ongoing life of the state. It affirms human dignity and individual liberty through an entrenched bill of rights. The Constitution, in other words, invests the individual with inalienable moral worth and primacy.

The individual citizen is indeed indispensable for the purpose of legitimate governance in every liberal democracy, pursued as it is through the framework of the rule of law. The rule of law assumes and, in fact, requires the consent of the governed, predicated on the belief that there is something sacred in every person. Some call it reason; others call it conscience. Either as reason or as conscience, this sacred entity is the essential attribute that defines humanity. This belief accounts for the voluntary character of all associations wherein humans are respected as morally responsible agents, capable of making decisions based on the exercise of their free will.

The state, too, could be seen as an association of individuals who voluntarily surrender certain personal rights in order to safeguard the inalienable rights of others. This provides an insight into the issue of the individual's acquiescence in the law as a manifestation of the state. The rule of law, Allan (2001:6) opines, constitutes 'an ideal of consent, wherein the law seeks the citizen's acceptance of its demands as morally justified: he is invited to acknowledge that obedience is the appropriate response in the light of his obligation to further the legitimate needs of the common good'. Without that consent, the rule of law loses its legal and moral legitimacy, and law, as a manifestation of the state, becomes mere barbaric force imposed on non-consenting subjects (So'o 2000; Malifa 1988).

I do not subscribe to the exaggerated notion of the individual as paramount, nor do I promote the sacrifice of the individual on the altar of the collective good. Rather, my position is at the middle point between the two extremes of atomistic individualism and claustrophobic collectivism. Negotiating a position in the middle, it may be argued that individualism and collectivism finally converge at the point of the individual citizen who is, after all, the final judge of what he or she wants, what is fair and just, relative to the legitimate interests and values of the community as a whole. But instead of promoting atomistic individualism, the existing rhetoric of individual rights in the Pacific would do well to seek to create a society in which individuals are accorded moral authority, *are morally and socially responsible* in the exercise of their liberties, and are respected accordingly. In that way, rights discourse could function as a powerful source for a constructive critique of traditional social arrangements and as a robust basis for working out alternative institutional practices that are appropriate to Pacific socio-cultural contexts with their varying degrees of socialism.

Rule of law and socioeconomic development

The urgent need for economic development in the Pacific is clear. The Eminent Persons' Group (2004:n.p.) aptly puts it in the following terms

> Improvement in the material well-being of Pacific people and the opportunities available to them will depend on expanding opportunities for the generation of increased wealth from the region's natural and human resources. Sustaining economic growth implies both macro and micro-economic policies that facilitate the creation of businesses and jobs, and also the development of a trading environment that allows equitable access to export markets and lower cost imports.

The issue for present purposes is not economic development *per se* but the proper use of the law as a vehicle of socioeconomic development. This is a central concern in legal theorisation. The danger envisaged here is the degeneration into an unprincipled legal utilitarianism, that is, the use of the rule of law as an instrument for the achievement of government policies without any moral or ethical justification—a mere means of achieving state control. When that happens, law becomes nothing more than naked government force.

The issues include the way in which the rule of law, either as principles or as legal rules, is used as an engine of development; the legal and moral underpinning of such use; and the extent to which the law could be legitimately used as such within appropriate constitutional limits and controls. The following theoretical discussion frames the issue in jurisprudential terms and underlines the appropriate limits and constraints on utilitarianism.

The utilitarian theory of law, historically associated with Jeremy Bentham and in contemporary legal theory with the proponents of the law and economics movement,[23] shows that the law can be made to serve legitimate functions. The utility principle in Bentham's censorial jurisprudence is one that either approves or disapproves of a particular course of action, depending on whether it augments or diminishes the happiness of the individuals whose interests are in question

(Bentham 1967). In terms of lawmaking, promoting the happiness of those individuals who make up the community 'is the end and the sole end which the legislator ought to have in view' (Bentham 1967:Ch.3, para 1).

Bentham's theory raises a number of issues. First, since the theory seems to have been predicated on an individualist ethic, it is a moot point whether the notion of the greatest good of the greatest number is really a communal good since Bentham himself appears to have reduced the community to a fiction that simply incorporates all individuals in society (McCoubrey and White 1993:26).

Second, while the utilitarianist ideal of maximising individual interests has its merits, it could—if wedded to the interests of a dominant group in society—result in the exploitation, oppression and deprivation of people without influence. This is especially true of societies with social classes, such as Tonga. In such situations, it is hard to ignore the Marxist jurisprudential conclusion that, since the dominant group has overwhelming political and economic power to influence the substance of laws and the lawmaking process, the law not only lacks autonomy but is, in fact, an instrument of class domination. In the words of the Soviet theorist Evgeny Bronislavovich Pashukanis (1978:146), '[p]ower as the "collective will", as the "rule of law", is realised in bourgeois society to the extent that this society represents a market'. Criticism of the economic determinism of classical Marxist thought and the reductionist explanation of the law in terms of class domination are fairly well noted. Marxist explanations of law are, nevertheless, important in that they seek to expose the entwinement of law in economic and political power relations that are apparently unjust, unfair and non-equitable when they result in economic and political exploitation, oppression and deprivation.

Also of interest is the 'law jobs' theory of the legal realist Karl Llewellyn, based on the premise that law is a legitimate means of achieving social objectives (for example, reordering society, maintaining law and order and facilitating the exercise of legal authority), and that law must be responsive to the changing needs of society (Llewellyn 1941). Llewellyn appropriately affirms the positive influence that law can bring to bear on society. Negatively, in addition to the arbitrary nature of Llewellyn's list of law jobs, legal pragmatism can be taken only so far. Reiterating Dworkin's criticism noted above, legal pragmatism does not take rights seriously. This points to an important constitutional constraint on the use of the law as a vehicle of socioeconomic change: individual and minority rights as a defence of the citizens against the fist of the state.

Whereas Dworkin's rights thesis appropriately underlines the significance of rights as a bulwark against arbitrary rule, and while he correctly opposes the arbitrary use of the law as simply an instrument for the achievement of political or economic goals, other important questions go unanswered. For instance, how viable is the judiciary as the protector of rights in a context where Dworkin's mythical judge, Hercules, does not exist (Dworkin 1977), and where the judiciary is not only conservative and timid but is at the mercy of an omnipotent parliament dominated by an exalted executive government (as in most Pacific nations)? To some extent, Dworkin addresses these issues with his doctrines of integrity in practice and community morality—an institutional morality embodied in the community's political culture that underpins the community's constitutional framework (Dworkin 1986b:214). The latter, interestingly enough, subverts the positivist distinction between law and morals, and extends the justification for the citizens' acquiescence in the law beyond rules to include the community's political morality as well. Thus Dworkin, in a very significant way, has underlined another constitutional constraint on the use of the law as an engine of socioeconomic change: the normative values and political morality of the community whose interests stand to be directly affected by the rule of law.

Morality as a constraint on the social practice of law is also a central plank in John M. Finnis' full-blown naturalist theory of basic human goods—life and the development of personal potential, knowledge, play, aesthetic experience, sociability or friendship, practical reasonableness (entailing the capacity to order and regulate life according to some rational scheme), and religion, which presupposes human awareness of a power beyond the normal run of things (Finnis 1980:86–9).

Evaluating Finnis' postulates positively, we find that morality and ethics constitute legitimate constraints on the utilitarian use of the rule of law. On a negative note, Finnis' list of goods is perhaps arbitrary. In common parlance, one person's treasure is another's trash, not only at the level of personal preferences but at the broader cultural level of multifarious community values. What is of ultimate concern to a Palestinian in the Middle East is not necessarily of the same value for a Tongan or a Fijian in the Pacific. Furthermore, since Finnis' basic goods are equally fundamental, this begs the question as to which goods should take precedence over others in cases where some of these goods are in competition or even incompatible. Finnis (1980:103–26) solves this paradox, to some extent, through his proposed tests of practical reasonableness, some of which are relevant for present purposes.

First, excluding arbitrary preferences regarding the pursuit of goods, individuals should not blindly pursue their interests to the exclusion or detriment of others, but should defer to the common good—the right to pursue one's personal preferences is not absolute. Put bluntly, utilitarianism is (and should be) subject to legitimate limits. Second, given Finnis' naturalist interests, his emphasis on the exercise of one's conscience is not unexpected. This is important in many respects; for example, citizens' have the moral right to judge the conduct of government, something that citizens can ill-afford to surrender to the state, and should exercise that right. Third, efficiency in terms of the pursuit of basic goods should be circumscribed by moral considerations, such as the good of others—efficiency should not be pursued as an end in itself. This legitimate concern is epitomised in the overriding principle of the inherent dignity of humans, a principle that precludes the reduction of people to mere functions of the system—legal, political, economic or cultural. This principle underpins Finnis' (1980:225) conception of natural rights as constitutional constraints on the use of the law as an engine of socioeconomic change.

Even Hart, despite his formalist sympathies, accepts that social values must influence the social practice of law. In keeping with his 'minimum content of natural law' as discussed above, Hart offered five truisms which are supposed to underlie and constitute the viability of a system of law. For example, there should be a condition of approximate equality which, taking into consideration the different capabilities of the members of any given society, ensures that no individual citizen will possess absolute and dominating power. This necessitates a 'system of mutual forbearance and compromise which is the basis of both legal and moral obligation' (Hart 1961:191). This system moderates extreme self-interest and engenders a state of limited altruism as a governing principle of social life. 'If the system is fair and caters genuinely for the vital interests of all those from whom it demands obedience,' Hart (1961:197) warned, 'it may...retain [their] allegiance...for most of the time, and will accordingly be stable. [Otherwise] a narrow and exclusive system run in the interests of the dominant group...may be made continually more repressive and unstable with the latent threat of upheaval'. The issue, extrapolating from Hart's postulates, is social and economic justice.

Certain aspects of John Rawls' theory of justice as fairness are also pertinent to present purposes. First, each person must be given equal rights within a system of equal basic liberties. Second, inequalities in social and economic status must be arranged in such a way that they are beneficial to the maximum extent possible to the least advantaged in society, but in a way that is consistent with the principle of just savings (Rawls 1973:302).[24] Rawls' propositions clearly impact on law and economic reform, that is, reform subject to community values and moral principles. As the critical legal studies advocate Roberto M. Unger (1984) has noted, the rule of law, wedded to capitalism, may become nothing more than the rule of the rich and the powerful.

Finally, two important matters deserve mention here. First, economic development must always be circumscribed by the proper protection of the environment in the interests of sustainable development. The Eminent Persons' Group (2004:n.p.) appropriately underlines the need for sustainable development in the Pacific as follows

> The greatest risk attached to economic development is that of destroying what one seeks to protect. The Pacific's natural resources are bountiful but fragile. Traditional subsistence approaches to farming and fishing have generally supported sustainability, but pressure from resource use has become intense. Non-sustainable resource use threatens not only the natural resources of the region, but also the livelihoods and traditional way of life of many Pacific people.

Second, in keeping with my interest in the relationship of legitimate governance to economic development, a case could be made for a position between the extreme left's centralised planning, which ultimately cripples economic growth, and the extreme right's unadulterated free-market capitalism, which exposes people alone to the cruel power of market forces. Advocating a leftist-leaning socialism that is left of centre and decisively to the right of full-blown socialism, Richard Rorty (1987:565) writes

> [n]obody so far has invented an economic setup that satisfactorily balances decency and efficiency, but at the moment the most helpful alternative seems to be governmentally controlled capitalism plus welfare-statism (Holland, Sweden, Ireland). There is nothing sacred about either the free market or about central planning; the proper balance between the two is a matter of experimental tinkering.

My point is that economic development in the Pacific must beware of extreme approaches. Getting rich at the expense of other human values should not be promoted. When the poor feed on crumbs of bread from the rich men's tables while the rich men's dogs have steak and milk for lunch, then there is clearly something wrong with society.

Perhaps this society has been reduced to nothing more than a market wherein human beings have become faceless cogs in a capitalist system that operates, without a conscience, according to the latent functional laws of market forces. An extreme-right capitalism is likely to create a rich few and a poor mass; we will merely change the face of poverty; and the poor usually become faceless. Fracturing social harmony is morally irresponsible, and the restoration of socioeconomic equilibrium is more economically expensive than sharing what you have with the have-nots. The revolutionary change of property rights from collective ownership into estates in fee simple, passionately promoted by some armchair academics, is theoretically intriguing but practically naïve. Some Pacific nations (like Samoa) do not need civil wars caused by unnecessary land disputes; the equal distribution of rent money from the lease of customary land remains a potentially divisive issue. Less government and more markets is indeed a desirable goal. But, first, government must be government for the people, not a private company of the élite. The legal, democratic, moral and ethical underpinning of the transformation of Pacific states into *de facto* corporations remains to be more clearly articulated and more convincingly debated as a public issue.

Conclusion

The rule of law is, and must remain, an essential human good. In using this notion as a mobilising theme, I do not follow the academic stream that slickly exploits the myth of inherent human lawlessness and presents a hopelessly fatalistic view of human nature with reference to Pacific peoples. My own interest is grounded in historical facts: past and present. When rulers flagrantly flout the principles of responsible and accountable government, when government haphazardly violates the rights of the citizens, and when the people's legitimate expectations of government continue to be frustrated, the most appropriate resort for the citizens is the rule of law—not the rule of the gun and the sword, as has been the case in some Pacific nations. The rule of law is absolutely essential to avert the relapse of the social order into the Lockean state of nature and the Hobbesian state of war. It must, therefore, be carefully safeguarded against the unwarranted exercise of executive discretion or the arbitrary caprice of parliamentary legislation. At stake is law and order, which must be maintained at all costs. While it might be simplistic to equate the rule of law with law and order (Jennings 1972), it seems certain that law and order is 'the primary meaning and purpose of the rule of law' (Walker 1988:23).

Also at stake is the construction and maintenance of 'an acceptable order of justice' (Allan 2001:15), especially in the arena of public power. While the attainment of government objectives is warranted, this must be subject to constitutional constraints 'that limit the pursuit of such objectives in the interests of individual autonomy and security' (Allan 2001:12). Although Allan's theory is primarily concerned with the protection of individual interests, his expressed recognition of contextual specificities in the sense of regarding a given polity 'as an integrated constitutional scheme' (Allan 2001:41) seems to underline the idea that justice exists (and is actualised) in the concrete context of a given society and intersects with community values, and hence is most effective when it takes these into account.[25] Either from the perspective of the individual or the standpoint of the community as a whole, justice is absolutely essential. For the purpose of legitimate governance, justice, putting it simply, requires hanging a bridle on capricious government action.

Notes

[1]   Apart from Tonga, which is a constitutional monarchy, all other Pacific nations are constitutional democracies pursuant to written constitutional mandates and hence the significance of 'writtenness' as a feature of Pacific constitutional making. Underlining the significance of the written Constitution of the United States, Chief Justice Marshall in *Marbury* v *Madison* 5 US (1 Cranch.) 137 (1803) at 178 referred to 'the greatest improvement on political institutions, a written constitution'. On written constitutions as products of an evolutionary political process see Lord Diplock's observation in *Hinds* v *The Queen* [1977] AC 195 at 212 regarding constitutions following the Westminster model of government.

[2]   This is also a common feature of Pacific constitutions, for example, the *Fiji Islands Constitution Amendment Act 1997*, chapter 1, section 2 and the *Constitution of Tuvalu 1978*, section 3. See also Austin's view of legal limitations on the sovereign as 'a flat contradiction in terms' (1955:254).

[3]   See, for example, Bickel (1962); also Elster and Slagstad (1988).

[4]   Note, for example, AusAID's (2000:3) definition

the competent management of a country's resources and affairs in a manner that is open, transparent, accountable, equitable and responsive to people's needs.

Good governance apparently entails 'the primacy of the rule of law, maintained through an impartial and effective legal system' (AusAID 2000:3). The UNDP (1997:2–3) definition of good governance refers to

the exercise of economic, political and administrative authority to manage a country's affairs at all levels. It comprises mechanisms, processes and institutions through which citizens and groups articulate their interests, exercise their legal rights, meet their obligations and mediate their differences.

On the diverse, even competing, definitions of the term note, for example, Hyden and Olowu (2000:6)

> [g]overnance was never allowed to become a conceptual straight-jacket but was expected to function as a rather loose framework within which each researcher could creatively explore political issues of significance. The problem that we encounter, therefore, is not the limitations stemming from the imposition of a confining concept, but rather the opposite. The challenge of making sense of the wide range of interpretations of governance that the authors bring to the agenda.

[5]   See, for example, Tucker (1978) for this view of the rule of law in the *Communist Manifesto*.

[6]   This proposition raises a whole range of questions about rule-following, for example, the authority, determinacy or indeterminacy and interpretation of rules, the correlation between rules and action, and the net effect of rules on action, whether direct or indirect. See, for example, Alexander and Sherwin (1994).

[7]   See also rule scepticism in the US version of legal realism and the critical legal studies movement. See, for example, Frank (1949:130); Hart (1961:144).

[8]   See, for example, Tyler (1990).

[9]   This seems to be another common feature of the jurisprudence of Pacific island nations. See, for example, the preamble, principle 2, of the *Constitution of Tuvalu 1978*; the preamble of the *Constitution of the Republic of Vanuatu 1980*; and the preamble of the *Constitution of Nauru 1968*.

[10]   See also Allan (2001) for an analysis of Hayek's theory of law.

[11]   It seems certain that there are cases where the use of coercive state powers is necessary, for instance, to accomplish legitimate public objectives. One example is the use by police of discretionary powers of arrest and search especially in cases where national security is at stake. Be that as it may, there is always a real danger of a breakdown in the rule of law and the emergence of the rule of force and a police state.

[12]   Legal positivism is generally favoured in formal theorisation, especially in Kelsen's proposed pure theory of law. See Kelsen (1934:474), who notes '[t]he pure theory of law is a theory of positive law. As a theory it is exclusively concerned with the accurate definition of its subject-matter. It endeavours to answer the question, What is the law? but not the question, What ought it to be? It is a science and not a politics of law'.

[13]   See also Allan (2001), whose liberal theory of the rule of law builds on Fuller (1969).

[14]   See also Allan's (2001) utilisation of Dworkin's notion of law as integrity.

[15]   See also note 9 above. Note further the preamble of the *Constitution of Kiribati 1979* which states: 'In implementing this Constitution, we declare that...[t]he principles of equality and justice shall be upheld'.

[16]   *Tariu Tuivaiti* v *Sila Faamalaga and Others* (1980–93) WSLR 17.

[17]   See also Hart (1963:7) on Hart's opposition to 'judicial moralism', citing Lord Mansfield in *Jones* v *Randall* (1774), Lofft (at 385), and *Shaw* v *Director of Public Prosecutions* [1962] AC 220 as authorities for his opposition to populist morality before which the unpopular minority in a given society would always be in danger.

[18]   On the internal/external perspective dichotomy in the social sciences see, for example, Winch (1958) and Dallmayr and McCarthy (1977).

19   The recognition of custom is required, for example, by the second recital of the preamble of the *Constitution of Samoa 1960*; Articles 100, 101, 103, 111(1); section 34(2) of the *Land and Titles Act 1981* (as amended by the *Land and Titles Act 1992*); and the *Village Fono (Council) Act 1990*.

20   The same requirement is found in most Pacific island constitutions. The recognition of custom as a source of law is therefore a common and fundamental dimension of Pacific jurisprudence. Consider, for example, schedule 2.1 of the *Constitution of Papua New Guinea 1975*. A notable exception is Tonga, where there is no recognition of an unwritten customary law. This is partly because of the precedence given to English common law and equity, and also because of the codification of Tongan traditions and custom over the years. Note, however, that the King and his so-called nobles are creatures of Tongan custom and tradition.

21   For a comprehensive analysis of this issue see Vaai (1999).

22   The security and protection of rights and liberties is a common feature of Pacific constitutions, for example, part II of the *Constitution of Nauru 1968*; chapter 4 of the Fiji Islands Constitution Amendment Act 1997; and chapter 2 of the *Constitution of the Solomon Islands*.

23   See especially Posner (1998). Concerning the divorce between constitutional analysis and economics, Posner (1998:675) notes, 'despite the fixation of American lawyers, and especially law students and professors, on the Constitution, there is relatively little economic writing on the subject. And this is not for want of topics that economic analysis might illuminate'.

24   See also Nozick's just entitlement theory in his *Anarchy, State and Utopia* (1974).

25   See, for example, chapter 5 of the Fiji Islands Constitution Amendment Act 1997 which mandates social justice and affirmative action 'to achieve for all groups or categories of persons who are disadvantaged effective equality of access to: (a) education and training; (b) land and housing; and (c) participation in commerce and in all levels and branches of service of the State'. This is perfectly congruent with Fiji's multi-ethnic, pluralist society.

2

Diluting parliamentary sovereignty and deprivatising Pacific executive paradises

This chapter extends the motif of the rule of law as an essential principle of legitimate governance. Providing the legal and moral warrant for government rule, the rule of law also mandates the strengthening of those bounds beyond which no free government ought ever go, and makes them limits beyond which no government whatsoever can ever legally go. We must make *ultra vires* all exorbitant acts of government to ensure that government is not only kept under control but in good order.

Doctrinal and institutional problems

The major focus of this chapter is on institutions that problematise the rule of law in Pacific jurisdictions. Of major concern is the doctrine of parliamentary sovereignty or supremacy that most Pacific jurisdictions are wont to follow. The problem is

> [a] study of constitutionalism in the context of the common law appears to face an immediate problem if the United Kingdom is regarded as one of the relevant jurisdictions for analysis: its doctrine of parliamentary sovereignty is widely thought to make both rule of law and separation of powers subservient to the wishes of a majority of elected legislators (or even, in practice, the executive government that wields the majority party whip in the House of Commons) (Allan 2001:13).[1]

Since most follow the Westminster system of government, it is little wonder that the institution of separated powers is underdeveloped, underutilised and even non-functional in many Pacific jurisdictions. When this institution is either ineffective or not functioning at all, it usually results in an ineffective system of checks and balances—a related tenet of constitutionalism.

It could be argued that the cumulative result of the interplay of these factors is the exaltation of Pacific executive governments—the modern manifestation of the English sovereign parliament and the self-fulfilling prophecy of Westminster's craving for a strong executive government. This exaltation of executive power seems to be the most demanding problem in Pacific jurisdictions that have inherited the Westminster model—the 'exaltation of executive power'[2] (Powles 1978); an 'unrestrained cabinet government [that] is the distinguishing mark of the Westminster system' (Mulgan 1995:268). The problem, in other words, is the creation of an 'executive paradise' (Palmer and Palmer 1997:10), a political heaven where members of the executive assume that they can do anything, unencumbered by constitutional limits and controls. Consequently, many modern executive governments have become 'elective dictatorships', an 'unaccountable and self-serving political élite' (Mulgan 1995:265, 269). Increasingly, the executive is seen as the political god of an élitist politics in which the same parliament empowers an executive with practically unfettered power. So much so that in the Pacific we can no longer legitimately speak of Pacific island paradises but of Pacific executive paradises. The problem, in short, is the privatisation of many Pacific states—captured, owned and exploited by an élite few.

The rule of law and parliamentary sovereignty

The issue is the romantic affair between Pacific jurisdictions and the Westminster doctrine of parliamentary sovereignty. This is evident in different ways. One is the judiciary's refusal to interfere in parliament's internal proceedings. I refer, for instance, to the Nauru Supreme Court case of *Harris* v *Adeang* [1998] NRSC 1; Civil Action No. 13 of 1997 (27 February 1998). The case related to a meeting of the parliament of Nauru on 12 June 1997, which the plaintiffs argued was held without the necessary quorum required by article 45 of the *Constitution of the Republic of Nauru 1968*. Pleading contravention of article 45, the plaintiffs sought from the court a declaration that the business transacted in parliament on the day in question was *ultra vires* and therefore null and void. The issue for the court was whether it had jurisdiction under the Constitution to inquire into parliament's internal proceedings and, in the event of a finding of parliament's non-compliance with article 45, could the court by order nullify the bills enacted on the day in question and which had been subsequently certified as law.

On the facts, Donne CJ held that it had no jurisdiction to do so, noting at 10, 'it has been emphasised in many cases that Parliament is "the highest Court in the land"', with the privilege to settle its internal disputes without judicial interference. According to Donne CJ at 2, the Nauru parliament inherited this common law privilege through its Constitution, which adopted 'the Westminster model, [and] also conferred on the legislature the power to declare its own privileges and immunities' by legislation, for example, section 21 of the *Parliamentary Privileges, Powers and Immunities Act 1986*. On that statutory basis, Donne CJ concluded at 4 that the 'common law privilege of non-impeachment was thereby inherited as a privilege of Nauru's parliament—there is nothing in the Constitution with which it is inconsistent'. And this, I need note, was permitted, despite the Nauru Constitution's authority as supreme law. Granted, non-impeachment was permitted, 'except any of such powers, privileges or immunities as are inconsistent with or repugnant to the Constitution or the express provisions of this act'. On Donne CJ's reading, however, the principle of non-impeachment in the context of Nauru's constitutional system would seem to be absolute.

The Tonga Privy Council Court of Appeal in *Sanft* v *Fotofili* [1987] TOPC 1; [1988] LRC (Const 110 (3 August 1987)) affirmed the principle of non-impeachment. The case related to irregular parliamentary procedures that, the appellants argued, rendered the *Bank of Tonga (Amendment) Act 1986* unlawful. Disavowing judicial interference in parliament's internal proceedings, the court declined to grant a declaration of *ultra vires* and said at 5, 'we are in the realm of "internal proceedings" of the house, and the court does not venture there'.

Likewise, the Court of Appeal of Samoa in *Sua Rimoni D. Ah Chong* v *The Legislative Assembly of Samoa & Others* [1996] CA 2/96 affirmed what the court at 13 described as 'the principle of non-intervention' in parliament's internal procedures, that

> the respective constitutional roles of the courts and parliament normally require the courts to refrain from intervening in parliamentary proceedings. Conflicts between the judicial and legislative organs of the state are to be avoided as far as possible.

The cases cited above reflect a broad approach by the Pacific courts.[3] However, while the privilege of non-impeachment or non-intervention might be a settled common law principle, it leaves open a number of issues. The viability of the promulgated distinction between judicial examination of acts of parliament and judicial non-interference in parliament's internal procedures is an issue. How viable is the distinction between what goes on in parliament and what comes out of it? If parliament can change the procedures whenever it suits the wishes of the majority in parliament, how secure, just, fair and reliable could the lawmaking process be? If what goes on within the walls of parliament is 'protected by the shield of parliamentary immunity' as the Court of Appeal in *Sua Rimoni* v *The Legislative Assembly of Samoa* observed at 16, the issue is that this shield could easily be turned into a parliamentary sword. And if non-compliance with procedure is acceptable, as some of these cases seem to suggest (for example, as Donne CJ in *Harris* at 7–8 put it, there 'is no enforceable duty owed by the parliament or its members to act constitutionally…The legislature cannot be restrained from passing an unconstitutional act'), the security and fairness of the lawmaking process comes into question.

The second issue concerns the doctrine of *stare decisis* which, as a critical mechanism of legal reasoning, requires the courts to follow precedents on the ground that this produces not only correct results but certainty, stability and continuity in the legal system. As we all know, some precedents are followed, others either distinguished or simply set aside. This raises a plethora of questions, for example, why do the courts follow some precedents and ignore others? In *Harris* v *Adeang,* Donne CJ followed the minority opinion of Casey J against the majority of the Court of Appeal in *Edward Huniehu* v *Attorney-General and the Speaker of the National Parliament of the Solomon Islands* (24 April 1997), who held that the court had jurisdiction to impugn and declare unconstitutional the failure of the Speaker of the Solomon Islands' parliament to adjourn the proceedings of the assembly when there was no quorum, as required by section 67 of the Solomon Islands Constitution.

In support of the proposition that the courts have no jurisdiction to review parliament's internal proceedings, Donne CJ cited quite extensively from the judgment of the Full Bench of the High Court of Australia in *Cormack* v *Cope* (1974) 131 CLR 432. The issue, in my view, is the accentuation of those parts of the Australian High Court's judgment that support the proposition to the detriment of those parts which either dilute or even undermine the proposition. An example is the following statement by Barwick CJ: 'it is not the case in Australia, as it is in the United Kingdom, that the judiciary will restrain itself from interference in any part of the lawmaking process of the parliament'. Qualifying that broad principle, Barwick CJ added the concession that the court would not interfere with parliament's internal proceedings. That qualification, however, was then framed within the latter part of the broad principle, that is, 'there is no parliamentary privilege which can stand in the way of this court's right and duty to ensure that the constitutionally provided methods of lawmaking are observed'. If my reading of Barwick CJ's statement is correct, it means that the privilege of non-impeachment is secondary, not primary, and that the court reserves the right to intervene where and when appropriate. There is no blanket preclusion of the court's jurisdiction to review parliament's internal proceedings. Interestingly enough, the Supreme Court of Victoria in *McDonald* v *Cain* (1953) V.L.R. 411 ruled that it had jurisdiction to declare that it was contrary to law to present a bill for assent if it had not been passed by the required majority under the Victorian Constitution as Menzies J noted (and then distinguished) in *Cormack* v *Cope* at 465.

This raises the issue of the courts' use of precedents to construct an 'idealised model of the legal process' (Kairys 1982:11). In *Harris* v *Adeang*, the court had a choice of precedents, some in point or *in toto*, others related by analogy; some binding, others merely persuasive. The fact that the court had a choice and did in fact make that choice is important in the respect that the court could logically decide the issue by adopting one possible interpretation and ignoring viable alternatives. This highlights the point that sometimes *stare decisis* is such an open-ended doctrine that one can do almost anything with it. But then again the doctrine is necessary to create a picture of judges simply declaring and applying the law, faithfully following precedents and thereby restricting their domain to law. Of interest is the extent to which this picture is a fairytale no longer tenable in the modern world (Reid 1992). Nor do we need to go along with the full panoply of the critical legal studies genre to support the view that sometimes the law can be 'radically indeterminate, incoherent, and contradictory' (Kress 1989:283). In the final analysis, despite its usefulness, the doctrine of *stare decisis* is certainly not perfect. As Thomas J (1993:15) has argued, it makes the law 'introspective and backward-looking', and that the judiciary should be free from 'the shackles of the doctrine of precedent'. Perhaps the courts should adopt an approach based more on substantive principles than syllogistic reasoning.

The combined effect of these issues is a parliament, following the Westminster system, that is ultimately sovereign (arguably within its own walls) in the face of a written constitution as supreme law. 'The sovereignty of Parliament is reinforced in the Constitution': *In re Article 36 of the Constitution and in re Bobby Eoe* (1988) 3 SPLR 225 at 228. The Pacific courts, deferring to settled common law practice or following precedents either treat internal parliamentary proceedings as, according to Donne CJ in *Harris* v *Adeang* at 8, 'sacrosanct and as such cannot be impeached,' or, otherwise intervene, as Gibbs J in *Cormack* v *Cope* counselled at 467, 'after the completion of the lawmaking process'. Such an approach, in my view, is tantamount to waiting for the concentration camps to stir the courts out of their acquiescence in the holy powers, privileges and immunities of Westminster parliaments.

The issue of the proper limits of parliament's lawmaking power arose in the Vanuatu Supreme Court case of *In re the Constitution, Timakata* v *Attorney-General* [1992] VUSC 9; [1980–94] VLR 691 (1 November 1992). The issue was the President of Vanuatu's constitutional power under article 16(4) to refer bills presented for his assent (in keeping with constitutional convention) to the Supreme Court for its opinion on whether a particular bill is inconsistent with the Constitution.[4] The case revolved around the Business Licence (Amendment) Bill 1992, which, according to the president, 'purports to give the minister wide and far ranging powers to grant or revoke a business licence and at the same time seeks to prevent any challenge of such grant or revocation in any court'.

On the facts, Charles Vaudin d'Imecourt CJ held at 31 that section 8A(2) of that Bill was inconsistent with article 5(1)(d) of the Constitution, which guarantees equal protection under the law, and was therefore unconstitutional. Central to the court's decision was the ousting of the court's jurisdiction by section 8A(2). While noting Vanuatu's adherence to the Westminster common law tradition, that 'the Constitution of Vanuatu is a constitution on the Westminster model', d'Imercourt noted at 8 that 'unlike the English court' the powers of Vanuatu's Supreme Court are also derived from the provisions of Vanuatu's written Constitution—for example, article 2 on the Constitution as supreme law and article 16(4), which vests power in the Supreme Court to review bills referred to it by the president (as in this case). The latter clause, in fact, mandates that a 'bill shall not be promulgated if the Supreme Court considers it inconsistent with a provision of the constitution'. Whether or not a bill that has already been passed by parliament but has not received the royal assent is part of parliament's internal proceedings is a moot point. What seems certain from this case is that the court had taken the initiative in curbing the lawmaking power of parliament. As d'Imecourt observed at 15, '[a]s far as I know, no other jurisdiction within the common law system is called upon to interpret the constitutionality of a bill as opposed to that of an act. Might this be the "French influence" within the Constitution of Vanuatu?'[5]

In theory, Pacific parliaments have limited lawmaking powers *vis-à-vis* entrenched constitutions as supreme law. In practice, there are problems, especially the unique authority wielded by bare majorities in Pacific parliaments. The issue is parliaments with lawmaking powers limited in theory but unlimited in practice. Making fundamental changes to the law shows how easy it is for Westminster parliaments to repeal old laws, enact new ones, and even change a nation's fundamental law with relative ease. As long as the changes are made in accordance with legal procedures for constitutional amendments, they are legally valid and legitimate. This makes the rule of law less than secure, manifested in the uneasy relation between the rule of law and the doctrine of parliamentary sovereignty as twin features of Westminster.

Under the doctrine of parliamentary sovereignty, parliament 'has supreme lawmaking powers' (Palmer 1987:219) and 'the lawmaker is supreme' (Kelsey 1993:192). According to the Diceyan doctrine, parliament has the authority and right to make or unmake any law and English law does not recognise the authority or right of any person or body to override or set aside parliamentary legislation (Dicey 1959). Paraphrasing Dicey, Geoffrey Walker (1995:190) states, '[a]ccording to Professor Dicey's theory of sovereignty, parliament had absolute power...Parliament...to use Leslie Stephen's example [could even] command that all blue-eyed babies be killed'. But if parliament can change existing laws and enact new ones, however oppressive those laws might be, then 'the rule of law is nothing more than a bad joke' (Walker 1995:192). A bad joke indeed if a government with a parliamentary majority can initiate the most fundamental changes in the law, unhindered and unfettered. Most certainly a bad joke when those who wield the powers of government under the rubric of parliamentary sovereignty enact laws that deprive people of their citizenship, violate citizens' rights and liberties, allow racial discrimination,[7] political injustice, and economic deprivation.

The situation is not aided by a judiciary that is conservative in approach and is unlikely to exercise its inherent review jurisdiction to limit legislative and executive actions. At best, we find judicial pronouncements of caution. Thus, Donne CJ in *Harris v Adeang* at 8 offered a timid reminder that privilege 'does not mean that Parliament is able, with impunity, to act unlawfully'. Being no more than an *obiter dictum*, the reminder was nothing more than conservative. Much more forceful was Lord Cooke's statement of possibility in *Sua Rimoni v The Legislative Assembly of Samoa* at 14, that there are possible limitations on the principle of non-intervention, for example, 'a written constitution such as that of Western Samoa [which] may place upon the courts some duty of scrutinising parliamentary proceedings for alleged breaches of constitutional requirements'. Unfortunately, having toyed with the possibility, the court then withdrew behind the doctrine of separation of powers and refused to question what actually went on within the walls of parliament out of deference to the principle of non-intervention.

This raises important jurisprudential and constitutional law issues. As noted in chapter one, relying on procedural justice alone is perhaps not sufficient protection against tyranny. The propriety of the legal positivist conception of law is always an issue: the Westminster, and the Pacific's adopted, sovereign lawmaker is not an angel without self-interest, prejudice, or malice. Regarding parliamentary sovereignty, perhaps, analysis of this doctrine needs to focus more on 'its wisdom [instead of] on points of law' (Fuller 1969:115). Further, Pacific courts need to be more proactive. Sometimes their approach is nothing more than cosmetic surgery of the Westminster sovereign parliament—taking the Diceyan substance and dressing it in a different form. These matters necessitate reconstituting Dicey's sovereign parliament. I will return to this issue below.

The institution of separation of powers

The following statement by Wilson J in the Samoa Supreme Court case of *The Honorable Tuiatua Tupua Tamases Efi v The Attorney General of Samoa* (1 August 2000) at 51–2 is programmatic for this section and warrants quoting in full.

> This court acknowledges the separate, independent and powerful roles of the parliament and the executive, and this court has no wish or intention, even in the slightest way, to challenge the notion of the separation of powers which is at the heart of Samoa's system of constitutional democratic government. But what this court can do, as the watchdog of the constitution, is do its best to do its duty 'without fear or favour, affection or ill-will' in the hope that right and justice will be done (and be seen to have been done). If, in addition, there are some benefits for constitutional government in some way, then well and good.

This section focuses on the institution of separated powers as an essential dimension of the rule of law, that is, the rule of law requires the arrangement of the branches of government in such a way that the arbitrary use of government powers by any one branch of the state is firmly opposed and checked by the others. Separation of powers means that government powers are dispersed and divided among three branches: parliament, the executive and the judiciary. Parliament makes the law, the executive carries the law into effect, and the judiciary interprets and applies the law.[8]

A complete separation of powers, however, is impractical and incompatible with the realities of contemporary political systems. For pragmatic reasons, such as, administrative efficiency, only a partial separation of powers is possible. The dispersed powers must be integrated into a workable system of government to enable government to function and execute its legitimate roles. Thus, there is separation and also interdependence. The American Supreme Court rejected the notion of a complete separation of powers for this reason, dismissing it as an 'archaic view of the separation of powers requiring three airtight departments of government'.[9] Nevertheless, the doctrine in its original form may serve as 'an ideal-type' (Vile 1967:10) used to measure changes, limitations or exaggerations made to the basic structure of government.

This dispersion of powers is essential for a whole range of reasons. Underlining its significance regarding absolute power, Madison (1961:322)warns,

> [t]he accumulation of all powers, legislative, executive and judiciary, in the same hands whether of one, a few or many, and whether hereditary, self-appointed, or elective, may justly be pronounced the very definition of tyranny.

Separation of powers is the antithesis of totalitarianism; it is 'a vital check against tyranny'.[10] It guarantees not only limited government but stable government because power is not monopolised, thus preventing the decline into despotism. For citizens, separation of powers equates to the safeguarding of liberty; the absence of arbitrary rule. The idea behind separated powers also seeks to preserve basic democratic values—justice, fairness, equal protection under the law, and so on. Economically, people are most creative and productive when they are free to pursue economic goals and enterprises. Separation of powers enables economic freedom by obviating totalitarianism and state monopolisation of economic activities and the means of production. Finally, and of equal importance, separation of powers protects judicial independence, which is absolutely vital to the rule of law.

In all, separated powers guarantee the constitutional order against the risk of violation that is naturally inherent in every constituted body. Herein lies its significance. As M.J.C. Vile (1967:2) has pointed out,

[o]f the theories of government which have attempted to provide a solution to this dilemma, the doctrine of the separation of powers has, in modern times, been the most significant, both intellectually and in terms of its influence upon institutional structures.

Pacific states exhibit a broad adherence to this institutional division of government into three branches: legislative, executive and judicial. While there are distinctive features and variations, the three-fold institutional division is followed very closely.[11] This three-fold division is enshrined in written constitutions and strictly adhered to. Parliament makes the law;[12] the executive carries the law into effect;[13] and the judiciary interprets and applies the law. There is also a conscious commitment to keep the judiciary independent from the other branches of government through the special procedures for appointment, tenure, salaries, and removal of judges. So important is judicial independence for the Fiji Islands that section 118 of the Constitution Amendment Act 1997 of Fiji expressly provides that the 'judges of the State are independent of the legislative and executive branches of government'. Whether or not that promise of independence is realised in practice is another matter.

Judicial recognition of the institution of separated powers as a legal and constitutional principle also seems certain. For example, in *Kenilorea v Attorney General* [1984] SILR 179; [1986] LRC (Const) 126, the Court of Appeal of the Solomon Islands held that section 5(d) and (e) of the *Price Control (Retrospective Operation and Validation) Act 1983* was void on the ground that the enactment violated judicial independence, as guaranteed by the Constitution, and was therefore inconsistent with the provisions of the Constitution.[14] The issue concerned an Act of Parliament that effectively required the court to dismiss all proceedings that challenged action taken to enforce certain price orders which had been made unlawfully, but which had been validated by that legislation.

The Samoan Court of Appeal took a similar approach in the case of *Attorney General v Saipaia Olomalu & Others* [1980–93] WSLR 41. While holding that the dual voting system then operating in Samoa (the *matai* franchise and universal suffrage) did not contravene the provisions of the Constitution (especially article 15 on equality under the law) and was therefore not void, the court expressed doubt about the justification for excluding those who are not cultural chiefs (*matais*) from direct participation in the election. But, said the court, '[t]hese…are questions of social policy: questions which, on our interpretation of the Constitution, are to be decided by parliament, not by the courts'. With that, the court confined its role to interpreting and applying the law in keeping with the institution of separated powers, thus leaving the political arms of government to their own devices.

This highlights a gnawing problem in Pacific jurisdictions—the institution of separated powers is static and is therefore underdeveloped, underutilised and even non-functional. The Pacific's association with the Westminster system allows only a partial separation of powers, wherein an independent judiciary, oppositional politics, coalition governments and other institutions, such as chief auditors and ombudsmen, are supposed to prevent the accumulation and misuse of power. More often than not, however, the emphasis is on cooperation and coordination among the three branches of government, thus neglecting the need for institutional scrutiny. The result in many cases is, perhaps, an unintentional concentration of government powers in one organ of the state, usually the executive. The danger in this is the exaltation of the executive, the vesting of wide discretionary powers in government officials, enlarging executive power, which then becomes a potential threat to the rule of law. Such a threat is exacerbated by 'the grant to official agencies of substantial powers to act for very broadly defined public purposes, subject to limited judicial control' (Allan 2001:16). Arbitrariness thus remains 'the distinguishing feature' of executive action; the operation of the executive 'carries an intrinsic danger of arbitrary treatment…Discretionary executive action in the interest of the public good as a whole must, then, be accepted as a necessary evil' (Allan 2001:14).

This evil is manifested in more ways than one. The more power one acquires, the more likely it is that one will abuse that power. Human nature remains humankind's own worst enemy. The issue of corruption in the Pacific could be explained, at least in part, along these lines. The effect of an exalted executive on the lawmaking process is equally adverse. The executive, given its domination of parliament, has the numerical power to even enact acts of attainder, *ad hominem* statutes, and *ex post facto* laws. In some cases, the executive deliberately extends its orbit and increases its reach through a wide range of special tribunals with quasi-judicial powers but which are ultimately subservient to the executive and are no more than vehicles of the executive will. And if oppositional politics is dysfunctional, if coalition government is nothing more than just a way of capturing executive power,[15] and if other checks and balances are not really effective, then curbing the increasing power of an exalted executive becomes an extremely difficult task.

Given the inherent dangers of executive power, it is therefore absolutely essential to subject the executive to 'the supervision of independent courts, bound to act on grounds of the general principles of common law, or constitutional law, that supplement the general rules laid down in legislation' (Allan 2001:15). Such legislation must stipulate the limits and the general purposes for which a grant of power is made. The judiciary, through its construction of the law, must ensure that executive action comes within the ambit of legislation and that it is consistent with constitutional principles. Going beyond those stipulated limits and purposes must attract judicial censure by way of judicial review of executive action and, in appropriate cases, a declaration of *ultra vires*.

Judicial control of the executive, nevertheless, is only possible if the judiciary is truly independent from the executive and also from parliament. This is essential if the courts are to be able to properly fulfil their role 'as servants of the constitutional order as a whole rather than merely as instruments of a majority of elected members of the legislative assembly' (Allan 2001:3). Taken in its totality, the control of the executive by the judiciary is vital to legitimate governance, to ensure that the use of public power by the executive is in keeping with 'a scheme of justice' (Allan 2001:32) wherein all citizens are treated equally, accorded moral dignity, and their rights and liberties protected. While it is conceded that executive actions can be carried out to attain public objectives, such actions must always be subjected to strict judicial scrutiny to ensure that the executive operates within the constraints of a community's 'scheme of justice' as democratically negotiated and publicly avowed.

The argument for a powerful executive has been made thus: a strong executive government is an essential component of a strong state; national development pivots on it; further, administrative efficiency justifies concentrating public power in the executive. Granted, the argument for a strong executive government has some credence; but it must be said that strong government does not necessarily equate to the rule of a minority with absolute power. The pressing challenge therefore is reining in the executive. This raises the issue: how effective are the legislature and the judiciary as checks on executive power?

Given the domination of parliament by a majority party, legislatures in many Pacific jurisdictions are being forced to acquiesce in this executive fiasco. Furthermore, in the name of strong government, legislatures cannot but favour executive decisions in order to facilitate the attainment of government goals. Yet, there is always the danger that the legislature and the executive are meshing into an undifferentiated super-executive body, 'an organised majority committed to a coherent plan of action' (Hayek 1979:23). The danger is that, when the legislature becomes the executive, there is no longer any separation of powers, which could have serious ramifications. The prospect of legislative control of the executive is therefore very slim, placing an onerous burden on the judiciary. That the judiciary itself could lose or sell its independence and become nothing more than an instrument of political power with which to grant legal legitimacy to executive interests is equally dangerous.

The theory of checks and balances

Related to, but not synonymous with, the institution of separation of powers is the system of checks and balances. The checks and balances theory holds that one branch of government should be able 'to prevent abuse of governmental process by another' (Harris 1985:50).[16] The pertinent principle here is that the stability of government and the successful achievement of its objectives 'are best accomplished by a delicate equipoise between equal powers, by mutual jealousies' (Pargellis 1968:47). This institutional checking amongst the organs of government seeks to protect the state against the arbitrary use of government powers by any one organ, or even by a public official or group of officials with sufficient influence to hold the state to ransom. However, the practical application of the theory could be problematic in jurisdictions with parliamentary executives where cabinet ministers are members of both the executive and parliament, as in most Pacific nations. The danger of power being concentrated in a few with a dominating influence in both parliament and the executive is real and immediate. Given that, it is imperative that effective checks and balances be set in place to curb possible abuses of power.

On balance, Pacific states have reasonable systems of checks and balances embodied in written constitutions and set up by statutes. The problem is that in most Pacific nations checks and balances have been dramatically eroded and are in danger of being dysfunctional. I refer, for instance, to the controller and chief auditor as a cornerstone of Samoa's system of checks and balances, a parliamentary watchdog acting as 'an important check against financial corruption and inefficiency' (Palmer 1987:18) in government. Established under Articles 97–99 of the Constitution and the *Audit Office Ordinance 1961*, the chief auditor, pursuant to a repealed clause (3), was to hold office 'until he reaches the age of sixty years', with the proviso that parliament could extend his term of office by resolution. The objective was to protect the independence of the chief auditor by security of tenure. His removal from office by a resolution of parliament carried by a two-thirds majority under a repealed clause (4) was likewise designed to place him under the jurisdiction of parliament. The prohibition under article 98 (still in force) against diminishing his salary during his time in office (unless such reduction is part of a general reduction of salaries) is also designed to secure his independence by placing him under the protective mantle of parliament. In the performance of his duties under article 99 he must 'feel completely free' (Constitutional Convention of Western Samoa 1960:Vol II, 667) to undertake his reporting role to parliament, drawing attention to any irregularities 'regardless of where they have occurred and of how unpopular he may become in some circles' (Constitutional Convention of Western Samoa 1960:Vol II, 667) for doing so is his 'duty, and his right, to inform the legislative assembly as soon as possible of these irregularities and not wait until the time arrives for his annual report' (Constitutional Convention of Western Samoa 1960:Vol II, 667).[17]

These constitutional provisions collectively make the chief auditor parliament's watchdog, overseeing the use of public funds and property, and promptly reporting—without fear of repercussions—on any irregularities wherever they may occur. In undertaking this constitutional role in an independent and impartial manner, the chief auditor constitutes a check against executive actions. Lord Cooke in *Sua Rimoni* v *The Legislative Assembly of Western Samoa* affirmed at 16, '[c]ertainly the intention of the constitution is that the chief auditor shall be independent and able to investigate and report freely within his proper sphere'.

The issue is, how effective could the present chief auditor, under the firm control of the executive, be as a parliamentary watchdog? The independence and effectiveness of Samoa's chief auditor is now an issue. The Constitution Amendment Act 1997 stipulates 'new conditions' for the chief auditor under a new article 97. Clause 2 of the new article stipulates a term of three years (though he may be reappointed) and is in marked contrast to the chief auditor's security of tenure under clause 3 of the repealed article 97, vital to the independence of the chief auditor. As Lord Cooke in *Sua Rimoni v The Legislative Assembly of Western Samoa* put it at 2, 'in the interest of the people of Western Samoa he [the chief auditor] is given security of tenure'. Nor is the chief auditor aided by clause 5 of the new article which provides for his suspension or removal from office by the Head of State on the advice of the prime minister, who is required by clause 6 to provide parliament with 'a full statement of the grounds' for his suspension or removal. Again, this procedure is in marked contrast to clause 4 of the repealed article 97 on the removal of the chief auditor on 'like grounds' and in 'like manner as a judge of the Supreme Court' (stated misbehaviour, or infirmity of body or mind) by the Head of State on an address by parliament carried by not less than two-thirds of the house requesting the chief auditor's removal on the aforementioned grounds. It may not be true anymore that, as Lord Cooke in *Sua Rimoni v The Legislative Assembly of Western Samoa* at 3 emphasised, 'in the performance of his [the chief auditor's] lawful functions he is not subject to any control by the government'. In theory, the chief auditor is parliament's watchdog; but a neutralised watchdog neither barks nor bites, and it is not surprising that no complaint is issued by the executive when the watchdog is silent.

The Constitution of Samoa embodies other equally important checks and balances which, if observed and properly utilised, could afford adequate protection against arbitrary power. Article 32(1) requires the executive to be collectively responsible to parliament.[18] The convention of collective ministerial responsibility means *inter alia* that parliament has power to pass a vote of no confidence in the executive's administration of government. Article 33(3)(b) provides for individual ministerial responsibility whereby cabinet ministers are held responsible not only for their own actions but for those of public officials in his department.[19] Such responsibility is predicated on the notion of employees as the minister's agents: 'everything they do, they do in his name. In the eyes of the law, the permanent official is an anonymous instrument of the minister' (Palmer 1987:47). The problem is that this convention is not legally enforceable and, as a consequence, could be casually ignored.[20]

The three interrelated aspects of ministerial responsibility—unanimity, confidence and confidentiality—also have the potential to produce 'strong executive control over parliament' (Palmer 1987:69). Unanimity, as 'the quintessential ingredient of the adversary system of politics generated by the Westminster system' (Palmer and Palmer 1997:70), can mask any disunity in cabinet from public scrutiny. Similarly, while unanimity can be used to inspire public confidence, it can also be used to obscure details and foster a culture of ignorance about government dealings. This is consolidated by the requirement for confidentiality in cabinet matters—the no-leaks rule. Ministerial responsibility, given its imperfections, cannot be seriously seen as a magic formula for executive accountability.

The ombudsman, established by the *Komesina o Sulufaiga (Ombudsman) Act 1988*, is appointed for a term of three years by the Head of State on the recommendation of parliament.[21] The placement of the ombudsman under the jurisdiction of parliament means that he is parliament's officer; the ombudsman owes 'no allegiance to the executive government, whose activities [he is] primarily involved in investigating' (Palmer and Palmer 1997:224); the ombudsman is 'a check on the power of the executive' (Palmer and Palmer 1997:224). Vested with wide discretionary powers of investigation, the ombudsman has jurisdiction to investigate acts or omissions by government departments and public officials. If the course of action recommended by the ombudsman is not heeded by the body or person under review, he has discretion under section 19 to report the matter to the prime minister or, as a final resort, parliament. The importance of this office is predicated on 'the right of every member of the public who is aggrieved by an act or decision of a government body…to have that grievance investigated by an ombudsman' (Kelsey 1993:175). It must be noted, however, that at present the ombudsman is only a statutory officer. It is unlikely that parliament will repeal this office in the future. But should parliament decide to do so, it needs only a simple majority to do that. Further to that, the ombudsman has no power of prosecution; he can only investigate, report and recommend. Whether or not that makes for an effective watchdog is a matter of opinion. My concern is that a watchdog with no teeth may find it convenient to consort with wolves and, in concert, slaughter the sheep he is supposed to guard.

General elections remain the major check on the abuse of government power, constituting the 'most important barometer of public opinion' (Palmer and Palmer 1997:14). But if elections are less than honest, the use of public opinion as a constitutional check is hardly of any value, being nothing more than 'a blunt instrument' (Government of New Zealand 1985:27). In some Pacific contexts, political indifference prevails. This involves viewing politics as a game of the less-than-mediocre, a profession unworthy of the idealist intellectual or the principled moralist. The effect is that politics has become the arena of self-seeking politicians who are left unchecked to exploit public office for private gain.

Going beyond constitutional and statutory checks and balances, the media, 'the fourth estate of government' (Palmer and Palmer 1997:16), and civil society organisations like non-government organisations, churches, civil liberties societies and so on have an equally important influence. The effectiveness of these civil society organisations as checks and balances ought to be gauged against their ability to foment positive change. The problem in the Pacific is that the media and civil society organisations are mute and therefore ineffective as checks and balances against the misuse of public power.

Further, facets of the international community—international bodies and organisations—have a vested interest in encouraging honest and peaceful political and economic change around the world without resorting to military power. But, by the same token, international bodies and organisations are too preoccupied with their own politico-economic agendas and bureaucracy. Where and when they do intervene in Pacific affairs, their interests are usually skewed in favour of achieving their own pre-determined objectives.

The issues canvassed above finally amount to the question: what sort of integrity do the systems of checks and balances actually have in Pacific jurisdictions? It has been demonstrated that they have been eroded to such an extent that a radical physical rebuilding is needed.

The reification of Pacific states

Taken to its logical conclusion, the exaltation of Pacific executive government ultimately manifests itself in the privatisation of the peoples' states—captured, owned and exploited by an élite few. Another cause behind the increasing privatisation of Pacific states is the complex interplay of cultural exaggerations, religious or theological engineering, historical miscalculations, philosophical blunders and misleading ideologies that are part of the Pacific mythmaking. These traditions are tenaciously transmitted through the communities, dogmatically perpetuated and jealously promoted for different reasons, resulting in the concentration of state powers either in one person or an élite few.

A clear example of the deification of leaders and their rule is the Kingdom of Tonga. Clause 41 of the *Constitution of Tonga 1875* sanctifies the person of the King ('the person of the King is sacred') and, by logical extension, his rule. Thus, Tonga has a sovereign King exercising divine rule in the manner of the Stuart Kings. This may be explained on a number of grounds. The Constitution of Tonga was drafted by a Reverend S.W. Baker (a Wesleyan missionary from England) at the request of King Tupou I. The resulting theological colouring of the Constitution is therefore not surprising. Furthermore, the move to formally deify the King suggests that the *volksgeist*, or 'spirit of the community', was conflated with state interests and embodied in the King. From the perspective of constitutionalism, the gnawing issue is the alarming extent of the King's power under the Constitution.

I refer also to the exaltation and reification of the State of Samoa (together with those who wield the powers of the state). There is something nationally sanctifying in viewing the state itself as something divine, an eternally ordained metaphysical reality. Central to that conception is Samoa's national motto, '*E fa'avae i le Atua Samoa*' (Samoa is founded or based on God), which, for most people, is an article of democratic faith. In the popular mindset, the state is, if anything, the unfolding of divine purpose on earth; the state exists by divine decree.

This concept of the state is perpetuated to serve different interests; for example, to legitimise state rule and justify the submission of the citizens to that rule. For ordinary Samoans, by contrast, the national motto is a valid truth espoused in good faith. Accepted *en masse* as a fundamental tenet of Samoa's jurisprudence, the motto constitutes the real (though *de facto*) 'constitution' of Samoa; it is more important than the national Constitution of 1960. Unfortunately—and this is pertinent to present purposes—this national declaration of democratic faith takes the state out of its earthly, existential moorings, away from the people, and converts it into a supra-mundane entity imposed from above. The question here is not the people's freedom of belief. The issue, rather, is that exalting, reifying or even deifying the state has serious ramifications.

A reified/deified state (wherever it may be) purportedly imposed from above is, by definition, not a mortal creation of, by, from and for the people. This is a frontal attack on basic constitutional principles: the people as creators, beneficiaries and owners of the state; the state as a servant of the people; and the sovereignty of the people as a legal and constitutional principle. Reified and deified, the state becomes a government of angels, needing no external or internal controls. Furthermore, in this schema, there is no need for the consent or the continuing concurrence of the governed as the proper basis of government. This is because (according to the deification rationale of power) the state first came into being by divine authorisation, it rules by divine right, and its authority is sacrosanct. When this happens, the democratic state is not really different from the totalitarian German state which Friedrich Hegel 'praise[d] as a god, and Marx curse[d] as a devil' (Kelsen 2000:172). The corollary of reifying/deifying the state is that citizens are reduced to cogs in a political machine; individual rights and liberties are not important, state interests take priority. A deified and therefore all-powerful state, an expression of 'the divine will' (Hegel 1952:85) with 'absolute authority' (Hegel 1952:81), is the polar opposite of a constitutional democracy with limited powers.

It is also arguable that Pacific misconceptions of the state are partly a debt bequeathed by colonialism. The fact that all Pacific countries were former colonies is critical here. It is not inconceivable that the peoples' colonial experience included viewing the state (whether under or from the colonial powers) as something imposed on them. This experience of something imposed from above—that is, according to the precepts of the time and space world of colonialism—is underscored by legitimating ideologies. An example of this is the idea that new forms of political organisation are superior to traditional forms; this idea spawned the mindset that the state does not really belong to the people and is beyond their influence or authority to control. The concomitant of such an estranged mindset—and the self-imposed alienation of the people it has engendered—is the exalted status of the state, above the people and beyond the normal run of things.

From a philosophical perspective, it may be argued that state reification/deification is reminiscent of the Hegelian conception of the state as a kind of spiritual entity—an omnipotent, all-embracing, all-powerful institution, 'an absolute end in itself' (Hegel 1952:80), deified as the 'march of God in the world [or even more aggressively as] this actual God' (Hegel 1952:141). This political god has 'supreme right against the individual, whose supreme duty is to be a member of the state' (Hegel 1952:80), wherein the citizen finds 'objectivity, genuine individuality, and an ethical life' (Hegel 1952:80). Taken to its logical conclusion, the deified state, undergirded by the doctrines of the power state and the Nietzschean 'will to power', is defined by power and is justified in increasing power. It is arrogant, cruel and brutish, as history has shown. It stands above civil society and deals with its own citizens in a condescending manner, as cogs, mere parts of a grand political machine (Lloyd 1915:630). Ultimately, the state becomes the embodied will to power.

Hegel was not a Samoan, nor did he ever set foot in Samoa. But his countryman, Governor Solf, spent significant time in Samoa. According to the records (Davidson 1967), Solf not only went out of his way to exalt himself as the paramount King of Samoa, he also exercised autocratic rule over the Samoan people. Not surprisingly, German rule in Samoa alienated the Samoan people in their own land. The people's experience of what government is could not therefore be described as gratifying or rewarding, and Solf's own condescending paternalistic attitude pushed the government over and beyond the people's influence and reach. The government, in other words, became an entity other than the people—an exalted, deified entity, something akin to Hegel's 'actual God'.

Misconceptions of what a state is (such as the above) are being reinforced and perpetuated by a Pacific postcolonial national bourgeoisie, an emerging *de facto* kind of ruling, upper/middle class (Ray 2003). This unorganised bourgeoisie speedily filled up the political vacuum left by the departed colonists, and they continue to advance colonialist ideologies. Central to such ideologies is the misconception of the state as the rule of an élite few and the assumption that people need strict rule because they are not enlightened enough to know how to rule themselves.

Most, if not all, Pacific governments must honestly face this alienation of the masses within their own states. From the standpoint of constitutionalism, constitutional democracy has degenerated into an oligarchy wherein power is monopolised by a few; constitutionalism has surrendered to totalitarianism. Embodied in the élite few who wield its power, the state is no longer an abstraction but an incarnate political monster feeding on the people over whom it has absolute power. Not surprisingly, the question 'who owns the state?' is forcing itself into public discourse and interest.

Reviving the rule of law: reconstitution, reconstruction and resurrection

To counter the danger of arbitrary rule by mortally-constructed states that are always seeking to exalt themselves over and above their mortal creators, we need to return to basic principles of government. And to reverse the theft of whole nations by an élite few, we need stronger basic institutions and principles that curb power aggrandisement.

Reconstituting Dicey's sovereign parliament

The detrimental effects of Dicey's notion of parliamentary sovereignty on the rule of law and the institution of separated powers necessitates a reconstitution of this doctrine. One way of resolving this doctrinal hiccup is to provide an alternative reading of parliamentary sovereignty, taking into consideration the sovereignty of parliament and the corresponding sovereignty of the judiciary as twin features with equal status in England's system of government. Lord Bridge of Harwich in *X Ltd* v *Morgan-Grampian (Publishers) Ltd* [1991] 1 AC 1 at 48 succinctly underlined this point in the following terms,

> In our society the rule of law rests upon twin foundations: the sovereignty of the Queen in parliament in making the law and the sovereignty of the Queen's courts in interpreting and applying the law.

In the light of Lord Harwich's pronouncement, Allan (2001:13) insists 'on a more plausible reading of Dicey' (also Goldsworthy 1999)[22] that takes into equal consideration Dicey's sovereign parliament and supreme rule of law as possessing equal status. One does not subjugate the other or render the other superfluous; most certainly, the rule of law is not rendered insignificant or impotent in comparison to parliamentary power.

It is possible that Dicey himself was aware of government coercion and the need to keep it to a minimum—that 'trust in a democratic parliament alone was a recipe for political disorder' (Mason 1995:118). It could be argued that Dicey accordingly sought to bolster the authority of the common law courts through his conception of the supreme rule of law. The principle that a person can be punished or lawfully made to suffer in body or goods only for a distinct breach of the law excludes punishment merely for disagreeing with the legislator. This is fortified by the principles that the rule of law excludes wide and arbitrary powers of constraint and that government powers conferred or sanctioned by statute are never really unlimited, for they are confined by the words of the statute itself and by the interpretation put upon the statute by the courts. In positing the law as a bridle on arbitrary power, Dicey thus accorded the courts the special role of protector of the rule of law. Through the interpretation of statutes and the construction of common law principles, the courts could thereby impose control on the power of the legislature. On balance, therefore, the sovereign parliament of the Westminster system is ultimately limited by law, and the Westminster judiciary is not at all powerless before an omnipotent legislature.

The alternative reconstitution of Dicey's sovereign parliament is through the more radical position advocated by Sir Edward Coke and, to some extent, Lord Cooke of Thorndon (former president of Samoa's Court of Appeal). I refer, for instance, to Sir Coke's 'judicial adventure' (Hodge 1995:97) and his 'most celebrated dictum' (Caldwell 1984:358) relating to *Dr Bonham's case* (1610) 8 Co Rep 114 at 118 which, perhaps, aptly expresses the power of the common law.

> And it appears in our books that in many cases, the common law will control acts of parliament, and sometimes adjudge them to be utterly void; for when an act of parliament is against common right and reason, or repugnant, or impossible to be performed, the common law will control it and adjudge such act to be void.[23]

In the Pacific, we find the *obiter dicta* of Lord Cooke (in a number of New Zealand cases) described as lying squarely 'in the tradition of and remarkably so of *Dr Bonham's case* and common right and reason' (Hodge 1995:109) as enunciated by Sir Coke. In *L v M* [1979] 2 NZLR 519, Lord Cooke at 527 noted '[t]hat there is even room for doubt whether it is self-evident that Parliament could constitutionally' confer on a public body (in this case, the Accident Compensation Commission) other than the courts, jurisdiction to decide whether or not a court action is barred. In *Brader v Ministry of Transport* [1981] 1 NZLR 73, Lord Cooke at 78 questioned the authority of Parliament to abandon the 'entire field of the economy to the executive'. In *Taylor v New Zealand Poultry Board* [1984] 1 NZLR 394, Lord Cooke at 398 affirmed that '[s]ome common law rights (freedom from torture) presumably lie so deep that even parliament could not override them'. Then in *Fraser v State Services Commission* [1984] 1 NZLR 116, Lord Cooke at 121 was much more direct in curbing the power of the New Zealand Parliament to act, noting that some common law rights (right to justice) 'may go so deep that even parliament cannot be accepted by the courts to have destroyed them'.

While confirming the 'constitutional role' (Cooke 1988:158) of the courts to give effect to the intention of legislative enactments, Lord Cooke also referred to legitimate limits to legislative power, for example, an act of parliament that purports to strip Jewish people of both their citizenship and property rights is contrary to common right and reason, morally repugnant, and should therefore be struck down by the courts. Ultimately, constitutional democracy demands fetters on the power of parliament and that 'one can no longer talk about "some vague unspecified law of natural justice" or resort to similar anodynes. One may have to accept that working out truly fundamental rights and duties is ultimately an inescapable judicial responsibility' (Cooke 1988:164).

For some people, this judicial activism is nothing more than 'judicial adventure' or even 'judicial glasnost' (Kelsey 1993:194). However it may be described, it does represent an informed judicial caution that, in 'taking Dicey undiluted' (Cooke 1988:164), an unlimited sovereign parliament may assume unbridled power and exercise arbitrary rule. This is not a lack of faith in the institution of responsible government and parliament's deference to that principle. It is, rather, a realistic assessment of the dangers a supreme parliament with unlimited powers poses to the citizens. When the citizens' rights and freedoms are infringed by legislative and executive action, the judiciary has a constitutional role to act according to the law.

From the point of view of Pacific constitutional systems, the position canvassed above is not a mere gloss on the principle of parliamentary sovereignty. It is, rather, constitutional law orthodoxy at its highest. In fact, when the Samoan judiciary declares void, in accordance with article 2, acts of parliament or executive actions that are inconsistent with the provisions of the Constitution of Samoa, it is certainly not judicial usurpation of the authority of parliament or a heretical assertion of judicial sovereignty. Such a declaration is, in fact, both constitutional, in the sense that it is in keeping with constitutional mandates as enunciated by the constitutional framers, and lawful, in the respect that it is within the powers and authority of the Constitution. Armed with article 2 and an open-ended Constitution that can be invoked to justify greater judicial activism, the courts can and should use them. After all, it is their constitutional role to ensure that government does not exceed its constitutional limits. Similarly, it is of note that, under the provisions of most Pacific constitutions, other Pacific courts, like the Samoan judiciary, are not impotent.

It is a moot point whether Pacific courts have been less adventurous than their constitutional position legitimately allows, or whether they have been less assertive than is allowed by the permissive juridical philosophy on which they are supposed to operate. If and when they are, judicial authority risks becoming a mere legal fiction, and the temper of members of the Pacific judiciary becomes an issue.

In conclusion, a valid case for judicial activism in the Pacific could be advanced. This argument is fortified by the common law position of the courts surveyed above, the role of Pacific written constitutions as supreme law, and the broad review jurisdiction of the courts to declare void legislative and executive actions that are inconsistent with constitutional provisions. There are, of course, issues and concerns. The question 'who guards the guard?' seems to follow inevitably. The notion of judicial sovereignty is not without its own ghosts. Indeed, there is always the possibility that the judiciary may itself become the greatest threat to the rule of law if judges assume and exercise unbridled power. These legitimate concerns warn against extreme judicial activism and call for a counterpoising measure of restraint on the part of the judiciary.

In the final analysis, however, neither judicial restraint nor judicial activism is of lasting importance *per se*. The really important matter is doing justice according to the law. The rule of law neither requires nor rejects judicial restraint or judicial activism; it simply requires justice according to law. This fundamental requirement needs to be undergirded by peace, welfare and good order issuing from the operation of the rule of law as a principle of legitimate governance. As Sir Laurence Street CJ has counselled,

> I prefer to look to the constitutional constraints of 'peace, welfare, and good government' as the source of power in the courts to exercise an ultimate authority to protect our parliamentary democracy, not only against tyrannous excesses on the part of a legislature that may have fallen under extremist control, but also in a general sense as limiting the power of parliament (Sir Laurence Street CJ 7 NSWLR:405).[24]

Reconstructing the institution of separation of powers

At the heart of the institution of separation of powers is the conviction that it 'enables the law to serve as a bulwark between governors and governed, excluding the exercise of arbitrary powers' (Allan 2001:3). The rule of law requires the arrangement of the branches of government in such a way that the arbitrary use of state power by any one branch of the state is firmly opposed and checked by the other two. The combined exertion of the rule of law and the separation of powers counteracts the sort of tyranny that portends the very probable collapse of the politico-legal order. This is not inconceivable when, in the absence of a separation of powers, there is one branch of government with absolute power to do as it wishes—legislate, execute and judge. This concentration of power, said Baron Montesquieu, 'would be an end of every thing, were the same man, or the same body, whether of the nobles or of the people, to exercise those three powers, that of enacting laws, that of executing the public resolutions, and of trying the causes of individuals' (Montesquieu 1748:Book XI, Ch VI).

The exaltation of Pacific executive governments urgently demands the resuscitation of the institution of separation of powers. Making this institution work necessitates cutting a sovereign parliament down to size and making the judiciary more proactive as discussed in the previous section. In some contexts, Tonga for example, there is an urgent need for constitutional change and a radical overhaul of the political order, including a thorough deconstruction of the ideologies that underpin the existing order.

A complete separation of powers is impractical, especially in jurisdictions with parliamentary executives where government ministers are members of both parliament and the executive. This overlap of personnel and functions is permitted on the ground that, despite the overlap, there are structures, processes and procedures (for example, professional ethics and the development of specialised interests along institutional lines) that provide some form of check against an unauthorised assumption of power. It must be noted, however, that there is always a real danger of one branch of government assuming powers not expressly granted, or usurping powers traditionally reserved to another branch, thus causing a major disruption to the balance of governmental powers, with serious consequences. The relevant test is whether a given law transfers a specific power from one branch to another, the extent of the power being transferred (whether substantial or not), and whether such transfer of power is accompanied by sufficient protections against concentrating too much power in one branch to the detriment of the other two.

The need for strong government is again acknowledged. Sometimes strong government requires and justifies some measure of concentration of effective public power in the executive. Be that as it may, the common concern—and a very pronounced one in some Pacific nations—nowadays is that the notion of strong government might be (and has, in fact, been) used as an excuse or justification by the executive to acquire freedom to rule, unfettered by a parliament that has been reduced to a rubberstamp and a judiciary that is too courteous to even complain. While conceding the need for the three branches of government to work cooperatively for the common good, the danger is that the balance tends to tip too far and too often towards cooperation and coordination. This is, of course, a question of degree. One thing seems certain though: interdependence must not be sought at the expense of separated powers and institutional checking. Responsibility for the public good, the efficient conduct of public affairs, public order and national security—

these idioms are usually part of an exaggerated rhetoric often used by the executive to drive the executive's own conception of the public good and to exalt itself as ruler of the social order, often at the expense of countervailing interests.

Strengthening the judiciary is therefore an imperative. In addition to the case for judicial activism mounted above, it is further argued that the courts must be firm in requiring accountability from parliament and especially the executive through the exercise of the courts' review jurisdiction, analysing every executive decision with cautious scepticism, ensuring that the executive acts according to the law. Important in this connection are the judicial functions of defining the content of legal rules and declaring what the law is. The use of legal precedents, despite its imperfections, is nonetheless important in that it gives judicial decisions legitimacy, certainty, predictability and stability. Judicial transparency through public scrutiny of judicial decisions is equally important. In addition, the mechanics of the court process are, on the whole, egalitarian, giving all parties in a case an equal footing and equal opportunity to present their cases. The presumption of innocence and the presumption against retrospective operation similarly ensure that justice according to the law is done and is seen to be done. In concert, these rules operate to subject both legislative and executive powers to legal limits, and to prevent the abuse of court processes.

The concentration of state power in the executive means the balance of power is disturbed, and the state increasingly inclines towards absolutism as a result. Restoring the balance and stability of government is therefore a political and moral imperative. The courts have a pivotal role to play in this process. When reliance on the ideological commitment of the rulers to justice, fairness and equality proves to have been a misplaced trust, when parliament is reduced to nothing more than a rubberstamp for the will of the executive, when the executive is so consumed by its own interests that those who wield executive power can no longer distinguish between personal ambition and public good, and when the people themselves are so politically apathetic that acquiescence in the status quo has become the norm, the judiciary is the last bastion of resistance against the certain decline of the social order into totalitarianism.

A pressing issue of concern is the diminishing influence of parliament in some Pacific states. Strengthening parliament (albeit as a limited sovereign) is therefore an urgent matter as well, an important means of counterbalancing the power of the executive government. Worthy of note are such practical strategies as the two-tier parliament and the multi-party cabinet structures adopted, for example, in the Fiji Islands. The passage of proposed bills through the two houses of parliament ensures, at least, open debate and scrutiny of those bills before they become law. Opposing views are expressed, heard and assessed in open debate, and the substance of proposed legislation is subjected to scrupulous analysis and critique in keeping with the interests of true deliberative democracy. Opposing views in both houses of parliament and in a multi-party cabinet are vital in checking, enhancing and enriching the lawmaking power of the executive by imposing constraints on that power. The system of coalition government, if it is not exploited as a ploy for capturing executive power, is an important way of keeping the executive under control.

The fundamental significance of the institution of separated powers is again emphasised. Law is a bridle on power; separation of powers reinforces the law's control of unbridled power. Pertinent to the limiting role of the rule of law and the separation of powers are basic democratic values such as justice and fairness, responsible and accountable government, equal subjection to the law, and the protection of citizens' rights and liberties against the tyranny of the state. Without the separation of powers 'there can be no public liberty' (Blackstone 1966:Vol.1, 142); with the separation of powers there is no minority rule and this is some 'guarantee of public freedom' (Hegel 1952:272). Separation of powers, in short, is 'essential for the establishment and maintenance of political liberty' (Vile 1967:1). These values are not self-executing. The rule of law, in concert with the separation of powers, provides an important means of realising those democratic values in practice.

Also at stake is the credibility and even survival of the political and legal order itself. In the absence of a separation of powers 'the destruction of the state is forthwith a *fait accompli*' (Hegel 1952:272). Usually there is fragmentation of the state from within when rulers self-destruct either when their power is spent or, as is more likely, when the citizens rise up in a violent revolution. Either way, the destruction of the state is a matter of course. Some Pacific states, particularly Papua New Guinea, the Solomon Islands, and Fiji, continue to straddle this fine line between the right to govern and the duty to govern in justice. The situation in Tonga (at the time of writing) is a clear illustration that the people will not put up with arbitrary rule for ever.

Resurrecting the system of checks and balances

The need to resurrect Pacific systems of checks and balances is demonstrable. General elections remain an important check and balance; the challenge lies in the reform of electoral systems and laws. Public referenda and other forms of direct democracy are also important on issues of major constitutional importance.

Strengthening parliament's watchdogs is an urgent imperative. Chief auditors are always a very important force for checking the power of the executive government. Critical to the effectiveness of a chief auditor is the independence of the office from the power of the executive government. This independence may be achieved through a number of means, such as the appointment and/or reappointment of office-holders being made by a unanimous decision of parliament, and removal from office being decided by more than two-thirds of parliament and based on limited grounds, such as those prescribed for the removal of judges of the Supreme Court. The reporting rights and fiscal position of the chief auditor also need to be strengthened and more precisely defined. Ombudsmen, too, could be an effective check on the power of the executive. The powers of this office may need to be extended and the constitutional position of the ombudsman more firmly grounded. A major problem with Pacific ombudsmen is financial. Their financial strength affects the scope and effectiveness of the work they do (Ombudsman of Western Samoa 2001).

Strengthening parliament clearly demands strengthening parliament's own watchdogs. One would like to think that the fortification of these offices and their investigative and reporting rights would buttress the authority and power of parliament vis-à-vis the executive. While making allowance for the achievement of legitimate public objectives, parliament must, at the same time, seek to guard the constitutional order against frivolous executive policy interests and departures from legal procedures in the quest for speedy solutions or ill-conceived strategies to frustrate and ultimately liquidate political opposition.

In the Pacific, strengthening parliament needs to be reinforced by strong party systems. Ideology espoused by political parties needs to be more clearly defined and more fervently encouraged. This would shift the focus away from self-interest and personal affiliations (cultural, religious, economic) towards strong ideological commitment and the perception of social issues as the basis of party politics. It would also shift the focus away from an interest-based democracy to deliberative democracy as the guiding norm. Of special interest is the category of a multi-party executive adopted in the Fiji Islands, as noted above. Although the Qarase government is at the time of writing seriously considering the abolition of that structure, there is no reason why the arrangement cannot work successfully if there is sufficient political will and resilience on the part of politicians to make a good structure work.[25]

Select committees in Pacific states also need support and strengthening. As a forum for members of the public to express views on proposed legislation, select committees are important barometers for gauging public opinion on issues that ultimately affect the lives of the citizens. But in order for select committees to become productive as public forums, we need to stir the people out of political apathy as is prevalent in most Pacific nations.

The convention of ministerial responsibility is arguably not legally enforceable or justiciable. The situation in Samoa and other Pacific jurisdictions is different: the convention is enshrined in written constitutions as the supreme and fundamental laws of these nations. Thus incorporated, this convention is therefore legally enforceable as part of the laws of these countries. Taken seriously and honestly (which, unfortunately, is not the case on many occasions) both collective and individual responsibility could ensure the accountability of public officials to the people. Failing that, ministerial responsibility is likely to remain a mere 'political axiom' (Palmer and Palmer 1997:46) or a fiction, an unworkable system whereby the minister is, 'in theory, accountable for everything and in practice accountable for nothing' (Palmer and Palmer 1997:81).

Then there is the media, which, when it is not preoccupied with sensationalism, has been and will continue to be the voice of conscience through honest and critical reporting of facts and situations that are genuinely in the public interest. The media's dissemination of information could also pique the interest of pressure groups like human rights organisations, churches and other non-government organisations. They too can bring pressure to bear on parliaments and executives on issues and situations involving arbitrary rule. The international community must also have a keen interest in what happens around the world, especially now with globalisation and internationalisation. Such interest should privilege peace and progress. And, I might add, in Samoa and the entire Pacific for that matter, we do not have any need for some president's militant ego to change the world.

Deprivatising and dereifying Pacific states

As noted above, the concentration of state power in an élite few ultimately results in the privatisation of the state. The need to deprivatise the state naturally flows on from the course of my argument. In light of this, I offer the following observations.

At the level of conceptualisation, myths are important for the social construction of reality. That also applies to the myths of reification and deification of rulers, their rule and states. However, beyond their constructive value and seductive appeal, their negative effects must be exposed, resisted and subverted. Against the notion of a deified state (with deified rulers), it must be emphasised that the state is a historical product: a mortal creation by mortal creators; a creation of, by, from and for the people. As such, it must continue to find its justification in the growing conviction of the people, its creators. Such justification must be sought in the value and usefulness of the state—through government institutions and personnel—to the development of the people's individual and corporate life, in the successful performance of those functions for which it was instituted—to secure the persons, property, rights, freedoms, defence and peace of the citizens.[26]

The state is really part of the superstructure of society, part of the citizens' experience of needs, interests and fears. It is, at worst, only an artificial construct. As Karl Marx (1975:85) put it, '[t]he state is an abstraction. Only the people is a concrete reality'. Bentham similarly emphasised the significance of the people over and above a political community which is only a fictitious body (Bentham 1970). The accent is clearly on real people, not 'straw men'. This motif clearly needs to regain currency in the current political climate.

These countervailing considerations are fortified by the notions of popular sovereignty, government by consent, and government as a trust for the governed. I will deal with these principles in detail in chapter three below. Suffice to note the following matters in this context. Deprivatising the state means rehabilitating the people as the creators, beneficiaries and owners of the state. It means giving back to the people what rightfully belongs to them: the state as a mortal creation of, by, from and for the people. This points to the fundamental significance of the people in constitutional systems of government, epitomised in the notion of popular sovereignty or the sovereignty of the people, including the people's legal title to rule.

The increasing privatisation of many Pacific states is contrary to, even a violation of, the sovereignty of the people, and the violation of this fundamental tenet of constitutional democracy is, in effect, a contravention of the people's right to rule. Hypothetically, if the present trend toward privatisation continues, Pacific states' dealings with arbitrary rule will soon no longer be playful experimentation. But then again, when states shoot into totalitarianism, citizens always have the 'liberty to disobey' (Hobbes 1960:ch 21) and to 'resume their original liberty' (Locke 1988:222). This is, of course, a perfect recipe for disaster. Pacific rulers and government officials would therefore do well to consider this alarming possibility. Sometimes the silence of the people can be very dangerous, as the events in Tonga (at the time of writing) clearly demonstrate.

Recourse to cultural institutions and protocols

When parliament and the judiciary fail to rein in an almighty executive, when the media, non-government organisations and churches are mute, introverted and therefore dysfunctional as public checks on government powers, and when the conventional means of protection are no longer working or effective, it is worth exploring the value of Pacific indigenous institutions, protocols, structures and values as limits and controls on state power and the exercise thereof.

By way of illustration, in the Samoan traditional universe of meaning, social practice and political organisation, the threat of absolute power and arbitrary rule is counteracted through the levelling effect of a whole range of cultural protocols—a complex network of overlapping institutions, beliefs, structures and reciprocal ties. The institution of the extended family imposes moral and psychological limits on the ambitious assumption of absolute power by a single individual through the threat of disinheritance (from the family titles and property) and social alienation. In the context of the village, the control of individuals and families is pursued within the framework of the council of chiefs and elders as a decision-making political body. An ambitious assumption of absolute power in the village readily attracts collective censure in the form of social control mechanisms such as fines, alienation, ostracism and, in the worst case scenario, banishment from the village. At the national level, an ambitious assumption of absolute power by an individual or group is controlled through the force of a collective socialism that resists and subverts every atomistic pretension to absolute power. This collective socialism is epitomised in and expressed through the *matai* (traditional chiefs) system, a ubiquitous feature of Samoan society, which guides, checks and controls the power (and the craving for more power) of individuals, families, groups and even villages.

In concert with those institutions, social structures like patronage and kinship (if they are not exploited in the service of sectional interests), cultural protocols like social civility and deferring to the wisdom and judgment of the elders, and cross-cutting ties based on historical, political, and economic alliances, all work to level out individual ambition and group excesses. In conjunction with, and undergirding the use of, those indigenous elements, traditional normative principles and rules need also be resurrected, strengthened and invoked as part of society's moral protection against the threat of arbitrary rule. The Samoan trait of being orientated strongly towards others, a trait manifested in the moral priority of the 'other' and their interests, is especially relevant in this connection. I will return to this matter in chapter four below. Suffice to note that these traditional traits and values, no doubt, would go a long way towards diffusing the current syndrome of extreme self-interest that seems to drive politics and guide democracy in the Pacific.

Worthy of note is the importance of public opinion as a court of reputation in the traditional Samoan worldview. This constitutes a powerful value judgment that can make a person into either a king or a friendless pauper virtually overnight. Consequently, anxiety about public opinion, ridicule and the negative estimate of one's fellows is a strong force of social control. Construed positively and used constructively, this traditional drive to avoid falling into disgrace has the moral and psychological force to check the degeneration of politics into a morally-neutral monopoly of self-seeking, exclusively self-interested, isolated monads. Resurrecting, strengthening and invoking public opinion as a check would help deconstruct the modern *laissez-faire* mindset that now afflicts Samoan and other Pacific politicians. As part of an honour/shame culture, the force of public opinion applauds, venerates, and confirms the honourable reputation of worthy people on the one hand, and decries, condemns, and rebuffs the unprincipled acts of ignoble people on the other.

These principles hang together in the construction of society where community power, politics, economics, laws, roles, objectives, interests and other institutions revolve around the principles of interdependence and interconnectedness. These inform, guide and govern interpersonal relationships. This accounts for a complex web of interlocking human relationships based on descent, sociopolitical alliances, economic associations and other cross-cutting ties. Out of those interrelationships emerge systems of duties and reciprocal obligations that bind together individuals and groups in lasting sociopolitical interdependent relationships which (couched in a metaphysical, even spiritual framework) could be epitomised in the term 'kin' and embodied in the institution of kinship.

In Samoa, interdependence and interconnectedness are moral and political imperatives. This is in line with the sociocultural emphasis on the collective good, maintaining the equilibrium of society and affirming the other instead of negating or dislocating him. Indeed maintaining and protecting social harmony is a first-order principle of social organisation and practice in Samoa, and is a major objective of traditional mechanisms of social control. This is reinforced by other equally important traditional protocols such as the requirement for civility and a compelling sense of respect for others, in both word and deed, subject to the following caveat of caution.

Negatively, in the context of modern cut-throat politics, speaking with respect makes political criticism somewhat difficult. Sometimes seen as discursive, even rebellious if the criticism is from the bottom upwards, criticism is seen as disruptive of social harmony within the group. This privileging of harmony at the expense of critical opinion is integrally related to consensual thinking. But when dissent from the consensus opinion is treated like treason, and seeking and achieving consensus is pursued to the exclusion of countervailing views and opposing interests, social harmony becomes a form of coercion and courteous speech becomes a method to maintain the status quo. Positively, the traditional protocol of speaking with respect for others resists the practice, again in the context of modern politics, of pedantic displays of arrogance in word and deed. Likewise privileging social harmony subverts the practice of causing public disorder to gratify idiosyncratic notions of political correctness.

Conclusion

The Pacific legal pendulum oscillates from Westminster to Washington to Paris and back again in a kind of self-confirming circularity, resulting in Pacific legal systems that are, at best, combinations of the best of many worlds and, at worst, hybrid constructs suffering from a split personality syndrome. In the final analysis, however, whatever lead the Pacific courts follow, the final test is this: the courts must uphold the rule of law; it is their sworn and holy duty to do so.

This necessitates reconstituting Westminster's sovereign parliament and thereby unleashing the full potential of the institution of separated powers and the related system of checks and balances as potent forces for constraining Pacific governments within constitutional limits and controls. These constraining forces constitute a bulwark against tyranny, totalitarianism and unbridled human ambition,[27] even serving to counteract 'the hydraulic pressure inherent within each of the separate branches to exceed the outer limits of its power'.[28] Allan aptly sums up this essential concerted opposition to government arbitrary rule in the following terms.

> At the heart of the ideal of the rule of law lies a traditional conception of 'law', implicit in the original understanding of the doctrine of the separation of powers. Arbitrary and capricious modes of government are excluded when the law consists mainly of general rules that are binding on all, including public officials and also members of the legislature in their private capacities (Allan 2001:32).

Notes

[1]   Most Pacific jurisdictions follow the Westminster system of government—for example, Fiji, Nauru, Vanuatu, Cook Islands and Tuvalu—by virtue of their historical association with England, New Zealand and Australia during the colonial period. Hence the adoption of common law and equity principles and practices in Pacific legal systems. In the case of Samoa, the adoption of a parliamentary form of government was 'the result of circumstance, rather than of conscious decision' (Davidson 1967:370). Tonga, of course, is more an imitation of the English feudal system under the Stuart Kings.

[2]   The comment was made with reference to the New Zealand government. In my view, the problem of the exaltation of executive power now afflicts many more countries following the Westminster system of government.

[3]   See further *The Honorable Tupua Tamasese Efi* v *The Attorney-General of Samoa* (Supreme Court, 1 August 2000); *Siale* v *Fotofili and Others* [1987] LRC (Const) 240; *Shaw* v *Commissioner of Inland Revenue* [1999] 3 NZLR 154. Most of these cases follow *British Railways Board* v *Pickin* [1974] AC 765, [1974] 2 WLR 208, [1974] 1 All ER 609, HL; also *Namoi Shire Council* v *Attorney-General for New South Wales* [1980] 2 NSWLR 639.

[4]   This is a common constitutional arrangement in Pacific jurisdictions. See, for example, article 73 of the Constitution of Samoa on the original, appellate, and revisional jurisdiction of the Supreme Court of Samoa; section 83 of the Constitution of Solomon Islands; section 88 of the Constitution of Kiribati; and section 123 of the Constitution Amendment Act of Fiji.

[5]   See also *Sope* v *Attorney-General No. 1* [1988] VUSC 11; [1980–94] VanLR 356 (2 August 1988). An interesting *obiter dictum* by G. Ward CJ amounted to the same effect. At 5, the learned justice noted as follows, 'I accept that these rules [on parliamentary privilege] were made under the doctrine of legislative supremacy

whereby the English courts cannot hold an act of parliament to be invalid or unconstitutional. Where, as here, there is a written Constitution entrusting the court with the interpretation of the Constitution and the determination of infringements, the situation is different. Thus, if it is shown to the court that any proceeding was in breach of a provision of the Constitution, it may make any order it considers appropriate to remedy the breach. That may include declaring any parliamentary business, including acts, to be invalid'.

7   *Oppenheimer* v *Cattermole* [1976] AC 249.

8   *M* v *Home Office* [1994] 1 AC 377.

9   *Nixon* v *Administrator of General Services*, 433 US 425, 433 (1977).

10   *Buckley* v *Valeo*, 424 US. 1, 121 (1976).

11   For a summary of these variations see Paterson (1999).

12   The most notable feature is the provision for a two-tier Fijian parliament under section 45 of the Constitution Amendment Act 1997, which vests lawmaking power in a parliament comprising the president, the House of (elected) Representatives (sections 50–63), and an appointed Senate (sections 64–66).

13   Notable variations for present purposes include the mandatory requirement for 'a multi-party cabinet' government for Fiji under section 99 of the Constitution Amendment Act 1997. In Kiribati and Nauru, ministers are appointed and dismissed by a president, not a prime minister as is usually the case in other Westminster systems of government. In both countries, however, the president must be a member of the legislature and is, thus, more like a prime minister than an executive head in the mode of the US president. Tonga is an extreme case. The Tongan executive is partly a parliamentary executive and partly a non-parliamentary one. Under clause 51 of Tonga's Constitution, the prime minister and cabinet ministers are appointed by the King from either inside or outside parliament.

14   See also the Solomon Islands Court of Appeal case of *Gerea and Others* v *DPP* [1984] SILR 161; In *re the Constitution, Timakata* v *Attorney-General* [1992] VUSC 9; [1980–94] VanLR 691 (1 November 1992); *Sope* v *Attorney-General No. 1* [1988] VUSC 11; [1980–94] VanLR 356 (2 August 1988).

15   See, for example, Windybank and Manning (2003) for an analysis of what the authors describe as the 'inherent instability' of Papua New Guinea coalition government, which has resulted in frequent changes in government through parliamentary no-confidence motions.

16   For a detailed account of the different checks and balances see especially Palmer (1987); also Palmer and Palmer (1997).

17   There are, of course, variations across Pacific jurisdictions in respect of the establishment and other matters relating to this office. For example, the auditor general of the Solomon Islands is appointed by the Governor-General on the advice of the Public Service Commission under section 108 of the Solomon Islands Constitution. In Kiribati, the director of audits is appointed by the Public Service Commission under section 100(2) of the Constitution of Kiribati. In Fiji, under section 167 of the Constitution Amendment Act 1997, the auditor general is appointed by the Constitutional Offices Commission in consultation with the standing committee of parliament. Differences aside, there seems to be a common interest in making the office of auditor general independent. For example, section 114(3) of the *Constitution of Kiribati* provides as follows: 'In the exercise of his functions under this section, the Director of Audit shall not be subject to the direction or control of any other person or authority'.

18   See also section 45 of the Constitution of Kiribati, section 97, on the constitutional
     requirement for responsible government, and section 102, on both collective and
     individual ministerial responsibility in the Constitution Amendment Act 1997 of
     Fiji, and article 17(2) of the Constitution of Nauru.
19   Section 102(2) of the Constitution Amendment Act 1997 of Fiji is more explicit
     and carries more weight in its demand: 'A minister is individually responsible to
     the House of Representatives for all things done by or under the authority of the
     minister in the execution of his or her office'.
20   See, for example, *Madzimbamuto* v *Lardner-Burke* [1969] 1 AC 645 in which
     recognition and enforcement of a convention was sought but declined; also *Re
     Amendment of Constitution of Canada* (1982) 125 DLR (3d) 1, where it was argued
     that conventions do crystallise into law and are therefore legally enforceable, an
     argument that was roundly rejected. In the final analysis, however, the distinction
     between laws and conventions is not really of fundamental importance.
     Conventions may not be really different from laws.
21   On the office of the ombudsman in other Pacific jurisdictions, see, for example,
     sections 157–65 of the Constitution Amendment Act of Fiji and sections 96–99 of
     the Constitution of Solomon Islands. The establishment of the ombudsman's
     office under the Constitution in the case of Fiji and the Solomon Islands contrasts
     with the establishment by statute of Samoa's ombudsman.
22   See also Allan's (2001) analysis of Goldsworthy's argument.
23   Understandably, Sir Coke's position has invited both criticism (that he either
     misquoted or misunderstood the authorities on which he relied and that,
     whatever merits his view had, it suffered an untimely death as a result of the
     constitutional changes brought about by the *Bill of Rights 1688* and the *Act of
     Settlement 1700*) and support. Thus, Allan (2001:204–5), notes that '[t]he nature of
     Coke's commitment to the "transcendental and absolute" jurisdiction of
     parliament has been much debated; but it is clear that he well understood the
     ability of judicial interpretation to tame potential excesses and abuses of
     legislative power'.
24   Similar requirements are found in Pacific constitutions. For example, article 28(1)
     of the *Constitution of Niue* (to be read with the *Niue Constitution Act 1974*); article
     16(1) of the *Constitution of the Republic of Vanuatu*; article 27 of the Constitution of
     Nauru; section 59(1) of the Constitution of Solomon Islands; section 66(1) of the
     Constitution of Kiribati; and section 44 (on social justice and affirmative action) of
     the Constitution Amendment Act 1997 of Fiji seem to encapsulate the
     requirement for good government.
25   Radio New Zealand International, 12 June 2003; as reported in the *Pacific Islands
     Report* (12 June 2003) under the heading 'Fiji 'Talanoa' to address multi-party
     controversy'.
26   On the functions of the state see Locke (1988); also Hobbes (1960).
27   Note also Bailyn: 'No one set of ideas was more deeply embedded in the British
     and the British-American mind than the notion, whose genealogy could be traced
     back to Polybius, that liberty could survive in a world of innate ambitious…men
     only where a balance of the contending forces was so institutionalised that no one
     contestant could monopolise the power of the state without effective opposition'
     (1990:76).
28   *INS* v *Chadha*, 462 US 919, 951 (1983).

3

Reinventing government: constitutional principles, ideals, realities and fictions

For a platonic idealist, government is the ideal expression of society. A contemporary pessimist, on the other hand, loathes government as nothing more than an insatiable political monster feeding on the body politic. For a classical Marxist, government is the manifestation of bourgeois rule. By contrast, a theocrat uproots government from its existential moorings and exalts it as the manifestation of some divine will on earth and, in some strange ontological sense, itself divine. Government, to the full-blown capitalist, is only a night watchman whose intervention in the deregulated world of market forces should be minimal.

This chapter instead argues that government is the government of the people. This is not mere pandering to the dictates of socialist thought; it is rather a reassertion of the proper status of the people in their mortal creation, the state, and a proper delineation of the often-nebulous connection between the government and the governed. In light of the problem of exalted Pacific executive governments, often manifested in the abuse of public power for private gain, my interest is in deprivatising Pacific governments and rehabilitating the people as the real locus of government authority. Warning of Papua New Guinea's decline into economic, political, and social chaos, Susan Windybank and Mike Manning (2003:1) write of the use of public monies to subsidise 'a small political élite' and how democracy has been 'hijacked by those responsible for and benefiting from the "systemic and systematic" corruption of public institutions'. As the authors of a report on security in Melanesia phrase the issue, the problem is the '[c]oncentration of political power in too few hands and for too long, with competition for power provoking violence and unethical management' (Anere et al. 2001:6). In Tonga, the problem 'is that the present system of government benefits a minority only, and it supports the fortunes of a few. The struggle for change is about freeing Tonga from that rule which is beneficial for a minority, and to allow people to share in the good fortune' (*Taimi o Tonga*, February 1996). In the words of the *Eminent Persons' Group Review of the Pacific Islands Forum*,

> [v]ariable standards of governance have produced at their worst instability, violence, corruption and a breakdown of the democratic process. These problems have exacerbated the generally slow pace of economic growth and, in some cases, led to economic decline. Poor governance has a direct impact on the lives of Pacific people. It affects not only their rights as individuals and as communities, but also the delivery of basic services such as health care, education and the management of scarce resources (Eminent Persons' Group 2004:n.p.).

The issue, for present purposes, is the alienation of the people from public power, influence, and physical resources in their own state, with the consequent loss of citizens' trust and confidence in government. Who owns the state? This is becoming an increasingly pressing question in the Pacific.

This chapter accordingly underlines the fundamental significance of the people, epitomised in the related principles of government as trustee for the governed, popular sovereignty, and government by consent which, taken together, provide a more basic and principled theory of government. These basic constitutional principles are underlined as the foundation and structure of the true relationship between government and governed, the proper basis of government, and the appropriate nature of government responsibility and accountability to the people. The implications of these principles are equally important: the structure and practice of government, lawmaking power, the phenomenon of political representation, government accountability in lieu of corruption, government protection of citizens' rights and liberties, judicial review of constitutional powers and roles, and judicial review of administrative decisions. I will address these issues throughout this chapter to expose the gap between theory and practice and gauge how much remains to be achieved.

Basic constitutional principles: ideals as benchmarks

The following discussion elaborates the overlapping principles of government as trustee for the governed, popular sovereignty, and government by consent. Collectively, these provide a more basic and principled theory of government. Each attaches government responsibility and accountability to the governed more firmly to the legal, political, moral and ethical values that should underpin, guide and govern the conduct of government. This is absolutely vital to legitimate governance.

Government as trustee for the governed: fiduciary powers and legitimate expectations

The principle of government as trustee for the governed is part of a body of ideas that seems to have been consolidated by the seventeenth century.[1] Its generation and evolution lay in the complex politics of uneasy alliances and opportunist usurpation of power that marked the relationship between the English monarchy, parliament, and people. Thus, disputing the House of Commons' assertion of authority in opposition to the King, the royalist Sir John Spelman in 1642 declared that their 'trust is limited by the writ to advise with the *King*, not to make Acts or Ordinances in any case against him' (Morgan 1988:62). The controversy between the King and parliament aside, it appears that by 1642 the power to govern and make laws was already conceptualised in terms of trusteeship and that the abuse of such vested power was being reviled as a breach of trust.

Evidently, also, the principle of trusteeship was being identified with the whole apparatus of government, and the expectation that parliamentarians would faithfully adhere to that trust in favour of the entire body politic had become a national sentiment (Morgan 1988:51, 62–3). So, when criticised for its actions, the English Long Parliament (1640–53) blatantly refused to initiate the reforms the petitioners were calling for on the ground that 'its status as trustee for the whole kingdom did not permit it to accommodate a part of the kingdom (that is, the petitioners)' (Morgan 1988:65). The Levellers saw fit, at this time, to impose limits on parliament by declaring through 'An Agreement of the People' that 'Parliaments are to receive the extent of their power, and trust from those that betrust them' (Morgan 1988:73). In opposing the 'Agreement', parliament reasoned that a 'parliament claiming omnipotent authority from the people could not afford to admit the possibility of the people being embodied anywhere outside the walls of Westminster' (Morgan 1988:73). And so Westminster's sovereign parliament was born. Its sovereign power was to be mitigated only by instruments such as the Magna Carta and the Petition of Right, and by basic constitutional principles such as the government acting as trustee for the governed.

The principle of popular trusteeship, of government as a trust, emerged from that complex politico-historical background. By 'the early 19th century a large body of law (criminal, tort and, to a lesser extent, equitable) was erected on this foundation governing the use and abuse of public office' (Finn 1995:11). The principle, however, has had an unhappy history. Within a few decades of its emergence into prominence, it faded into the background of legal and political thought, eclipsed by the notions of representative and responsible government, cabinet government, the convention of ministerial responsibility, and, in some cases, the enactment of comprehensive public service legislation. These developments—believed to allow a more robust (though limited) role for the people—led to the subversion of the principle of government as trustee and the dismissal of the idea that parliament itself could be a trustee for the people as nothing more than 'a "political metaphor"' (Maitland 1911:Vol. 3,403), that parliament is not 'in any legal sense a "trustee" for the electors' (Dicey 1959:75).

But the balance of thought has changed again. In recent times, the principle of popular trusteeship has re-emerged as a very important category for defining the nature, end, and functions of government. A number of factors have prompted this shift of opinion: the failings of representative democracy, the defects of oppositional politics, the exaltation of the executive and the emergence of élitist rule, the dysfunction of the institution of separation of powers and the related system of checks and balances, the unenforceability of the convention of ministerial responsibility, and the development of modern governments into *de facto* corporations (Finn 1995:12). These problems in contemporary political systems have critically raised the issues of the true nature and end of government, the proper nature of the relationship between government and governed, the appropriate exercise and limits of public power, and the basis and legitimacy of government rule. In this context of political experimentation, the principle of government as trustee has re-emerged, providing important answers to searching constitutional, legal, political and public ethics questions.

In keeping with that revived interest in the principle of government trusteeship, it should be emphasised that government is a trust; public offices are offices of trust and confidence concerning the public; and public officials are officers who discharge duties in which the public has a vested interest.[2] Government powers belong to and are ultimately derived from the people. Public officials are simply 'the trustees, the fiduciaries' (Finn 1995:14) of those powers. Institutions, officers and agencies of government 'exist for the people, to serve the interests of the people and, as such, are accountable to the people' (Finn 1995:14).

The central tenet in this edifice is that the relationship between government and governed is essentially a fiduciary one that imposes a very high standard of care and responsibility on government officials. Paul D. Finn (1995:9) thus underlines, 'the most fundamental fiduciary relationship in our society is manifestly that which exists between the community (the people) and the state, its agencies and officials'. Here the word trust is used as a synonym for fiduciary, and the accent is on the idea that government powers are the fiduciary powers conferred by the people (Finn 1995). The transfer of power is thus significant as the basis of a fiduciary relationship that not only confers rights but defines corresponding duties as well. Government institutions, officers and agents are charged with fiduciary duties to the people. As trustees, they are 'the servants of the people' (Finn 1995:11).

All this amounts to the people's legitimate expectation of a high standard of conduct and practice on the part of public officials in the public arena—a duty of care, loyalty, honesty, responsibility, prudence and good judgment, and a responsibility to act in the best interests of the people and in good faith. This has a significant levelling effect on government and what it can do. Thus, Locke (1988:221) wrote, 'the legislative acts against the trust reposed in them when they endeavour to invade the property of the subject, and to make themselves, or any part of the community, masters or arbitrary disposers of the lives, liberties, or fortunes of the people'. This limitation on the exercise of government powers points to 'the core idea of trusteeship—that government exists to serve the interests of the people and that this has a limiting effect on what is lawfully allowable to government' (Finn 1995:13). Put differently, government cannot abrogate the citizens' rights without legal and/or moral justification, take away their property by force or without adequate compensation, discriminate against minorities in society, deprive the judiciary of its inherent jurisdiction, assume powers not expressly given, or abuse powers given and thereby exercise unbridled rule. When government does any or all of the above, it acts contrary to the terms of its creation. It is, in a broad sense, a breach of trust.

This raises the point that trust, both institutional and inter-personal, is vital to the health of every democracy.[3] It is a vital component of society's social capital and a powerful integrating force for civil society.[4] A healthy social capital and a strong, robust civil society are essential to a good, wise and trustworthy government. Trust, understood in ethical and interpersonal terms, means that citizens have confidence in their rulers as honest, frank, open and responsive to their needs. It means, in simple terms, that one can trust one's member of parliament to act in one's best interests. Where ethical trust in politicians obtains, trust in government prevails. Where it is either low or even absent, trust in government declines and citizens view government institutions with an increasingly negative sense of apathy. This points up the important correlation between ethics and politics: ethical trust in government officials engenders political trust in government. Both involve a basic evaluative and cognitive view of whether government is functioning to meet the people's normative and legitimate expectations.

And while parliament might not be a trustee for the electors in a strictly legal sense, government is. This is variously manifested. The public trust doctrine makes government responsible for public land and other resources as trustee for the people as beneficial owners. In Samoa, for example, the state is made a trustee of customary or native land.[5] In some jurisdictions, the state is guardian of indigenous estates, as in the case of the American Indians.[6] There is also evidence that the courts might be increasingly prepared to impose fiduciary duties on government, even in cases where no proprietary interest is affected and where the state acts as guardian of the interests of a section of the people. Anthony Mason (1994) observes that interests protected by fiduciary principles could be extended beyond narrow legal and economic ones to include fundamental human and personal interests as well (also Batley 1996; Sweeney 1995; Bartlett 1995). The idea that categories of fiduciary relationships are not closed is an interesting one.[7]

In the Pacific, trust in most politicians and governments is at very low levels and in some cases non-existent. Corruption, mismanagement of public resources, deficit financing, poor fiscal planning, economic waste, institutional failure, political instability manifested in the failure to provide basic public services, the neglect of government infrastructure, and the inability to maintain law and order—these are some of the hallmarks of poor governance in many Pacific nations. This has had a debilitating effect on the people who, placed in an amorphous fiduciary relationship of trust with their rulers, feel betrayed and misled when their rulers do not act within the terms of the trust relationship. Not surprisingly, trust (understood in both ethical and political terms) is sadly lacking.

In most cases, apathy ensues, and citizens become indifferent to the affairs of government. Viewing politics as a game of the worse-than-mediocre, unworthy of the idealist intellectual or the principled moralist, the governed indiscriminately surrender their state to the governors and, more and more, politics becomes a monopoly of self-seeking politicians who, as a result, are left unchecked to exploit public office to further their private interests. Herein lies a familiar problem, a very real and gnawing one in the Pacific: the real danger in any democracy is internal decay spawned by the indifference of citizens in matters affecting their government. When citizens are indifferent, democracy quickly degenerates into any of its polar totalitarian opposites. It can become an odious autocracy or rapacious oligarchy overnight, and both can maintain the façade of democratic institutions. Indifference, in short, means the end of democracy, which signifies more than just the death of a principle.

The principle of government as trustee presupposes, requires and constructs, active political subjects, citizens who are rational enough to either trust or distrust their own government, citizens with an active and vested interest in what happens to their government. This is a powerful combatant against apathy. It is the citizens who make or unmake governments, give them fettered powers, hold them accountable, reform or remove them when they are not responsible, accountable and responsive. This prerogative lies in the sovereignty of the people.

Popular sovereignty: 'We the People'

The principles of government as trustee and popular sovereignty are integrally related. Popular sovereignty forms 'the core idea of trusteeship'; government as trustee constitutes 'the inexorable logic of popular sovereignty' (Finn 1995:15). The accent is on the fundamental significance of the people, epitomised in the notion of popular sovereignty as an 'emerging legal and constitutional principle' (Finn 1995:5) that underlines the priority of the people over the state. Before there was a state, there were people who, by and with their consent, brought the state into existence. Since the people created the state to serve their interests, the state is therefore a means to an end, not an end in itself. It is the servant of the people.

But what is this amorphous category called 'the people'? Is it a mere fictional entity, 'existing as a people only in the actions of the Parliament that claimed to act for them', as Edmund S. Morgan (1988:49) describes it? Ultimately, the existence of this body—the people—is vital to the credibility of the principle of popular sovereignty itself: the people cannot conceivably possess or exercise sovereignty if it does not exist in fact. And how should we view and treat the people? A rude, useless, unwieldy agglomeration of ignorant, irrational and deluded souls who need to be ruled because they do not know how to rule themselves and should not therefore be entrusted with their own welfare—a condescending, élitist view that some Pacific parliamentarians and rulers continue to negligently entertain?[8] If this is the case, then there is a fundamental flaw in the principle of popular sovereignty—namely, the people's inability to rule.

Moving on from such crude perceptions, it must be said that, if the principle of popular sovereignty has taught us anything, it is that 'the people' is not an abstract notion but one that has real, tangible effects. If we take Samoa as an example, we are able to look at the politico-historical antecedents of the formulation 'We the people', as presented in the written Constitution of 1960, to chart the emergence of 'the people' as a political force. From 1900 to 1914, Samoa was a German protectorate. Its administration was then handed to New Zealand, first as a mandate of the League of Nations and subsequently as a trust territory of the Trusteeship Council of the United Nations. In 1961, the United Nations dissolved the Trusteeship Agreement for the Territory of Western Samoa 1946 and New Zealand enacted the *Western Samoa Act 1961*, section 3 of which provides, 'It is hereby declared that on and after Independence Day [1 January 1962] Her Majesty in right of New Zealand shall have no jurisdiction over the Independent State of Western Samoa'. And so, on 1 January 1962, Samoa became the first independent nation in the South Pacific.

At the centre of Samoa's legal-political order stands the Constitution of 1960. Marking a decisive rupture with the colonial past and the birth of an independent nation, the Constitution serves as the linguistic expression of the compact 'of the people with each other, to produce and constitute a government' (Paine 1979:209), a compact antecedent to the state. Behind the Constitution's enigmatic words, terse clauses, crisp imperatives, succinct injunctions and noble intent stand the constitutional framers of the 1960 Constitutional Convention, all but a few of whom were Samoans by birth. In the final recital of the preamble, the framers declared: 'NOW, THEREFORE, we the people of Samoa in our Constitutional Convention, this twenty-eighth day of October 1960, do hereby adopt, enact, and give to ourselves this Constitution'. On 9 May 1961, in a plebiscite conducted under the supervision of a UN plebiscite commissioner, the Samoan people voted overwhelmingly in favour of independence.

It seems certain that the historical emergence of 'we the Samoan people' occurred in important paradigmatic stages. As a process, the political evolution of Samoa involved a social contract among the people themselves to form a government. The 1960 Constitutional Convention, the adoption of the Constitution pursuant to the final recital of the preamble of the Constitution 1960, and the plebiscite of 1961 are very important in this regard. Cast in terms of Thomas Hobbes' version of the social contract theory, by that contract 'the multitude so united in one person, is called a COMMONWEALTH' (Hobbes 1960:Chapter 18; also Hampton 1986; Goldsmith 1980). The basis of the sovereignty of the people thus lies in the will of the people themselves, in keeping with article 21(3) of the Universal Declaration of Human Rights 1948, which was one of the major defining documents in the Constitutional Convention 1960. Important in this vein is the notion of a written Constitution as an act of the people, 'an act of popular self-government' (Rubenfeld 1998:210). Central to that act of the people is the constitutional declaration: 'We the people of Samoa'. This is obviously much more than a pedantic shout that the Constitution emanates from the people. It is instead more fundamentally an assertive claim of popular sovereignty; a declaration of the people's authority to create the government of Samoa and 'to specify the forms and limits of government powers' (Kay 1998:30).

The incorporation of the principle of popular sovereignty in Samoa's written Constitution is important. In common law, the sovereignty of the people is regarded as simply a political notion. Dicey's distinction between legal sovereignty and political sovereignty saw to that.[9] In the case of Samoa, it could be argued that legal sovereignty and political sovereignty have coalesced in a written Constitution, thus making the common law distinction superfluous and converting the notion of popular sovereignty into a legal and constitutional principle, enshrined and embodied in a written text. Consequently, the declaration 'We the people of Samoa' is much more than mere political rhetoric. It is, in fact, a public declaration of the people's right to rule. This has important ramifications for the structure and practice of government. In the words of Finn,

[b]y sourcing the power of government in the people, by acknowledging its
devolution in a general scheme of government on to institutions that exist for
the people to serve the interests of the people, they give an importance to the
general scheme in which, and the purpose for which, power is entrusted to
government...the people, not the parliament, are sovereign (Finn 1995:20).

That said, there is always the gnawing problem of how the people
could exercise 'effective control over a government that pretended to
speak for them—a form of tyranny that popular sovereignty continues
to bring to peoples all over the world' (Morgan 1988:83). The root cause
of the problem is the contradiction inherent in the status of the people
as both governors and governed at the same time. When parliament
becomes the people (in a sense, the self-fulfilling prophecy of the
principle of popular sovereignty itself), when opposing parliament is
seen to be not merely destructive but wicked since parliament can do
no wrong, and when parliament is in fact oppressive, who protects the
people? Herein lies the irony of popular sovereignty.

It has been said that, when there are serious issues affecting
government, the rights and entitlements of citizens in England, the
people look to parliament for solutions. In a sense, popular sovereignty
yields to parliamentary sovereignty. In France, the people look to
themselves for solutions and the general will prevails. In the United
States, citizens look to the Supreme Court and the exercise of its review
jurisdiction. In Samoa (and, I might add, most Pacific states), a case
could be made that citizens should look to the judiciary, notwithstanding
the Pacific's love affair with Westminster. This is demanded by the
Constitution as supreme law, interpreted and applied by the courts
with a very wide review jurisdiction under article 2.

Furthermore, as hitherto argued, democracy does not simply mean
majority rule, but majority rule subject to the rule of law. Democracy,
argues Allan (2001:261), 'is erroneously equated with majority rule; and
the corresponding idea of popular sovereignty should be understood
to embody the claim of every citizen to equal respect'. On that basis, a
majority decision that permits the torture of a citizen, denies an
aggrieved citizen access to the courts, or deprives him of his
constitutional rights, 'is not to be understood as an exercise of popular
sovereignty, however great the majority or passionate its specious claim
of legitimacy' (Allan 2001:261).

There remains the issue of the people's seemingly momentary
sovereignty, that the people are sovereign only at the moment of
adopting their written Constitution and declaring themselves 'We the

people'. Thereafter, they are no longer sovereign, at least, not until the next major constitutional moment, when the people will again declare themselves the creators of the state. The people, in other words, are sovereign only at certain constitutional moments, and the exercise of popular sovereignty is only periodic and fairly rare. By implication, for long periods of normal politics the people lie dormant, mostly passive, largely manipulable, and thoroughly at the mercy of their rulers.

This is a major issue in the Pacific. Parliaments not only pretend to 'speak' for the people, politicians and public officials have also hijacked the sovereignty of the people. An élite few own and treat government monies as if they were private property as, for example, in the case of Papua New Guinea (Windybank and Manning 2003). In some cases, rulers and their cohorts have a monopoly over the ownership of both private and public lands; citizens without power or political influence have been reduced to squatters in emerging Pacific ghettos outside city precincts, as in Suva. In other cases, governments (sometimes in the form of one or two persons) in concert with multinational firms have a monopoly over public resources, for example, the telecommunications sector.

> Increasingly, these monopolistic arrangements are joint ventures between governments and private sector partners. Moreover, the governments have been induced to sign exclusivity agreements with the private sector partner that lock those arrangements in place for many years (Duncan 2004:130).

The result is socioeconomic alienation of the people, especially when ownership of resources is vested in a few people. In the arena of political representation, politicians are elected on promises that the people accept in good faith. Yet it is usually the case that, once elected, politicians readily forget their promises and rule as they please. Thus, representation in the Pacific remains a predominantly beautiful fiction. Between elections, the sovereignty of the people is captured, owned and manipulated by an élite few.

History has shown, however, that the people will not eternally abandon their right to rule to a dictator or tyrant. What happened in the Solomon Islands and the current situation in Tonga provide clear examples of this. Quite appropriately, the *Eminent Persons' Group Review of the Pacific Islands Forum* (Eminent Persons' Group 2004) strongly encourages forms of governance and development that focus on the people, who are government's own greatest asset, in every society with right-minded rulers.

Government by consent: the people's legal title to rule

Inherent in the principles of government as trustee and popular sovereignty is the related principle of the consent of the governed and hence government by consent. 'Put another way', observes Morgan (1988:13), 'all government rests on the consent, however obtained, of the governed'. I concede that the historicity of this consent is an issue. In the absence of conclusive evidence regarding such matters as the unanimity of the consent and the weight given to opposing views, the notion of consent is, at best, a graphic way of expressing the values of trust and popular sovereignty. At the risk of repetition, I note the following matters given their pertinence to the interests of this chapter.

The consent of the governed provides the explanation and justification of popular government. 'Self-government, as we almost invariably understand it', writes Jed Rubenfeld (1998:211) 'consists ideally of government by the will or consent of the governed. This holds for the most cynical as well as the most romantic depiction of self-government'. Abjuring brutal force as a way of securing the consent of the governed to the rule of governors, consent should be obtained by the power of ideas. 'Human beings, if only to maintain a semblance of self-respect, have to be persuaded. Their consent must be sustained by opinions' (Morgan 1988:13). Whether or not such opinions are true and honest is another matter. What seems certain is that the principle of government by and with the consent of the governed is commonly adopted as a viable explanation of how the many are governed by the few.

In the case of Samoa, government by consent is anchored in the people's declaration 'We the people of Samoa' as an essential term of the constitutional agreement of the people to constitute a government. It is also rooted in what Bruce Ackerman (1991:51) calls important 'constitutional moments' expressing popular will and voice, culminating in the 'commanding voice of the People', the 'supreme and original will' of the people, as CJ Marshall in *Marbury* v *Madison* 5 US (1 Cranch) 137 (1803) put it at 176. This consent not only authorises the creation of the state but also legitimises and maintains its existence and rule. 'What creates that legitimacy in a regime founded on the consent of "the people"', says Richard S. Kay (1998:35), 'is the agreement of a sufficient number of people whose representative capacity makes their joint will an acceptable surrogate for "the people" itself'. Accordingly, the declaration 'We the people of Samoa' is really an affirmation of popular rights, which the people have surrendered upon submitting to the rules of civil government with the understanding that only by surrendering their rights to govern and defend themselves can there be peace and security for their property and persons. However the consent of the governed is understood—whether as popular will, or popular voice, or 'popular authorship' (Rubenfeld 1998:214)—it seems certain that the consent of the governed must and does constitute the basis, authority and legitimacy of government and constitutional rules.

The temporal reach of that consent is a matter of debate though. Consent could be construed as continuous, inferred from the people's acquiescence both in major constitutional moments and in ordinary politics. Alternatively, we could treat the original framers of a written Constitution as rational and responsible agents acting with care and foresight such that their decision could be deemed to be acceptable over a long period of time, even though that acceptance can never be permanent. Rubenfeld (1998:211) gives an apt summation, arguing

> [w]hether we understand the will of the governed through a hyperdisintegrative lens such as public choice or through a hyperintegrative lens such as fascism, in either case, and in all the intermediate cases, we begin by understanding self-government as, ideally, government by the will of the governed *here and now*.

The importance of government by consent is also axiomatic. Absent the consent of the governed and we have a body politic of slaves who are at the mercy of self-appointed rulers and who have to be moved by naked force at the rulers' behest. Without the consent of the governed, the state loses not only its right to govern but also its authority as the state of the people. The consent of the governed is therefore indispensable as the proper basis of government rule.

The function of government in this scheme is to protect the persons, property, rights and freedoms of the citizens. In the philosophy of John Locke, finding life in the state of nature unsatisfying, people eventually come to an agreement to resign certain rights proper to them in their natural state 'to join or unite into a community for their comfortable, safe and peaceable living one amongst another' (Locke 1988: Ch. 8, 95). The objective is to acquire security of person and property against internal and external threats. In return for that security, 'every man by consenting with others to make one body politic under one government, puts himself under an obligation to every one of that society to submit to the determination of the majority' (Locke 1988:Ch. 8, 97). We find the same motifs in the philosophy of Thomas Hobbes. Since life in the state of war is literally hopeless, humans eventually come to understand that the first fundamental law of nature is 'to seek peace, and follow it' (Hobbes 1960:Ch.13). From this is derived the second law of nature: that humans must be willing to renounce their natural rights to govern themselves (as in the state of war); to covenant or contract with one another to surrender their natural rights to a sovereign power; and by that contract, the said sovereign power, vested in either one person or an assembly of persons, is instituted for the purpose of securing the peace and defence of all.

All this highlights the fundamental importance of the people not only in their priority over the state but in their status as the creators and therefore owners of the state. As creators, the people are therefore sovereign. '[I]t seems safe to say', argues Kay (1998:35), 'that we as we actually are do not recognise the title of anyone save the people of a country to rule it. Democratic sovereignty is the only sovereignty we accredit'. The people, according to Finn (1995:1), sustain the 'authority and legitimacy' of the state. Popular sovereignty means that the people 'are constituted the owners, not merely the beneficiaries' (Finn 1995:5) of government.

In addition, as rational and responsible subjects, the people have the moral authority and the intellectual ability to choose, insist upon, and enjoy the form of government they want. 'The principle of popular sovereignty', says Jeremy Waldron (1998:272), '—basic to liberal thought—requires that the people should have whatever constitution, whatever form of government they want'. It could be argued also that the people did not create just any government but a particular form of government, that

> in constituting the very possibility of "the will of the people", the members of a society intend to commit themselves not just to any old form of majoritarianism but to a particular form of majority decision, namely the sovereignty of a popular will formed in vigorous and wide-open debate (Waldron 1998:293).

The principle of government by consent fundamentally challenges what some Pacific public officials have been doing to the peoples' states. Corruption, with its multifarious manifestations and detrimental effects, sums up a very bad situation in some quarters of the Pacific. Corruption, in the words of the *Eminent Persons' Group Review of the Pacific Islands*, is

> [the polar opposite of] a style of governance that is respected for its inclusiveness, effectiveness and freedom from corruption...[It is] people-centred and democratic in spirit. It needs to reach into communities and address the issues that are important to them. These include poverty in all its forms, the position of women and youth in society, education, 'lifestyle diseases', and the growing threat of HIV / AIDS. The Pacific Way [the Forum's proposed guiding philosophy]

should deal openly, honestly yet respectfully with problems including failures of governance and corruption (Eminent Persons Group 2004:n.p.).

Corruption, the use of public power to exploit public office for private gain, violates citizens' trust reposed in government officials. It is a frontal attack on the people's entitlement as owners of government monies, property and resources. It is also worth noting—to set the record straight—that the corruption of some public officials is not a mandate from the people. Equating corruption with a whole nation, as is the wont of some irritable academics, is therefore absurd and repugnant, logically fallacious and empirically barren.

Constitutional principles: ideals, realities and fictions

The question is whether the constitutional principles articulated above have normative value in practice in the Pacific. The issue is the discrepancy between theory and praxis, with the difference between ideal and reality being, at best, an optimistic fiction denoting what remains to be achieved. This issue is further examined by reference to the following matters: lawmaking power; electoral representation; freedom of thought and expression; the accountability of government; judicial review of constitutional powers and roles, and judicial review of administrative decisions. The Lockean formula noted above provides a broad test

> the legislature acts against the trust reposed in them when they endeavour to invade the property of the subject, and to make themselves, or any part of the community, masters or arbitrary disposers of the lives, liberties, or fortunes of the people (Locke 1988:221).

Lawmaking power: when the law becomes a sham

Lawmaking power is sometimes arbitrary. Unlimited, it becomes menacing and oppressive. In some Pacific jurisdictions, lawmaking power is characterised by an inherent tendency towards totalitarianism, engendered by the political ideologies of corporate states. Central to the political setup of a corporate state is the principle of leadership that places the leader at the top of a hierarchy of authoritarian structures that organise all dimensions of national life. The nation is accordingly organised in such a way that each level in the hierarchy is controlled by the next level above it, with the whole edifice being controlled by a single leader. The logic here is that the leader not only represents the people, the leader is the people; the will of the leader naturally becomes the will of the people who are, in many cases, no more than a mere object of leadership. Perhaps people could still vote in elections, exercise their rights, and sometimes criticise politicians, but those things do not make them a political factor with any significant influence—their opinions and actions will not change, let alone influence, anything. Ultimately, the leader is functionally all-powerful.

Herein lies the problem of lawmaking in corporate states. Because the will of the leader is the will of the people, the will of the leader is therefore law. Parliament, the executive and the judiciary are all subservient to that law. This usually leads to the danger of synchronising parliamentary enactments, executive decisions and even judicial judgments with the wishes of the leader. This synchronising process (subtle in many cases) is usually predicated on the fabricated notion that the will of the leader is always right and should therefore be law. When the leader's will meets with resistance of already enacted laws, the substance of the laws can always be changed at any time and in any direction, often on the absurd ground that it is the role of the leader to protect the law. This is undergirded by the constructed appearance that the rule of the leader is just and merciful. This ideological transformation of the law entails adverse ramifications. For example, it effectively cancels out the judicial function of interpreting and applying the law in an independent, impartial manner. Parliament keeps producing legislation; the courts continue to sit; but the law and its operation are, at all times, manipulated, sometimes grossly, in order to serve the ruler and his cohorts' interests.

To what extent the lawmaking process in some Pacific states, especially Tonga, fits into this model is a moot point. Ideally, the principle of leadership of the crown is democratised in practice through conventions, such as representative government, which require the crown to follow the decisions of the elected representatives of the people. The problem remains that, in some Pacific cases, democracy still means the arbitrary rule of either a single individual or an élite few. But then, again, all forms of government are inherently totalitarian. Some assume a totalitarian posture simply because they are bastard imitations of outdated feudal orders. Others evolve into totalitarianism through a gradual usurpation of powers. That aside, the adverse effects of a corporate model of government cannot, and should not, be explained away. I refer, for instance, to the effect on land ownership, the institution of property rights and the progress of under-privileged classes. The choice of this rubric is based on the ground that the corporate political order is ultimately grounded in property rights and the regime of land ownership, with all land being made the property of the leader.[10]

In such scenarios, control over land and the prerogative to grant or withhold estates lies with the leader. Given that there are always some people whom the leader favours more than others, the possibility of the others getting little or nothing is not remote. And more often than not, the others deprived of estates in land are usually those at the bottom of the pecking order. This either creates an under-privileged class or reinforces the plight of an already entrenched under-privileged class. Either way, the institution of estates (and the grant or withholding thereof) is an uncanny way of maintaining the dominance of a monopolising and élitist group.

This raises serious questions about the lawmaking power of a state organised on the corporate model. The alliance between law and class power is a very real concern. Likewise law's imbrication in unfair property relations, legitimated by the law itself, raises serious concerns about the law being nothing more than a façade masking shams and inequities, as nothing more than an instrument of class ideology.

In light of the above, I offer the following observations predicated on the principle of government as trustee and measured against the Lockean test noted above. First, law is deeply embedded in the productive arrangement, forces and relations existing in every society. In a political order arranged on the corporate model and governed by social classes, as in Tonga, lawmaking power is particularly amenable to manipulation by dominant groups. Adopting a critical legal studies perspective, the danger is the possible reduction of the law to a mere 'instrument of the *de facto* ruling class: it both defines and defends these rulers' claims upon resources and labour-power...Hence the rule of law is only another mask for the rule of a class' (Thompson 1975:259).

Second, while it may be an exaggeration to claim that the law is nothing more than an instrument of the dominant groups in those types of societies, it is certainly true that the law mediates and legitimises existing class relations, accords rights and entitlements based on social status, determines and defines peoples' perceptions of the social order and their place in it, and maintains the status quo. Whenever that happens, the law's rhetoric of justice and equity is empty; its forms and procedures actually hide ulterior injustices and inequities. Put bluntly, the rule of law becomes a sham.

Finally, even in jurisdictions where lawmaking power is exercised by a duly elected parliament, there is always the danger of unjust deprivation when the state takes land, either without adequate or any compensation, or in violation of the property rights of an individual or a section of the body politic. This was the issue in the Samoa Supreme Court case of *Western Samoa Trust Estates Corporation* v *Tuionoula* [1987]. The court held that the taking of customary land for a national airport was in accordance with an agreement concluded between the Crown and the owners of that land in 1942. However, the issue remains—was the level of compensation adequate? Article 14 of the Constitution 1960 provides for rights regarding property and, under clause 1, prohibits the compulsory taking of land except by law subject to 'the payment within a reasonable time of adequate compensation'. The issue still stands unresolved.

Paraphrasing the Lockean test, rulers and lawmakers (both totalitarian despots and democratically constituted parliaments) violate the trust reposed in them when they deprive citizens of the right to property, or acquire land without adequate compensation or, in a mighty act of naked state compulsion, without any compensation at all. Such acts contravene the constitutional principle of government as trustee broadly construed in legal, ethical and political terms. Sometimes, the principle of identification of rulers and ruled is a trick used by dictators to justify the rule of a few over the many.

Political rights and the power of representation: the few and the many

This section addresses political rights and political representation as central tenets of the constitutional principles of government as trustee, popular sovereignty and government by consent. To what extent is representation in the Pacific nothing more than 'a make-believe…a fiction' (Morgan 1988:13) designed to make possible and justify the rule of a few? And to what extent has representation been converted into a self-evident truth, which, as such, is insulated against scrutiny or criticism since challenging the so-called self-evident truths might rend the fabric of society? The following analysis exposes the gap between ideal and reality, and broaches the issue of rulers acting as 'the masters or arbitrary disposers' of the civil liberties of the ruled.

'Many of the small island democracies of the South Pacific', comments Benjamin Reilly (2004:n.p.), 'are natural laboratories for constitutional and electoral experimentation'. Experimentation is a risky business; it could be productive, sometimes; but more often than not, it is fraught with disaster. Problems range from 'a wave of relief at the removal of a government, and a rush of optimism after each new government is formed' in Papua New Guinea (Standish 2004) to adopting indigenous-friendly electoral systems in the Pacific generally. The alternative voting system in Fiji continues to cough up problems of its own. The Solomon Islands electoral system of first-past-the-post has provided 'a major link in the chain contributing to the "social unrest" period the country suffered during its 1998–2003 years' (Roughan 2004).

In most Pacific states, bribes and electoral fraud mar general elections. Politicians bribe other politicians to acquire a majority in coalition governments—perceived as 'tactics of survival' in Papua New Guinea (Okole 2004). The system of coalition government is being hijacked and reduced to a means of capturing executive power. Politicians are playing the part of political gods. In Fiji, the promise of the alternative voting system is yet to be realised. The evidence, thus far, shows that 'there are clear limits to electoral engineering for managing conflict in divided societies' (Stockwell 2004). Voters now expect that their elected representatives will return favours. Politicians, in turn, expect the government to pay 'for electors' rising expectations from them', as in the Cook Islands (Crocombe and Jonassen 2004). This scenario, commonly explained by attributing blame to Pacific custom, has an alternative explanation. The electors are not drunk or stupid. They know very well that, after the elections, the political world reverts back to its usual psychology: their elected representatives benefit from government resources at the expense of the masses. The trick, therefore, is to get a share of the politicians' fortunes before they become masters of the world.

Samoa's system of parliamentary representation presents its own interesting issues, for example, the considerably long life of parliament (Salevao 2004). In November 1991, parliament amended the Constitution and by article 63(4) extended the life of parliament from three to five years. The propriety of such an arrangement is questionable. The rationale is political stability and that the longer term will enable the government to pursue more responsible policies. That may be true. Still, the longer parliamentary term is an élitist solution that creates an élitist democracy. Lacking faith in the capacity of the common citizen to make a positive political contribution, politicians deem it their noble duty to remain in power for as long as they possibly can. Yet, in truth, the longer the term, the longer the political élite holds citizens to ransom. Thus, the adoption of élitist solutions could be construed as an attempt to avoid 'the restraints imposed by constitutional checks and balances and by the pressures of almost constant electioneering' (Walker 1995:185). While the five-year life of Samoa's parliament is nothing compared to England's Long Parliament of 1640 to 1653, the fact that Samoa has only two general elections in a whole decade is somewhat disturbing.

Another issue of importance concerns parliament's imposition of disqualifications in respect of parliamentary candidature. In the Samoa Court of Appeal case of *In re the Constitution, Mulitalo v Attorney-General of Samoa* [2001] WSCA 8 (20 December 2001), the appellants challenged the lawmaking authority of parliament (pursuant to article 45 of the Constitution 1960 and the *Electoral Act 1963*) to change constantly the disqualifications—twice in the same year—with the effect of excluding the appellants from seeking parliamentary election in 2001. On the facts, the court held that the changes were validly enacted by the *Electoral Amendment Act 2000* and that they were correct under the Constitution. However, the court's approach is troubling in light of the following *obiter* statement by the court at 10.

> Essentially, this was a case about the appellants' sense of grievance that parliament had changed the qualifications to be a member of parliament with the result that some people who had lived overseas [as the appellants] and who would have been eligible to stand under the previous legislation could no longer do so. *Whether that is unfair is not a matter for the courts to judge.* If what parliament did was within the powers vested in it by the Constitution, there is no basis for court intervention [emphasis added].

In my view, either the court had abdicated its constitutional role of protecting rights and liberties out of deference to the institution of separated powers, or it had taken the doctrine of parliamentary sovereignty undiluted in apparent contradiction of the Constitution as supreme law and the court's power of review of constitutional roles and powers under article 2. Once again, the Samoan judiciary is faced with the problem of reconciling Westminster, Washington, Paris and Samoa as noted in chapter two above.

In Tonga, political representation is clearly an issue. Clause 17 empowers the King to govern on behalf of all 'his people'. The use of the possessive pronoun 'his' is remarkable in its connotation of ownership. The people belong to the King, perhaps in the limited, mythical sense of the King as the father of the nation (Koloamatangi 2004; Campbell 2004), but even that patriarchal reading does not take away the compelling sense of the people's subjection to the rule of the King. The qualification in the second half of clause 17, that the King will not rule 'to enrich or benefit any one man or any one class but without partiality for the good of all people of his Kingdom', must descend to the level of empirical reality.

Clause 41 is central to the whole constructed edifice of the King's rule. In addition to deifying the person of the King, the clause also expressly vests sovereign power in the King: 'The King is the sovereign of all chiefs and all the people'. The King, not the people, is sovereign. This is hardly surprising since the Constitution of Tonga 1875 was granted by the King to the people; it did not emanate from the people. There is, therefore, no assertion of popular sovereignty in the Tongan Constitution. The King created the government of Tonga, not the people.

Clause 51 vests extensive powers of appointment and dismissal in the King. The King appoints the cabinet or ministers of the King (including the prime minister, minister of foreign affairs, minister of lands, minister of police and any other minister) whom the King 'may be pleased to appoint' (the King's prerogative) and who hold office 'during the King's pleasure' or for the duration of their commissions.

Clause 38 extends the power of the King over the Tongan parliament. The King has power to convoke the legislative assembly 'at any time' and prorogue it 'at his pleasure', and then command the election of new representatives of the nobles and the commoners. Clause 61 vests power in the King to appoint the speaker of parliament, thus extending his power over parliament. There is also the issue of the domination of parliament by the privy council (appointed by the King), cabinet ministers (appointed by the King and sitting as nobles and members of the privy council), the prime minister and speaker of the assembly (both appointed by the King), and representatives of the nobles. This is because under clauses 59 and 60, the assembly shall consist of members of the privy council, cabinet members, nine nobles as representatives of the nobles and nine representatives of the commoners elected on universal suffrage under clause 64. The dominance of the King, privy council, cabinet, and nobles is much more than a matter of statistics.

A further restriction on the political rights of the nine representatives of the commoners is imposed by clause 67 which provides that: 'It shall be lawful for only the nobles of the legislative assembly to discuss or vote upon laws relating to the King or the royal family or the titles and inheritances of the nobles…'. Clause 71 further provides that

> [s]hould any representative of the nobles be guilty of conduct unbecoming his position whether during the session of the legislative assembly or not he may be tried and deprived of his office by the nobles of the legislative assembly but the representatives of the people shall not take part in his trial.

These restrictions inevitably split parliament in half, alienating not only the representatives of the commoners but the commoners themselves, seriously compromise the effectiveness of parliament as a check on the power of the executive, and function to undermine the constitutional order.

In light of the Tongan situation, I note with interest Morgan's observations about fiction-making in England. First, monarchy 'has always required close ties with divinity'. Second, the alliance between Christian/Jewish theology and Christian/English politics 'created a theomorphic king'. Finally, '[t]he divine right of kings had never been more than a fiction, and as used by the Commons it led toward the fiction that replaced it, the sovereignty of the people' (Morgan 1988:17). Quite frankly, some Pacific nations may well need to re-examine how their fictions came about and to reorganise their legal, political and moral priorities.

Freedom of thought and expression: 'I think, I speak, therefore, I exist'

Freedom of thought and expression is an issue everywhere. The Pacific is no exception. Again the test is government's trust duty to guarantee and protect that freedom (subject to reasonable limits), even if the exercise of that freedom involves criticism of government and its policies. Put simply, government or the ruling political party in government has no trust to act as the master or arbitrary disposer of 'the lives, liberties or fortunes of the people'.

Freedom of speech and expression is the cornerstone of human liberty and the condition for nearly every other freedom. Without it, other rights are liable to die and wither away. This is embodied in Mill's dictum that the act of silencing the expression of an opinion is tantamount to robbery. It is robbery not only of the truth produced through the subtraction of error but robbery of important values vital to a free society which freedom of speech entails. 'Historically, we have viewed freedom of speech as indispensable to a free society and its government'.[11] Truth, self-fulfilment (when citizens are able to realise their full potential as humans if they are not deprived of the right to express what they think, praise or even criticise their government) and the advancement of knowledge—these values are indispensable and must be protected at all costs.

Freedom of the media is critical to the realisation of freedom of thought and expression.

> Freedom to distribute information to every citizen wherever he desires to receive it is so clearly vital to the preservation of a free society that, putting aside reasonable police and health regulations of time and manner of distribution, it must be fully preserved.[12]

There is a political environment that is optimal for freely distributing information. Factors that are conducive to this environment include the government performing its work in public, and a media sector capable of publicising this work. Since information is the life-blood of the political process, freedom of the media is absolutely vital.

> Absent such freedom of communication, representative government would fail to achieve its purpose, namely, government by the people through their elected representatives; government would cease to be responsive to the needs and wishes of the people and, in that sense, would cease to be truly representative.[13]

I need emphasise that an informed and enlightened citizenry is much more productive in government affairs than a dull and uninformed one. Unless, of course, the government is bent toward tyrannical rule—tyrannies thrive on mass ignorance.

An environment that allows for freedom of expression inevitably enables the publication of critical views on political issues. This is important for the government. Informed of what citizens think, the government would then respond accordingly. Ideally, unfair criticisms are corrected; criticisms with substance are heeded. Other than that, those who wield the powers of government must be open to public criticism. 'In a free democratic society it is almost too obvious to need stating that those who hold office in government and who are responsible for public administration must always be open to criticism. Any attempt to stifle or fetter such criticism amounts to political censorship of the most insidious and objectionable kind'.[14]

While freedom of thought, expression and the media is guaranteed under Pacific constitutions,[15] there is a marked discrepancy between the constitutional ideal and what occurs in practice. In Tonga, the struggle for freedom of expression and the media goes on. As the author of the Tongan newspaper *Taimi* understands it, 'the role of the media in Tonga is the same role that the media perform in other countries...There is a watchdog role and a responsibility to provide people with information' (Koloamatangi 2004:n.p.). The issues, in his view, include the bias of other Tongan media outlets towards the government.[16]

The Samoa Supreme Court case of *The Honourable Tuiatua Tupua Tamasese Efi* v *The Attorney General of Samoa* (S.Ct., 1 August 2000) provides another illustration and is used here to tease out the pertinent issues and principles. The plaintiff, a former leader of Samoa's opposition party, sued the attorney-general on behalf of the former prime minister, the present prime minister, the board of directors of Televise Samoa Corporation, the Broadcasting Department and others. He alleged that the ruling party (the Human Rights Protection Party, HRPP), since coming into power in 1989, had pursued or permitted a policy of denying him (as leader of the opposition) fair access to the government-controlled media; that the policy in question was a reaction against his political views and was designed to interfere with the performance of his constitutional duties as a parliamentarian and leader of the opposition; and that that policy violated of article 13(1)(a) of the Constitution which guarantees freedom of speech and expression,[17] and article 15(2) on freedom from discriminatory legislation.

On the facts, Wilson J held that the former prime minister, by his conduct and words, placed a restriction on the plaintiff's access to the media. Such restriction created a fetter on the plaintiff's freedom of expression and was, in effect, an infringement of the plaintiff's rights under articles 13 and 15. Further, Wilson J held that under the current administration, the present prime minister, Tuilaepa Malielegaoi, publicly announced on 4 March 1999 that no restraint on the access of the plaintiff or his party to the media 'is now in existence'. Wilson J thus held at 54 that 'nothing in the conduct of the Tuilaepa Administration since late 1998, which has been reviewed in these proceedings, violates either of those guarantees' under articles 13 and 15.

This case raises important constitutional questions relating to the practice of prior restraint and the courts' role of declaring void such restraints.[18] On a functional theory of the press, the public has the right to be informed of government actions, and freedom of the press serves that right. Upholding the legal prohibition against prior restraint, Wilson J at 52 noted that the policy under the former prime minister amounted to 'a pattern of exclusion' and was, in fact, 'a ban'. It seems certain from the facts that the former prime minister was of the opinion that it was in the public interest to deny the plaintiff access to the media, that the plaintiff's conduct threatened to incite public disorder and cause division, and that such conduct justified denying him access to the media.

Part of the problem is that notions such as public order and public interest are subjective concepts, representing a subjective assessment of the danger speech or conduct is likely to create. But as Mason CJ observed in *Australian Capital Television Pty Ltd* v *The Commonwealth* (1992) at 145, the history of freedom of expression is characterised by attempts to restrict that freedom 'in the name of some imagined necessity'. Adopting the test in *Schenck* v *United States* 249 US 47, 39 Sup. Ct. 247, 63 L. Ed. 470 (1919) at 52, it should be said that, on the facts, the plaintiff did not shout 'fire' in a theatre and cause panic, and his words did not create 'a clear and present danger' that might have justified banning him from the media.

Following the more stringent test in *Jacob Abrams* v *United States* 250 US 616, 40 Sup. Ct. 17, 63 L. Ed. 1173 (1919) at 627, the plaintiff's words neither produced nor were 'intended to produce a clear and imminent danger' of bringing about any substantive evils. Unlike Schenck's attempted insubordination of the US military when the United States was at war with Germany, and unlike Abram's publication of leaflets which were accused of, among other things, encouraging resistance to the US war with Germany, the plaintiff's criticism of Samoa's executive government was made in time of peace and was directed at the government's lack of accountability. His allegations might have had some substance, or they could have been baseless, but he was certainly entitled to express them.

Measured against the test in *Brandenburg* v *Ohio* 395 US 444 (1969) at 447 where the court held that the constitutional guarantees of free speech and free press do not permit a state 'to forbid or proscribe advocacy of the use of force or of law violation except where such advocacy is directed to inciting or producing imminent lawless action and is likely to incite or produce such action', the plaintiff's criticism of the Samoan executive was not in the mode of Brandenburg's advocacy of crime, sabotage, violence and terrorism. Criticising government cannot be reasonably equated with incitement to acts of rebellion. And, unlike Brandenburg, who was a Ku Klux Klan leader, the plaintiff was the recognised leader of Samoa's opposition party in parliament.

In the final analysis, banning the plaintiff was, in effect, silencing opposing political views simply as a matter of personal predilection on the part of the former prime minister. When he denied the plaintiff access to the government-controlled media, he excised from public discourse what he saw as unacceptable speech. This was based on the theory that such speech was inherently likely to cause division, and the facile assumption that it was the executive government's role to act as guardian of the social order. This assumption is often employed as a guise for banning opposing, unpleasant political views.

Perhaps the plaintiff's speech was culturally repugnant to members of the executive government. In the realm of politics, however, the plaintiff's criticism was uttered as part of his role as leader of the opposition. Within 'reasonable restrictions', freedom of speech is vital in the face of executive governments so keen to extend their orbit and increase their powers. Freedom of speech, since it is not absolute, must therefore be carefully guarded against official depredations. When executive governments assume the power to decide who can speak, where, when and what they say, freedom of speech is flagrantly violated. We may disagree with what a member of the opposition says; it is our moral right to disagree. But, pursuant to articles 13(1)(a) and 15(2), we also have a constitutional duty to defend his right to say what he or she has to say—however ill-informed that might be in our view.

Government accountability: parliament, the executive and the judiciary are servants of the people

The constitutional principles enunciated above ultimately define the nature and scope of the accountability of all institutions and officials of government, and provide the overarching legal and constitutional framework within which government should be conducted. As noted above, the re-emergence of principles such as government as trustee has been prompted by the failings of representative and responsible government, the uncertain force of conventions like ministerial responsibility, the exaltation of the executive, and the development of modern states into *de facto* corporations. These factors have posed the need to hold government more strictly accountable, reassess the capacity of the principle of representative and responsible government to hold government to account, and reappraise our basic constitutional principles. With reference to the Australian situation, Finn (1995:13) observes, '[f]or so long as we remain committed to the system of responsible government, Westminster principles will continue to provide an integral part of our theory and practice of government. But they are second order principles, not the basal principles of our system of government'.

To what extent this applies to other Pacific jurisdictions is a moot point. In the case of Samoa, it may be reiterated that parliament, the executive and the judiciary are creatures of an entrenched Constitution—created by the Constitution, governed by the Constitution, and subject to the authority and control of the Constitution as supreme law. And since the Constitution is an act of the people, the accountability of government is therefore demanded and justified by the sovereign status of the people as the creators, owners and beneficiaries of government in keeping with the principles of government as trustee, popular sovereignty and government by consent.

Parliament, naturally, belongs to the people—elected and owned by the people, accountable to the people. Part of its fiduciary obligations is to adhere faithfully to the terms upon which the people have entrusted their powers of government to it. Similarly, the executive belongs to the people and is ultimately accountable to the people. While entrusted with the important role of administration and the efficient conduct of government affairs, there is no term (whether expressed or implied) in the people's transfer of power to the executive that the executive should exalt itself as the protector of the social order at the expense of countervailing interests, including the exercise of rights to criticise and organise opposition to government policy. Like parliament and the executive, the judiciary too belongs to the people; judges should exercise judicial power for the people (Mason 1993a). Underpinning the exercise of judicial power is the citizen's right not only to invoke the jurisdiction of the courts, but to insist on the exercise of the courts' jurisdiction. That jurisdiction, and the requisite power to exercise it, is fortified by the presumption against depriving the courts of their inherent powers and preventing an unauthorised assumption of jurisdiction.

The review jurisdiction of the Samoan judiciary deserves further mention in this connection. Samoa's constitutional arrangement places an onerous burden on the jurisdiction of the courts to review legislative and executive actions pursuant to article 2(2) of the Constitution 1960 as supreme law by virtue of article 2(1). Underlining the significance and force of article 2, Davidson in Samoa's Constitutional Convention 1960 explained, 'clause 2 makes it clear that because this is the supreme law no other laws may be made that contradict anything that is set out in the constitution itself' (Constitutional Convention of Western Samoa 1960:Vol. I, 67). Whereas article 2 might not have been intended to create judicial supremacy, it does permit judicial review of constitutional powers and roles. This, in itself, raises a host of issues as US constitutional jurisprudence has found out since *Marbury v Madison* (Alfange 1993; Corwin 1963). I offer the following comments in addition to the analysis of this issue in chapter two above.

First, judicial review points up the significance of a written Constitution like that of Samoa and is related to constitutionalism as the imposition of fixed limits on the powers of government. This engenders a measure of trust in the way government is conducted. Obviously, the trust that men repose goes beyond trust in a mere written text designed 'to keep a government in order' (Hamilton 1931:255). It is, more basically, trust in the power of the rule of law to constrain the conduct of both government and governed within prescribed limits and controls, that both rulers and ruled would and should act according to the law.

Second, constitutional constraints, like judicial review, are a form of the people's own precommitment to be bound by and within constitutional limits. They are the people's own necessary precautions against hasty and irrational acts of self-destruction.[19] Such precommitment may be characterised as an act of popular sovereignty in the sense that the people have the right to decide on their own form of government, that is, without necessarily condoning dictatorships even if democratically elected. Samuel Freeman (1990:353) describes this as 'a kind of rational and shared precommitment among free and equal sovereign citizens at the level of constitutional choice'. It is the electorate's collective decision 'to bind itself in advance to resist the siren charms of rights violations', to protect and prevent themselves from shipwreck (Waldron 1998:275). The decision of Samoa's constitutional framers to arm the Samoan judiciary with review powers is very important in this respect.

Third it is possible to reconcile judicial review and democracy. For instance, judicial review may be viewed in terms of popular choice in keeping with popular sovereignty. Furthermore, the 'counter-majoritarian difficulty' (Bickel 1962:16) could be overcome by reference to the courts' constitutional duty of protecting the rights of minorities and individuals. This is important given the danger of arbitrary rule that is always inherent in majority power. In addition to the democratic justification of judicial review based on normative or fundamental values (Dworkin 1977), it could also be argued that, in most cases, judges are more principled, reasonable and reliable than most legislators. Taken together, these arguments carry the cumulative effect of removing the democratic objection to judicial review.

Fourth, judicial review demands a strong, independent and impartial judiciary. The judiciary in a truly constitutional system is thus 'the primary keeper of the rule of law' (Mason 1995:119) and judges themselves the 'guardians of the rule of law' (Mason 1995:116). Being the 'least dangerous branch' of government, because it has no influence over either the government's sword or the government's purse, the judiciary is most likely to diligently execute its constitutional role without fear, favour or ill-will (Hodge 1995).

In jurisdictions following the Westminster system, the judiciary has a critical significance in the face of the exalted executive governments that now dominate most parliaments and the general tendency towards super-executive bodies. Indeed, the institution of separated powers presupposes that two, or even all three, branches of government will not cooperate to circumvent legal rules to achieve illegal objectives through a system of trade-offs. Be that as it may, there is always the risk of the three branches acting in concert to monstrous, illegal effect. This poses the real need for a branch of government with no incentive to make deals to enhance its own authority, one that could be trusted to restrict political departments to their constitutionally defined powers and enforce the substantive constitutional limits on the exercise of those powers. This is the special constitutional role of the courts: to declare, elaborate and enforce constitutional limits and controls. In this manner, the judiciary is and should be 'the primary keeper of the rule of law' (Mason 1995:116).

But the judiciary, too, is subject to constitutional limits and controls. First and foremost is the subjection of the judiciary to the control of a written Constitution. Furthermore, when judges do not comply with the rules of their profession there will be consequences. Removal from office in cases of serious misconduct is available as a last resort. The less formal censure of public and professional criticism is also available to keep judges on the side of the law. When judges refuse to exercise the courts' jurisdiction—even though that jurisdiction is clearly authorised by law, and a citizen has invoked and insists on the exercise of that jurisdiction—they unconstitutionally abdicate their judicial responsibility to the people. When that happens, judges themselves are subject to legal and political sanctions.[20]

I refer also to the courts' review of administrative actions jurisdiction, that is, the inherent powers of the superior courts to review the decisions of public officials in the administration of government and to grant appropriate orders. First, there is a central conceptual connection between administrative law and the principle of government as trustee. Administrative law is, in fact, one of those bodies of law that are fiduciary in character though not professing to be such in express terms. '[M]odern administrative law…from its earliest days,' writes Mason (1993a:3) 'has mirrored the way in which equity has regulated the exercise of fiduciary powers'. The correlation between equity and administrative law is encapsulated in the principle of government trusteeship defined as

> the 'architectural principle' of our [Australia's] institutions and a measure of judgment of their practices and procedures [and] a principled foundation for the new generation of 'corruption laws' now being imposed on public officials; and more generally, for the standards of conduct to be expected of public officials of all stations (Finn 1995:15).

This is important. The recognition of government's fiduciary relationship with the governed underlines the role equity plays in the rule of law. It is an essential principle of legitimate governance, in terms of the exercise of fiduciary powers.[21] Originating from the Courts of Equity, the fiduciary concept was partly designed 'to prevent those holding positions of power from abusing their authority' (Owen 1996). This is in keeping with the overriding purpose of equity as a system of law designed to redress wrongs, provide justice rooted in conscience, and to protect the vulnerable from abuse by persons with power over them. Since 'the inflexible procedures surrounding the common law writs made justice an elusive goal' (Evans 1993:1), equity as developed by the Court of Chancery sought 'to correct defects in the law' (Evans 1993:2) and to provide an additional avenue of recourse for aggrieved citizens whose actions did not satisfy one of the common law causes of action.

Second, public sector reform in the Pacific, the 'fourth institution' (Larmour 2004:107; also Teuea 2004; Ives 2004), now involves the corporatisation and privatisation of public sector bodies and the enactment of corporate legislation governing those bodies. The economic arguments for corporatising and privatising public enterprises are fairly well-known.[22] For public sector reform to deliver its desired results, its economic benefits and effects must be carefully balanced, especially where, for example, reform involves downsizing the public service. Aggravating the unemployment situation is a real possibility, especially in developing countries where the private sector may not be large or strong enough to absorb public servants put out of work in the downsizing process (Mellor 2004), as in the Pacific. Public sector reform also requires 'a major change in "public expectations" to generate the motivation for reform' (Ives 2004:90). In the Pacific, it is not clear that public expectations are high enough to absorb the shock of change given the lack of trust in government policies and conduct in most jurisdictions.

My specific interest is in the legal issues which public sector reform has raised, particularly the increasing importance of administrative law in the Pacific, especially in light of 'the enlargement of executive power as a potential threat to the rule of law' (Allan 2001:16). Dicey's concern with 'the existence of arbitrariness, of prerogative, or even of wide discretionary authority on the part of government' (Dicey 1959:202) is still with us. For instance, Samoa now has legislation creating government-owned corporate public bodies that provide goods and services in the manner of private sector companies but which operate at arms length from government. These public bodies now have boards of directors with chief executive officers, corporate structures, a measure of autonomy, clear operating objectives, and are charged with statutory duties—to provide full financial statements and earn a commercial rate of return, be subject to any relevant regulation, have performance targets, and comply with community service obligations. The overall objective is to improve the focus, efficiency, service performance, operating flexibility, financial returns, accountability and transparency of public bodies.

The *Samoa Public Bodies (Performance and Accountability) Act 2001* was enacted to 'promote improved performance and accountability in respect of public bodies' and, to this end, (a) specify principles governing the provision of the operation of public bodies; (b) specify the principles and procedure for appointing directors to public bodies; (c) establish requirements concerning public bodies' accountability; and (d) provide support for directors of public bodies. Section 4 provides that '[t]he purpose of this act is to enhance the performance and accountability of public bodies so that they provide the best possible service for the people of Samoa and as a result contribute to Samoa's social, cultural, economic and commercial development'.

In the first instance, this new breed of legislation, combining aspects of public and private law, is a significant step in improving the accountability, integrity and efficiency of public bodies and officials. Its aim is to exact strict standards of practice and conduct in the exercise of public power; it is founded on the principle that government was created to serve the interests of the people. This kind of legislation also forms part of the push to recapture public trust in government institutions and officials. These measures are in keeping with the principles of government as trustee, popular sovereignty and government by consent which, taken together, provide a more basic and principled theory of government.

It remains to be seen, however, how the courts will construe Samoa's public bodies legislation. It is nonetheless important to refer, albeit hypothetically, to the broad implications of such legislation. First and foremost is the issue of accountability. Section 6 of the Act 2001 sets out a chain of accountability.

> (5) The shareholding ministers shall be responsible to parliament for the performance of public bodies under this act. (6) The Board [of directors] of a public trading body shall be accountable to the shareholding minister. (7) The Board [of directors] of a public beneficial body shall be accountable to the responsible minister.

Interestingly enough, section 25 of the Act 2001 mandates the responsible minister to dismiss a director who has failed to perform his or her duties. There is no statutory provision under the act requiring the dismissal of a responsible minister who fails to perform his or her own duties. The issue of an accountability deficit needs to be addressed not only in the context of this act, but in the broader context of the unenforceability of the convention of ministerial responsibility.

The viability of the accountability arrangement is also an issue in the sense that accountability models for commercial entities fundamentally differ from those that apply in the public/administrative law arena. For instance, to what extent should public law accountability mechanisms be imposed on public bodies without defeating their principal objective as required by section 8(1)(a) of the Act 2001 which states that the principal objective of a public trading body is to be 'as profitable and efficient as comparable businesses that are not owned by the state'.

The situation, no doubt, will be complicated if the public trading body is competing with a private sector provider of similar services not subject to public law accountability mechanisms.[23] Even if the competitive neutrality principle applies in this instance, the issue of the operation of a public body as a revenue-generating entity remains.

In addition, section 8(1)(b) and sections 9–13 of the Act 2001 require community service obligations from public trading bodies. Section 9 defines 'community service obligation' in broad terms, including the 'provision of a good or service by a public trading body to a consumer or user on any terms other than normal commercial terms applying from time to time'. Section 10 vests a discretion in the responsible minister to direct a public trading body to provide a community service obligation if the performance of the obligation is necessary to ensure any of the following

- universal access to a necessary good or service
- the promotion of a policy vital to the national interest as declared by the head of state, acting on the advice of cabinet

- proper and timely response to a local, regional, national or international emergency
- correction of an injustice as declared by the ombudsman.

This is important in the respect that public bodies operating as business enterprises are charged with social responsibilities and community service obligations, thus giving a human face to the pursuit of commercial interests.

This new type of legislation will, however, put increasing strain on the courts' review of administrative decisions jurisdiction.[24] The purpose of judicial review in this particular area of law was aptly stated by Lord Chancellor in *Chief Constable of North Wales* v *Evans* [1982] 3 All ER 141 at 144

> The purpose of judicial review is to ensure that the individual receives fair treatment, and not to ensure that the authority, after according fair treatment, reaches on a matter which is authorised or enjoined by law to decide for itself a conclusion which is correct in the eyes of the court.

But new questions are bound to arise.

The class of decision-makers may become an issue given the corporate structure of public bodies and the legitimate expectations for public trading bodies to operate as successful businesses at arm's length from government.[25] In the event of a breach of fiduciary duties, apart from the dismissal of a director who has failed in the performance of his duties, it is a moot point whether the existing common law writs (*certiorari*, prohibition, *mandamus*, *habeas corpus* and *quo warranto*) and equitable remedies (injunction and declaration) are sufficient to provide redress to aggrieved citizens.

The appropriate grounds of review may also become an issue given the increasing blurring of the distinction between public/administrative law and private/corporate law. For instance, a board of directors' decision that privileges profit over community service obligations is likely to throw the *vires*[26] and bias[27] tests into confusion. Natural justice, framed by Lord Cooke in *Daganayasi* v *Minister of Immigration* [1980] 2 NZLR 130 at 140 as 'fairness writ large and juridically, fair play in action', would be very hard to find given the ambiguous distinction between business profit and providing 'universal access to a necessary good or service'.[28]

The reasonableness test as Lord Greene MR in *Associated Provincial Picture Houses, Ltd* v *Wednesbury Corporation* [1948] 1 KB 223 put it at 229 requires the decision-maker to 'call his own attention to the matters which he is bound to consider. He must exclude from his consideration matters which are irrelevant to what he has to consider. If he does not obey those rules, he may truly be said, and often is said, to be acting "unreasonably"'. But which is more reasonable? Profit or social responsibility? After all, the Act 2001 mandates both as having (seemingly) equal value.

In the final analysis, the increasing development of modern governments (including Pacific nations) into *de facto* corporations, as well as the growing trend toward a managerial form of governance, call for a more stringent application of the courts' judicial review of administrative decisions jurisdiction. This is of particular importance if the rule of law is not to degenerate into the rule of men. The danger envisaged here is unfettered administrative discretion[29] and the reductionist use of the law as nothing more than an instrument of executive government policies. Indeed, the tendency towards arbitrary rule is always an attendant threat of the exercise of government powers, and the sacrifice of justice and equity on the altar of economic progress is always an easy option, especially in developing economies. While the rule of law retains its character as the governance of rules, it is a rule of law at the service of policy interests.

Conclusion

In conclusion, I need briefly reiterate what was said in chapter one. The rule of law as an engine of socioeconomic development brings its own challenges. The extent to which the law can be so used without compromising the law's own authority and legitimacy is of concern, the danger being that law may be subsumed by politics or economics. There is always the lurking danger that the law so used would harbour distortions and subtle forms of 'coercion in the guise of passive acceptance of the existing world within the framework of capitalism' (Russell 1986:19). While the utilitarian theory of law legitimately allows for the use of the law as a vehicle of development, there is always the substantive concern that '[p]ower as the "collective will", as the "rule of law", is realised in bourgeois society to the extent that this society represents a market' (Pashukanis 1978:146).

This calls for the following enjoinder. First, the Madisonian reminder must always be taken seriously—we must first empower the government to govern and, in the next place, 'oblige it to control itself' (Madison 1961:322). The challenge is having a democratic government and keeping the same government under control and in order.

Justice and equity are essential to legitimate governance.

Second, government must adhere to the normative demands of the rule of law. This demands and justifies a cautious adoption of legal pragmatism,

> [p]ragmatism does not rule out any theory about what makes a community better. But it does not take rights seriously. It rejects what other conceptions of law accept: that people can have distinctly legal rights as trumps over what would otherwise be the best future properly understood. According to pragmatism what we call legal rights are only the servants of the best future: they are instruments we construct for that purpose and have no independent force or ground (Dworkin 1977:22).

Third, legitimate governance demands and justifies the rejection of legal positivism. The rule of law, from a normative perspective, entails significant substantive demands. For example, the use of coercive government powers must be publicly explained, debated, justified and defended on legal and moral grounds, such as on the basis of a conception of the common good that is both publicly accepted and open to public debate and moral scrutiny. The crude positivist notion that the law is whatever the sovereign lawmaking power lays down as law, while important for descriptive analysis, is hardly of any use for the purpose of legitimate governance.

Fourth, executive discretionary action is

> a necessary evil...[T]he inherent dangers of unfair treatment must be acknowledged and contained; and the executive is rightly made subject to the supervision of independent courts, bound to act on grounds of the general principles of common law, or constitutional law, that supplement the general rules laid down in legislation (Allan 2001:15).

The challenge is finding the balance between a strong executive government and curbing executive excesses. Maintaining the line of compromise between those two legitimate aims is a matter of democratic debate and judgment based on the common good. The issue of an accountability deficit is an ongoing concern.

Finally, in respect of the corporatisation of modern governments, I reiterate my preference for a position between the extreme left's centralised planning which ultimately cripples economic growth and the extreme right's unadulterated free-market capitalism which exposes people, unprotected, to the cruel power of the market forces. Rorty (1987:565) describes it in the following terms,

> Nobody so far has invented an economic setup that satisfactorily balances decency and efficiency, but at the moment the most helpful alternative seems to be governmentally controlled capitalism plus welfare-statism (Holland, Sweden,

Ireland). There is nothing sacred about either the free market or about central planning; the proper balance between the two is a matter of experimental tinkering.

The enjoinder I am promulgating is inherent in the rule of law which presupposes 'an acceptable order of justice' and mandates that government must adhere to 'a general scheme of just governance' (Allan 2001:41). Here, justice, as an external standard of evaluation, is understood from the perspective of legitimate governance and is accordingly defined in broad terms—government's just treatment of its citizens; just and fair promulgated laws; the proper exercise of government powers within prescribed limits and controls; honest performance of the functions for which government was instituted and in keeping with the terms on which the people have entrusted their power of government to it; reasonable gratification of the citizens' legitimate expectations; and the secure protection of the rights and liberties of citizens.

Notes

[1]   '[B]y the middle of the 17th century…the trust concept had become an established mode of thought' (Gough 1950:161).

[2]   *R* v *Whitaker* [1914] 3 KB 1283, 1296.

[3]   On trust as a necessary condition of social integration see, for example, Arrow (1972); also Barber (1983); Braithwaite and Levi (1998); Woolcock (1999).

[4]   On civil society (that is, the intermediate realm situated between the state and the household, occupied by organised groups or associations separate from the state and enjoying some autonomy from the state, and are formed voluntarily by citizens to protect or extend their interests) see, for example, Salamon and Anheier (1998).

[5]   *Western Samoa Trust Estates Corporation* v *Tuionoula* [1987] WSSC 1; [1987] SPLR 437 (19 January 1987).

[6]   *United States* v *Mitchell*, 445 US 535, 100 S. Ct. 1349 (1980); *United States* v *Mitchell*, 463 US 206, 103 S.Ct. 2961 (1983).

[7]   *Hospital Products Ltd* v *United States Surgical Corporation* (1984) 156 CLR 41.

[8]   See, for example, Morgan (1988) for some politicians' interesting pejorative characterisations of the English people.

[9]   With reference to the effect of the Diceyan distinction on Australia, see Finn (1995:2–3), who notes that 'the troubling distinction drawn by Dicey between "sovereignty" in its legal and in its political senses (a distinction unknown to the jurisprudence of a republican United States) produced the fissure which was to divorce the legal and political identities of the Australian people for much of this century. And…it gave a prominent place, though not primacy, to British constitutional thought, in the Australian legal consciousness'.

[10]   See also clause 104 of the Constitution of Tonga 1875. The first part of the clause provides that 'all land is the property of the King and he may grant to the nobles and titular chiefs or matabules one or more estates to become their hereditary estates'.

[11] Rehnquist J in *Smith* v *Daily Mail Publishing Co* (1979) 443 US 97 at 106.

[12] Black J in *Martin* v *City of Struthers* 319 US 141 (1942) at 146.

[13] Mason CJ in *Australia Capital Television Pty Ltd* v *The Commonwealth* (1992) 177 CLR 106 at 138.

[14] Lord Bridge of Harwich in *Hector* v *Attorney General of Antigua and Barbuda* (1990) 2 All ER 103 at 106.

[15] See, for example, section 30 of the Constitution Amendment Act 1997 of the Fiji Islands; section 12 of the Constitution of Solomon Islands 1978; and, section 24 of the *Constitution of Tuvalu 1978*.

[16] Clause 7 of the Constitution of Tonga is something of an anomaly and therefore deserves to be set out in full.

> It shall be lawful for all people to speak write and print their opinions and no law shall ever be enacted to restrict this liberty. There shall be freedom of speech and of the press for ever but nothing in this clause shall be held to outweigh the law of defamation, official secrets or the laws for the protection of the King and the royal family.

See further the Tonga Court of Appeal case of *Utoikamanu* v *Lali Media Group Ltd* [2003] TOCA 6; CA 04 & 10 2003 (25 July 2003) where clause 7 was the main legal issue.

[17] Clause 2 of article 13 authorises the imposition (by law) of 'reasonable restrictions' on freedom of speech and expression: national security, friendly relations with other nations, public order or morals, protecting the privileges of parliament, preventing the disclosure of information received in confidence, preventing contempt of court, defamation, and inciting offence.

[18] The *New York Times Co* v *United States* 403 US 713 (1971).

[19] See, for example, Waldron (1998), which is really a critique of the notion of constitutional constraints as a form of precommitment.

[20] Note, for example, the significance of the English *Habeus Corpus Act 1679* designed to make judges personally liable when they refuse to exercise certain powers expressly allowed by law. Thus Sharpe (1989:19–20) notes that 'the legislators had learned that the judges could not always be trusted to act according to the law'.

[21] For example, article 111 of the Constitution of Samoa defines law as follows

> Law means any law for the time being in force in Samoa; and includes this Constitution, any Act of Parliament and any proclamation, regulation, order, by law or other act of authority made thereunder, the English common law and equity for the time being in so far as they are not excluded by any other law in force in Samoa, and any custom or usage which has acquired the force of law in Samoa or any part thereof under the provisions of any Act or under a judgment of a court of competent jurisdiction.

After independence in 1962 common law and equity principles still apply unless they are inconsistent with the Constitution, acts of parliament or subsidiary laws, or are inappropriate to the circumstances of Samoa (section 349 of *Samoa Act 1921* and articles 111 and 114 of the Constitution).

[22] Supporting arguments include allowing market forces to facilitate better consumption decisions, better production decisions, and hence a more efficient economy. This is part and parcel of the commercialisation of government's provision of goods and services usually pursued through competitive tendering and contracting out, and based on principles such as value for money, and improving the quantity and quality of goods and services. The proclaimed benefits include giving consumers more control over how much of the good or

service they need given the price, better matching of products to the needs of users, and thereby minimising costs and increasing production efficiency gains. Where privatisation is allowed, the delivery of products or services is transferred from the public sector to the private sector, sometimes involving the sale of government-owned businesses, outsourcing of the functions of public agencies, and private financing of public infrastructure. The stated benefits include efficiency gains, removing constraints of public ownership, freedom to explore new markets and products, and enabling commercial strategic alliances which are more difficult for government-owned enterprises.

23   For an analysis of this issue in the Australian context, see Mulgan (1997).

24   See, for example, *Associated Provincial Picture Houses Ltd* v *Wednesbury Corporation* [1948] 1 KB 223; also Royal Commission on Thomas Case [1982] 1 NZLR 252.

25   But see *R* v *Panel on Takeovers and Mergers* ex p Datafin [1987] QB 815; also *Council of Civil Service Unions* v *Minister of State for the Civil Service* [1985] AC 374.

26   See *Animistic Ltd* v *Foreign Compensation Commission* (1969) 2 AC 147, as per Lord Reid at 171; *Racal Communications Ltd* (1980) 2 ALL ER, as per Lord Diplock at 637.

27   But see, for example, the reasonable and real danger or possibility of bias test (in cases of apparent bias relating to the exercise of the powers of a tribunal) adopted by Lord Goff of the House of Lords in *R* v *Gough* [1993] AC 646, at 670; followed by the New Zealand Court of Appeal in *Auckland Casino Ltd* v *Casino Control Authority* [1995] 1 NZLR 142. On bias by predetermination, especially involving a pecuniary interest, see, for example, *CREEDNZ Inc* v *Governor-General* [1981] 1 NZLR 172; at 192, Richardson J noted 'The general principle captured in the Latin *nemo iudex sua causa* is that no one should be judge in his own cause'.

28   For instance, in *Yarmirr* v *Australian Telecommunications Corporation* (1990) 96 ALR 739, the High Court of Australia held that a legislated community service obligation required of Telecom (now Telstra) to provide standard telephone services to all citizens of Australia on an equitable basis did not entitle the complainant (who resided in a remote area of Australia) to compel Telecom to provide any service at all on the ground that the object of the empowering statute was expressed in very general terms and that there was no legislative intention to confer any private legal rights on individuals such as the complainant.

29   See Schauer (1991) for the view that discretion is nothing more than a mask for bureaucratic control and the pursuit of policy interests. See also Allan (2001:128), who notes that

> [a]dministrative discretion is not [and must not be] merely a tool of efficient government…but a crucial resource for reconciling the attainment of public purposes with the fair treatment of individuals.

4

Rights and liberties: the individual, the collective and the clash of ideologies, values and institutions

This chapter examines government's role of protecting rights and liberties in the concrete normative contexts of Pacific communities with their distinctive universes of meaning, social practice and discourse. The violation of individual rights and liberties in the Pacific in the name of any number of gods provides the foil for the discussion.[1]

The state's duty of protecting citizens' rights and liberties as required by the *Universal Declaration of Human Rights 1948* is my point of departure.

> Whereas recognition of the inherent dignity and of the equal and inalienable rights of all members of the human family is the foundation of freedom, justice and peace in the world,
>
> Whereas disregard and contempt for human rights have resulted in barbarous acts which have outraged the conscience of mankind, and the advent of a world in which human beings shall enjoy freedom of speech and belief and freedom from fear and want has been proclaimed as the highest aspiration of the common people,
>
> Whereas it is essential, if man is not to be compelled to have recourse, as a last resort, to rebellion against tyranny and oppression, that human rights should be protected by the rule of law.

The *Eminent Persons' Group Review of the Pacific Islands Forum* (Eminent Persons' Group 2004:n.p.) is similarly emphatic on the need to protect rights and liberties: 'The Forum should support the work of members in developing national human rights machinery. As part of this process, those Leaders who are not already engaged with the Asia Pacific Human Rights Forum might consider becoming so'.

Rights violations and Pacific gods

When rights violations are perpetrated in the name of religion, we read each other out of the kingdom of heaven, beat the toms-toms of our religious rituals as well as the heads of our religious opponents in the name of some god. When undertaken in the name of custom, we acquiesce in the violent worship of the tribal deity of cultural chauvinism and the philosophical god of essentialism. And when undertaken in the name of the modern state, most people happily follow Socrates' lesson on the value of silence, unlike the ignorant sheep that complained that the watchdog was doing nothing.

The danger, in short, is the progressive whittling away of rights and liberties. In due course, small sins will become big sins. As underlined in *Thomas* v *Collins* (1944) 323 US 516 at 543, 'it is from petty tyrannies that large ones take root and grow. This fact can be no more plain than when [restraints] are imposed on the most basic rights of all. Seedlings planted in that soil grow great and, growing, break down the foundations of liberty'.

Promulgating a rights jurisprudence as a mobilising theme, my objective is not to promote the apotheosis of the individual but to avoid a collective nightmare of paralysed Pacific individuals. This position requires steering a middle course between the two evils of claustrophobic collectivism and egocentric individualism. And grounding rights and liberties in the normative contexts of Pacific communities requires balancing individual rights with the custom, traditions, social structures, values, and protocols of the Pacific peoples themselves. We find a major overture to this balancing exercise in the Samoa Court of Appeal's constitutional approach in the case of *The Attorney General* v *Saipaia Olomalu* [1980–1993] WSLR 41.

> [T]he Constitution should be interpreted in the spirit counseled by Lord Wilberforce in *Fischer's case*. He speaks of a constitutional instrument such as this [the Constitution of Samoa] as *sui generis*; in relation to human rights of 'a generous interpretation avoiding what has been called the austerity of tabulated legalism'; of respect for traditions and usages which have given meaning to the language; and of an approach with an open mind. This involves, we think, still giving primary attention to the words used, but being on guard against any tendency to interpret them in a mechanical or pedantic way.

This is essential in the respect that rights and liberties do not arise, or are practised, in a vacuum or in a manner divorced from the social context in which they operate. Dworkin (1977:369) notes, '[t]he rights people have depend on the background justification and political institutions that are also in play, because the argument for any particular right must recognise that right as part of the complex package of other assumptions and practices that it trumps up'. More fundamentally, as Judge Learned Hand has pointedly emphasised,

> liberty lies in the hearts of men and women; when it dies there, no constitution, no law, no court can save it; no constitution, no law, no court can even do much to help it. While it lies there it needs no constitution, no law, no court to save it (cited in Rishworth 1998:133).

This underlines the point that rights and liberties are more than mere constructs of the mind; they are more fundamentally habits of the heart and moral convictions of the soul. For rights and liberties to trump, they must be embedded in the community's culture and *Volksgeist*, ingrained in the people's hearts as it were.

This chapter also underlines the inevitability of change, true democratic change that is sometimes very slow, change of the two steps forward one step back type. Abjuring a Machievellian overthrow of the institutional order, change requires established Pacific verities, institutions, protocols and practices to be constantly revised. If we cannot counterpoise reverence for national and cultural symbols with freedom of revision, Pacific societies will ultimately decay either from anarchy or from the slow atrophy of a life smothered by irrelevant cultural, religious, and political forms. Stated bluntly, we need to change what needs to be changed and retain what should not be changed. Sometimes that means transcending cultural prejudices, parochialism, and chauvinism.

Pacific constitutions as entrenched bills of rights: reinforcing and renegotiating the culture of individual rights and liberties

The propriety of a bill of rights, whether incorporated and entrenched in a written Constitution as in US constitutional jurisprudence or as an ordinary act of parliament as New Zealand's *Bill of Rights 1990*, continues to be a matter of debate.[2] In most Pacific jurisdictions, bills of rights have been incorporated and entrenched in written constitutions.[3] This seems to have been guided by the understanding that rights and liberties will be securely protected if they are incorporated and entrenched in a written constitutional text. In this, Pacific jurisdictions appear to be following US constitutional practice.

In defence of an entrenched bill of rights, I refer to Justice Black's justification of the US Bill of Rights in *Adamson* v *California* 322 US 46, 91 L. ed. 1903 (1946),

> I cannot consider the Bill of Rights to be an outworn 18th Century 'strait jacket'... Its provisions may be thought outdated abstractions by some. And it is true that they were designed to meet ancient evils. But they are the same kind of human evils that have emerged from century to century wherever excessive power is sought by the few at the expense of the many. In my judgment the people of no nation can lose their liberty so long as a Bill of Rights like ours survives and its basic purposes are conscientiously interpreted, enforced and respected so as to afford continuous protection against old, as well as new, devices and practices which might thwart those purposes.

A bill of rights is a shield against arbitrary rule. It demands the state to protect citizens' rights and liberties, sometimes through 'the use of the physical force of the state' (Glanville 1957:259). Part II of the Constitution of Samoa 1960, for example, is an entrenched bill of rights. This guarantees and protects fundamental rights and liberties: life; personal liberty; a fair trial; freedom from inhuman treatment; freedom from forced labour; rights concerning criminal law; freedom of religion; rights concerning religious instruction; rights regarding freedom of speech, assembly, association, movement and residence; rights regarding property; and freedom from discrimination. These are subject to reasonable restrictions such as national security, public order, and community morals.

Underlining the fundamental importance of part II, Professor Aikman in the Constitutional Convention of Samoa 1960 emphasised that '[t]he intention of part two of the Constitution is, of course, that no part of the Government of Western Samoa, whether it be the Head of State, Cabinet, Parliament or any other authority, shall infringe the rights set out in this part of the Constitution' (Constitutional Convention of Western Samoa 1960:Vol I, 73). Leaving no state institution outside the reach and demand of part II, the term 'State' is therefore defined in article 3 of part II as follows: 'In this Part, unless the context otherwise requires, the State includes the Head of State, Cabinet, Parliament and all local and other authorities established under any law'.

Clearly, the guarantee and protection of rights and liberties was meant to be comprehensive, perhaps reflecting the constitutional framers' awareness of the danger an all-powerful state would pose to the citizens. While government has been empowered by the citizens themselves to govern on their behalf, part II is a clear statement that the citizens have retained certain rights and liberties, and that power to take them away has been withheld from government. Significantly, the bill of rights is more than just a parchment barrier or a pedantic lesson on community ethics. It is, in fact, intended to be a shield against arbitrary rule, a constitutional limit on the power of the state.

Critical in this connection is article 2(1) which makes the Constitution the supreme law of the State of Samoa. The supremacy clause is buttressed by the inconsistency clause in article 2(2): 'Any existing law and any law passed after the date of coming into force of this Constitution which is inconsistent with this Constitution shall, to the extent of the inconsistency, be void'. Explaining the practical application of article 2, Professor Aikman emphasised that '[i]f the Legislative Assembly were to pass an ordinary law which denied [fundamental rights], that law would not be valid—in other words, it would not be a law at all' (Constitutional Convention of Western Samoa 1960:Vol. I, 68).

To protect rights and liberties given under part II, article 4(1) provides for their enforcement by application to the Supreme Court, which is authorised by article 4(2) 'to make all such orders as may be necessary and appropriate to secure to the applicant the enjoyment of any rights conferred under the provisions' of part II. 'Because the Supreme Court is the most important Court in this sense,' said Professor Davidson in the Constitutional Convention 'it has been described and referred to in article 4. It is felt that these matters of fundamental rights are so important that they should be taken directly to the Supreme Court or to a Judge in the Supreme Court' (Constitutional Convention of Western Samoa 1960:Vol. I, 86). Article 81, though placed outside part II, is structurally related to article 4 discussed above. Extending the jurisdiction of the courts in respect of fundamental rights and liberties, article 81 provides that '[a]n appeal shall lie to the Court of Appeal from any decision of the Supreme Court in any proceedings under the provisions of Article 4'.

Article 15(1), placed in part II, mandates equality before the law and equal protection under the law, and proscribes special treatment or discrimination. This is captured by article 15(2), which provides that '[e]xcept as expressly authorised by this Constitution, no law and no executive or administrative action of the State shall either expressly or in its practical application, subject any person or persons to any disability or restriction or confer on any person or persons any privilege or advantage' on the grounds of race, sex, and so on. The exception to this general principle is a concession to the custom and traditions of Samoa. There are cases where 'preference [must] be given to certain people to enable certain posts in the government to be filled by those who ought to fill them in accordance with Samoan custom' (Constitutional Convention of Western Samoa 1960:Vol. I, 221). Taken in its entirety, article 15 is critical to the guarantee and protection of fundamental rights and liberties—the framers were well aware that the protection of rights and liberties would depend very much on 'the impartial administration of justice' (Constitutional Convention of Western Samoa 1960:Vol. I, 221) by the courts.

Finally, article 109(1) is significant in that it entrenches the provisions of the Constitution. Accordingly, any of the provisions of the Constitution (except article 102 which prohibits the alienation of customary land) may be amended or repealed, and new provisions added, only by means of a special procedure. First, a bill for any of the purposes referred to above must be supported at its third reading by votes of not less than two-thirds of the total number of members of parliament (including vacancies). Second, the third reading of the bill comes 90 days after the second, to give citizens ample time in which to assess the merits or otherwise of the proposed legislation. On the overall significance of entrenching the provisions of the Constitution, Professor Aikman underlined the legal status of the Constitution as a list of the 'basic and fundamental [laws which should therefore] be protected by a special procedure for amendment' (Constitutional Convention of Western Samoa 1960:Vol. I, 55). In mandating that special procedure, the framers thereby firmly secured the protection of rights and liberties, and limited the power of parliament, the executive, or any other institution of the state to take away citizens' rights and liberties.

A final observation. The end of colonialism gave Samoa its independence; independence gave Samoa a Constitution; and the Constitution gives Samoa a bill of rights. Embodied and entrenched in the Constitution, the bill of rights is a fundamental dimension of Samoa's jurisprudence. Each of the articles in part II sets a standard, and those standards collectively constitute, in a very significant sense, the measure of Samoa's success or failure as a constitutional democracy. When rights are violated, the question arises: does the list of rights and liberties provide sufficient guarantee in practice? If not, the constitutional guarantee of rights and liberties becomes nothing more than a misleading literary conceit or just an empty promise.

Rights violations also highlight the issue of the clash of ideologies, ethics, institutions, and objectives which is a perennial problem in the Pacific. The clash between Western ideologies, ethics, institutions, and objectives and their Pacific indigenous counterparts is a complex issue. Occurring at critical points of the body politic (in the family, schools, churches and government), this clash continues to cause uncertainty in virtually all levels of society. Unravelling this perennial clash of epistemologies and its consequences, with particular reference to the institution of rights and liberties, is the major focus of the remaining part of this chapter.

Liberal-individualism versus communitarianism in the existing rights discourse

This section briefly sketches the individual/collective dichotomy in the existing rights discourse, couched, as it is, within the framework of the liberal-individual position, on the one hand, and communitarianism or collectivism, on the other. This discussion provides the context for my discussion of Samoa's negotiation of the individual/collective dialectic in the next section.

The polarisation of liberal-individualism and communitarianism is such that they 'are not to be thought of as liberal bedfellows who have already settled the basic terms and conceptions of their association. They are tensions at a deep philosophical level' (Waldron 1995:99). This tension is tied up with conflicting modernist, postmodernist, and poststructuralist assumptions about selfhood, human dignity, emancipation, the nature of the community, transcendentalism or contingency, and so on.

The liberal-individual position naturally focuses on the individual in keeping with liberalism's privileging of individual rights and liberties.[4] Postulating a plurality of interests in the community, liberalism

> grants people a very wide freedom of choice in terms of how they lead their lives. It allows people to choose a conception of the good life, and then allows them to reconsider that decision, and adopt a new and hopefully better plan of life (Kymlicka 1995:80).

At the centre of liberalism's cosmology is the Kantian autonomous self: unique, inviolable, sacrosanct, an end itself and not a mere means to an end. This conception of the self is predicated, to some extent, on the Cartesian dualistic notion that the individual can have a transcendental (metaphysical) self—the core self—that, somehow, can be separated from one's contingent self, which is tied up with a particular culture or socio-historical context (Descartes 1979; Kant 1964). Adding to the postulated priority of the self, John Rawls (1973:560) speaks of the self as something 'prior to the ends which are affirmed by it'. And pushing the individual into the international arena of the global village, Waldron (1995:111) speaks of a cosmopolitan self with multiple associations and attachments, a kind of 'cosmopolitan manager, standing back a little from each of the items on the smorgasbord of its personality'. This process of extending the cosmopolitan self's horizons, Waldron (1995:110) claims, is 'a richer, more honest, and more authentic response to the world in which we live than a retreat into the confined sphere of a particular community'.[5]

Underpinning the individualist ethic are important principles such as the moral primacy of the individual over the interests of the collective, and that only the individual (not the group or the collective) has moral standing for right-holding purposes. And given that the community is not an abstraction but a community of persons, its interests and objectives have significance only in so far as they promote the welfare of its individual members. Furthermore, the moral legitimacy of the community lies in the consent and acquiescence of its individual citizens in community interests and objectives. Without that consent, we have a community of slaves acting under coercion and who have to be moved by naked force, thereby plunging the legal and moral legitimacy of the political order into chaos. In the final analysis, whatever importance the community has, that should be understood as essentially derived from the importance of its individual members.

So pervasive and compelling is this liberal version of social reality that it has been said that 'we seek to escape it at the cost of becoming historically irrelevant' (Bowles and Gintis 1986:62). The hegemony of liberal discourse aside, in a positive sense, liberalism's 'discourse of rights has framed the hopes... of ordinary peoples' for centuries (Bowles and Gintis 1986:25) The individual, to put it bluntly, is not (and should not be reduced to) a mere cog in the system, whatever the system.

While confirming the foundational importance of the individual and his inalienable rights and liberties, the inherent danger in liberalism's view of the world is its atomistic bias, the exaltation of the individual, that usually fails to give adequate consideration to peoples and societies for whom communal life is central, even vital, and often sacrifices the traditional ethic of self-restraint and duties to others, thus creating the beasts of isolationism and egocentrism, sustained by the ethic of the maximisation of individual interests. The issue is not, to use Waldron's (1995:101) pointed critique of communitarianism, cultural immersion or 'hiding in Disneyland…and evading the complex actualities of the world as it is'. The issue, rather, is that liberalism's individualist premises often preclude proper consideration of the communal dimensions of life, which are clearly much more important than some liberals recognise.

This is the basic thrust of the criticism of liberalism by proponents of communitarianism.[6] Richard Flathman (1976:49) argues, 'writers of a communitarian persuasion argue that rights (indeed rights of all kinds) encourage an individualistic, even an egoistic, ethos that is destructive of the most valuable kinds of human relationships, and productive of an anomic and politically vulnerable society'. Methodologically, the liberal-individual position is clearly skewed in favour of a particular political ethic. But, of course, it is 'shrewd of the philosophers of liberalism to insist that their world of private values is the only possible world. So long as they…maintain that fiction, dissatisfaction with the ideals of liberal society can be dismissed. Once the ideals of affective, productive, and rational community are defined, however, we see quite clearly that the dissatisfaction stems not from the poverty of human experience… but…from the poverty of liberalism' (Wolff 1968:194–5). Indeed, the real danger is that of fracturing social harmony and destroying human relationships, and of the individual arrogating to himself rights without limits or duties.

The communitarian position, in contrast, naturally focuses on the community and its vital role in the emergence, meaning construction and acquisition, identity formation, and even survival of the individual. Since the individual is ultimately rooted in the community, his interests and actions are therefore meaningful only within the collective context from which he emerges—not outside it. This is not mere sentimental attachment to a particular spiritual view or background. Rather, it is about the community providing the frame within which people 'can determine where they stand on questions of what is good' (Taylor 1989:27). Whether or not the community could reasonably be seen as ontologically prior to its members in 'a non-ethical ontological' (Jones 1999:372) sense is a moot point. It seems certain though that the community was there before the individual was born and it will be there after the individual is gone. In a sense, therefore, the community is cognitively prior to the individual.

Critical to the communitarian school of thought is the notion of the self as an entity that is always concretely situated, embedded in, and constituted by a particular culture, language, and history.[7] Louis Althusser (1971:218–9) perhaps aptly summed up the negation of a transcendental self (that is, the non-immersion of the self in a particular context) in the following terms

> Since Marx, we have known that the human subject, the economic, political or philosophical ego is not the center of history—and even, in opposition to the Philosophers of the Enlightenment and Hegel, that history has no center...In turn, Freud has discovered that the real subject, the individual in his unique essence, has not the form of an ego—that the human subject is de-centered, constituted by a structure which has no center either.

Problematising the Cartesian ego, Madan Sarup (citing Claude Lévi-Strauss) describes it as the 'spoiled brat of philosophy' (Sarup 1989:1). Applied to the holding and practice of rights, Flathman (1976:65) decries the

> notion of a purely individual or private practice of rights, whether by a Robinson Crusoe living apart from other men or by an individual living in a society but asserting to himself that he has rights against himself (e.g., against his better or worse self) [as] metaphorical. If taken literally it would have the same well-rehearsed difficulties as the notion of duties to oneself.

Add them all up and we find the cumulative argument that the notion of the self on which the liberal-individualist position is predicated is too disembodied and atomistic to capture the actual needs and interests of real people in the real world. Even Will Kymlicka (1995:105; 1989), despite privileging individual choice, insists that

> liberals should recognise the importance of people's membership in their own societal culture, because of the role it plays in enabling meaningful choice and in supporting self-identity...Cultural membership provides us with an intelligible context of choice, and a secure sense of identity and belonging, that we call upon in confronting questions about personal values and projects.

Disputing the proclaimed virtues of liberalism, John Gray (1989:235) proposes that

> the sustaining myths of liberal modernity—myths of global progress, of fundamental rights and of a secular movement to a universal civilisation—cannot be maintained even as useful fictions in the intellectual and political context of the last decade of our century .

Communitarianism or collectivism, however, faces its own distinctive problems, for example, what is a group for right-holding purposes, and what is a group or collective right? On Peter Jones' (1999:354) characterisation, '[a] right is a group right only if it is a right held by a group qua group'. On the 'collective' conception of group rights (associated with Raz and others),[8] three conditions must be met: (1) individuals (as a group) share a common interest; (2) that common interest relates to one specific matter; and (3) that collective interest is sufficiently significant to justify creating duties for others. On this view, the defining feature of a group right is a common interest—identified, shared, pursued, and sufficiently significant to impose duties on others. Rejecting the collective conception as too generous and too broad, Jones (1999:365) proposes the 'corporate' conception of group rights, according to which, 'a right-holding group has a clear identity as a group'.

Unlike the collective conception which takes the collective moral standing of the members of the group as its only moral and legal warrant, Jones' corporate conception posits that the group itself 'has a pre-existing moral identity as a group,' that is, a moral standing that does not depend on the collective moral standing of the members of the group. Importantly, investing the community with moral standing and treating the group as a moral community in its own right entails treating the community as an ethical unity with moral and ethical imperatives which guide and sustain the community as a whole.

The principal problem with communitarianism, despite its virtues— for example, it appropriately emphasises the importance of the collective and the embeddedness of the self—is that it, too, tends towards exaltation. That is to say, while liberalism exalts the individual, communitarianism exalts collective. Even Jones (1999:375), notwithstanding his passionate defence of group rights, concedes that '[a]t the limit, a group as a corporate entity may possess a moral standing so inclusive and complete that it deprives the group's individual members of any independent moral standing: the group becomes everything, the individual nothing'. Perhaps, in view of that danger, it could be argued that the group must not be recognised as a subject for right-holding purposes where such rights would conflict with and potentially override the claims of individuals, at least, not without legal and/or moral justification.

It could be argued that both the 'collective' and 'corporate' conceptions of group rights stand or fall on this issue. Whereas there may not be any credible impediment to the notion that a group can have rights, there is no legitimate legal and/or moral justification for the violation of the rights of the individual by the group simply because the group is bigger and stronger. Without such justification, individual citizens may legitimately withdraw their assent to and acquiescence in the rule of the group, thus creating law and order problems and throwing the group into legal and moral confusion.

In summary, the two extremes of liberal-individualism, on the one hand, and communitarianism, on the other, have their pitfalls. Preaching either of the two with ideological dogmatism (some liberals, on the one hand, and most Pacific conservatives, on the other) often produces supporting arguments that are simplistic in the extreme and which, unfortunately, drive an insurmountable wedge between the individual and the collective.

The individual and the collective in Samoa's universe of meaning, social practice and discourse

Using Samoa as a case study, it is argued that some societies conceptualise and approach the relationship between the individual and the collective in ways that are more complex than either liberal-individualism or communitarianism recognises. This underlines the point that the world view and system of ethics a particular society adopts depend on a complex range of cultural, moral, psychological, and other factors, and that the character or temperament of a people is not an academic lesson in abstract principles but a community enterprise to reinforce community values and virtues which are taught and practised in everyday interpersonal interactions. After all, virtues are not mere thoughts of the mind but habits of the heart which persons acquire, practise and develop by acting out those virtues in their everyday lives.

The existing framework of rights discourse set out above usually polarises the issue as a conflict between the individual and the collective. This has two unacceptable results. First, it misconceives the debate as a conflict between individual rights and group rights. The debate is rather more correctly conceptualised as a conflict between different types of individual rights which need different types of collective protection and enforcement. For instance, the right to freedom of movement needs the government to restrict its reach and scope by imposing limits on the exercise of that right such as through the law of trespass to land. By comparison, there are individual rights with social and communal dimensions like the right to belong to and share in one's indigenous culture. These rights also need collective protection and enforcement, such as through affirmative action laws or through the adoption of customary means of governance, customary laws, and traditional means of dispute resolution. The two types of rights view the individual and the role of the community from different perspectives, and in both cases, the individual and the collective are mutually interactive.

Second, the individual/collective debate is usually viewed through the classical prism of liberalism versus communism. And, usually, all non-Western societies are haphazardly lumped together in the communist/fascist camp of illiberal, oppressive collectivities. Contradicting this common misperception, the Samoan normative worldview occupies a position somewhere in between the two extremes of egocentric individualism and claustrophobic collectivism. It takes the individual as a primarily political animal who could live a meaningful and full life only in the *polis/nu'u* which, empirically, was there before the individual came on the scene. Although this does not make the collective superior to the individual, it does mean that human nature cannot be properly defined without reference to community meanings and values.

That said, there may sometimes be an intrinsic bias slightly in favour of the collective in Samoa's traditional thinking and praxis, especially when individuals make idiosyncratic assertions of their rights and liberties to the exclusion of everything and everybody else. While that may be the case sometimes, the Samoan individual and collective—for legitimate reasons and for the most part—are not pitched against each other in a winner-takes-all tug of war. In fact, the individual and the collective do and must cooperate, thereby avoiding a survival of the fittest scenario which reduces everyone else to either a competitor or a mad enemy who must be defeated or, better still, eliminated.

It needs to be acknowledged as well that Samoa's normative view of the individual/collective relationship has undergone fundamental structural changes (both good and bad) over the last 50 years. I will deal with this issue below. Suffice to note at this juncture that the inevitability of change raises the important point that we must allow for the possibility of the balance between the individual and the collective being able to shift—without causing intolerable conflict—as ideas, interests, and needs change in response to internal and external influences.

Treating the individual/collective relationship as less a matter of intellectual abstraction and more primarily a pragmatic issue, I advocate the view that, for pragmatic reasons, the Samoan individual and collective should not be promoted as mutually exclusive but must rather cooperate for the mutual benefit of all. Among other things, this involves a reaffirmation of Samoa's normative conceptualisation of the individual/collective relationship, minus the exalted individual of liberalism and the exalted, reified collective of sociological/cultural determinism. The appropriateness of this position for the Samoan people themselves is predicated on moral, cosmological, structural, sociological, psychological, economic, and property considerations rooted in Samoa's own symbolic universe, social structure, and interpersonal intercourse.

First, the Samoan self has always been and will continue to be embedded in multiple groupings: the immediate/extended family defined by blood ties; the tribe defined by titular and property relations; the village defined by titular, political and property associations; the traditional district defined by titular and political affiliations; and the nation defined by ethnicity. The Samoan individual, therefore, is not some kind of disembodied and atomistic self but an individual embedded in kinship structures, some of which entail a very important relativising effect. This problematises, even subverts, egocentric individualism as an acceptable axis of value in the cultural script of Samoan society, one centering on the collective good and on a culture of responsibilities to the family, the tribe, the village, the district, and the nation.

The individual is indeed fundamentally important, not as an isolated organism but as a member of the collective. This is defined by Samoa's structural positioning of the individual at the centre of the world. But this is not simply a privileged position. The individual is not only placed at the centre of the world but at the centre of a network of duties and responsibilities. Accordingly, the individual not only has rights but corresponding duties and responsibilities. When he exercises only his rights and disavows his duties, there is a disruption in the equilibrium of the social order with serious consequences for both the individual himself and others. And this is incompatible with the social and moral imperatives of a community which prioritises social harmony and equilibrium.

Second, that notion of the self is underpinned by the social construction of the individual. From birth to death, the Samoan individual is oriented very strongly towards others in the individual's multiple groupings. It is also underpinned by the constitution and social construction of society whereby the whole, the community, the collective is seen as prior to its constituent parts, that is, without ascribing to the community 'a non-ethical ontological status' as noted above. This is in line with the socio-cultural emphasis on the common good and collective well being. While the individual is ultimately important, the notion of the interest-maximising individual is a second-order axis of value in traditional thinking and practice. The main emphasis is on one's others. This is a moral imperative in Samoa's normative view of life and reality.

Third, the cumulative effect of the above is the generation of a Samoan personality that may be broadly described as dyadic. That is, Samoans are oriented very strongly towards others. This is not the Dr Jekyll/Mr Hyde split personality syndrome that the word dyadic (from δυο, meaning two) seems to imply. Nor is it a case of extroversion which empties the self of any meaning or value. Likewise, the negative implication that an other-oriented personality is one that depends somewhat forlornly on others to provide that person or group of persons with a sense of worth and identity is undercut by the fact that Samoans (as individuals and as an ethnic group) do not need non-Samoans to provide them with a sense of worth or identity. Nor do Samoan individuals hopelessly prostrate before other Samoans or the Samoan collective begging for appreciation, approval, or a sense of identity. Already rooted in multiple social attachments and human associations, every Samoan individual knows where he comes from and who he is. Rather, dyadic personality means that Samoans are, by nature and through socialisation, other-oriented in their interests, objectives, and actions. This moral imperative is fully in keeping with the socio-cultural emphasis on the common good and Samoans' sense of collective well being.

Fourth, this highlights the significance of a Samoan's 'significant others' (Berger and Luckmann 1967:151)—family members, those in authority, village elders, *matais*, fellows, and so forth who constitute one's chorus of significant others. This is manifested, to some extent, in social structures like patronage. As a social imperative, patronage binds the individual to the extended family, the tribe, the village, the district, and the nation. Operating reciprocally, patronage also binds the extended family, the tribe, the village and others to the individual in a network of reciprocal relations manifested in social structures like kinship, that is, a complex web of interlocking human relationships based on blood-ties, socio-political alliances, and economic ties. As a self-adjusting system based on shared values such as benevolence and gratitude, patronage defines and governs the relationship between the individual and the collective as a pragmatic question, not an academic or philosophical issue.

Finally, human interdependence that binds together the individual and his multiple groupings takes place within the context of a broader holistic cosmology that conceptualises humans in their totality (that is, as people with bodies, minds and spirits) and connects humans not only with other humans, but with their physical environment (the land/earth, the sea, the sky) and the spirit, supra-mundane world. This spiritual connection between the individual and his physical environment is grounded in the Samoan conception of the land as a kin that is more than a commodity to be exploited, but something that must be cared for and protected. The notion of kinship amongst humans and their physical environment manifests itself in the institution of communal ownership of customary land held by the *matai* (the head of a Samoan family) as a *de facto* trustee of that land subject to the state's trusteeship of such land.

Mention of Samoa's *matai* (traditional chiefly) system, the heart of Samoa's symbolic universe and a ubiquitous feature of Samoan culture (Vaai 1999), is warranted in this connection. Significantly, the *matai* system encapsulates the Samoan negotiation of the individual/collective polarity and the Samoan individual's other-orientation. The term *matai* comprises the noun *mata* (meaning eye as a proper noun or the more abstract noun seeing or looking) and the preposition *i*, which, in the accusative case, connotes direction towards someone or something. Taken together, the term *matai* denotes the act of looking towards or at someone or something, that is, away from oneself. It defines the individual as an 'I' in community with 'others'; the one and the many are mutually interactive and interdependent.

The term *matai* thus evokes a cosmology and is expressive of the disposition of the Samoan people, manifested in the Samoan dyadic personality discussed above and the privileging of the individual's significant others. The *matai* system as a whole and individual *matais* operate within this traditional worldview of cross-cutting social relationships, political alliances, mutual expectations, and economic ties as their *modus operandi*.[9]

Essentially a servant, a *matai*'s role is that of a *de facto* trustee (*tausi mea*) of his family's title and lands, the caretaker of the family property. The *matai*, in other words, is bound by fiduciary duties to his family. The land of which the *matai* is trustee is, in traditional cosmology, the *fanua* which belongs to the whole family. It follows that the *matai* has no authority in law or custom to alienate family lands, at least not without the consent of the members of his family with legal interests in those lands.

As an individual, the *matai* is not without bridles. As the family representative in the village council of *matais*, a *matai*'s views on the governance of village affairs are supposed to be informed by the perspectives and interests of family members. In a speech at the United Nations General Assembly on 18 December 1960, the first prime minister of Samoa aptly characterised the true nature of the *matai* system as 'a system of representation; not one of domination' (United Nations General Assembly 1960). The *matai* as an 'I' is not a self-centred, isolated, atomistic individual.

Through the process of selection, a person is appointed by extended family members to be the holder of the family title (the *matai* title) with its ascribed social status, authority and corresponding duties. In most cases, the appointment has to be endorsed by a wider cluster of extended families with connections to the *matai* title and by the village council of *matais*, whose consent is vital in conferring legitimacy on the title-holder for the purposes of village affairs. The appointment of a *matai* is therefore a process of election over more than two stages, and the consent of innumerable others is indispensable. That is to say, the individual does not exalt himself to the status of a *matai* through usurpation, deceit, or by sidelining his significant others.

Underpinning the *matai*'s power of representation are important democratic principles: trust reposed in the *matai* as a decision-maker; the transfer of authority from the many to their representative; the exercise of that authority within prescribed limits and in accordance with the principles of justice, fairness, love and service; and the consent of those with a vested interest in how the *matai* exercises their representative authority. Put differently, the *matai* as an individual is embedded in a complex web of social relationships, organisation, powers, rights and corresponding duties, mutual expectations, property relations, and group morals and ideals.

Against that backdrop of Samoa's normative worldview, I offer the following caveats of caution. First, as already noted, Samoa's normative conceptualisation of the relationship between the Samoan individual and collective defined above is indeed changing. One of the main effects of liberalism has been the increasing privatisation, and, in some cases, dislocation of the Samoan self. Samoans, too, have been caught up in the conflict, the competition between the individual and the collective. The Samoan individual and collective are becoming increasingly alienated from each other. This is perhaps inevitable since all societies (Samoa included) are susceptible to the multiform conflicts (external and internal) that regularly accompany the construction and maintenance of social worlds. This also challenges the somewhat one-sided view of the social order as an integrated system without problems, disagreements and conflicts. Internationalisation and globalisation have likewise propelled Samoan individuals into the arena of the global village, with its own milieu of ideologies and cosmologies. Those forces have significantly influenced the way in which Samoan individuals now see themselves in relation to their collectivities.

For some people, the Samoan collective is now too restrictive, even oppressive. Induced to conform to the majority by a society of consensus ruled within the parameters of paternalism and deference, the liberal individual naturally finds her right to choose or dissent seriously compromised. Consensus politics indeed has its benefits, but conducted within an aristocratic framework it seems inevitable that a sadistic, authoritarian cast of mind will arise and exert control. The right to choose or dissent is most likely to suffer as a result. And this calls for a fresh negotiation of the individual/collective relationship, one that is decisively in favour of the individual over the collective, as some have argued. The alternative danger—and the point must be emphasised—is an unnecessary and unwarranted alienation of the individual from the collective, and the emergence of a Samoan self which has

> arrived at freedom by setting aside all external obstacles and impingements [and which is therefore] characterless, and hence without defined purpose, however much this is hidden by such seemingly positive terms as 'rationality' or 'creativity' (Taylor 1978:157).

Second, given that, I underline the point that the more appropriate position is that which neither condemns the individual to the arbitrary will of the collective nor sacrifices the collective good to gratify the idiosyncratic whims of the individual. As Allan Hutchinson (1988:88) has correctly reminded us,

> whereas communitarianism sacrifices the individual to the collective will, liberalism worships the individual at the expense of the collective good. An individual is more than an automatic functionary of some holistic society and less than an obsessive egoist in an alienated world.

Avoiding the two extremes, I offer the following points of reference to the ongoing search for balance.

On the one hand, the danger is exalting and reifying, even deifying, the collective.[10] But worshipping a sanctified collective in the spirit of the tribe which prays to idols of its own making is as heinous a sin as worshipping the individual. The concomitant corollary of exaltation and reification is the reduction of the individual to nothing more than a cultural dope, a mere 'tape recording of his culture' (Chinoy 1968:128), a mere actor playing out the role in a script provided by society. Society, when exalted and reified, becomes a reality that thickens and hardens, an objective entity that confronts the individual as a fixed reality, a society either devoid of humans or, otherwise, 'a forbidding prison' or 'a gigantic Alcatraz' from which humans cannot escape (Berger 1976:110).

We need, therefore, to take seriously the individual as an acting subject with a choice, 'an active being who…possesses the capacity for innovation and deviation and may through his actions significantly influence and change the nature of his culture or society' (Chinoy 1968:129). We need to affirm that humans are active participants in social life; that social life is not just a product but a process, an active engagement in social life; and that humans can create ideas, construct meanings, live and often fight against social structures that oppress them. This is an affirmation of the wealth of social life and of the 'ingenuity human beings are capable of in circumventing and subverting even the most elaborate control system' (Berger 1976:129).

Rejecting altruism as too convenient a rationale for individual actions, it may be argued that the 'great majority of good actions are intended not for the benefit of the world, but for that of individuals, of which the good of their world is made up' (Cohen 1961:344). In terms of world construction, individuals externalise themselves and project their 'own meaning[s] into reality' (Berger and Luckmann 1967:122). As they externalise themselves, they thereby construct a social world. Through externalisation as 'an anthropological necessity' (Berger and Luckmann 1967:70), individuals become and remain human. And being human means breaking out of one's idiosyncracies, the 'closed sphere of quiescent interiority' (Berger and Luckmann 1967:70), and continually externalising oneself in meaningful activity.

On the other hand, the problem with the liberal-individual position is the apotheosis of the individual at the expense of the community. But, quite frankly, the community is an essential variable in the social construction of reality. After all, world construction is a social enterprise; people work together to produce a human environment. Just as it is impossible for a person to develop as a person in isolation, so it is impossible for one person to produce a human environment all by himself. 'One cannot be human all by oneself and, apparently, one cannot hold on to any particular identity all by oneself' (Berger 1976:118). Nor can 'the organism and, even more the self...be adequately understood apart from the particular social context in which they were shaped' (Berger and Luckmann 1967:68).

In terms of the individual's consciousness of who and what he is, this does not result from the 'autonomous creations of meaning by isolated individuals, but begins with the individual "taking over" the world in which others already live' (Berger and Luckmann 1967:150). Knowledge, or what individuals accept as reality, is not produced by 'passively perceiving individuals, but by interacting social groups engaged in particular activities' (Barnes 1977:18–9). Individuals acquire the concepts that they use 'within a social context' (Toulmin 1972:96). This underlines the importance of the individual's chorus of 'significant others' who are indispensable to the maintenance of the objective and subjective reality of society. It also underlines the fundamental significance of the institutional order of the community.

> On the level of meaning, the institutional order represents a shield against terror. To be anomic, therefore, means to be deprived of this shield and to be exposed, alone, to the onslaught of nightmare (Berger and Luckmann 1967:119).

Taking the middle position between the two extremes of atomistic individualism and claustrophobic collectivism, it is argued that, in the final analysis, the individual is neither a Robinson Crusoe living alone on some uninhabited island nor a mere function of the collective. Reiterating Hutchinson's (1988) characterisation, the individual is 'more than an automatic functionary of some holistic society and less than an obsessive egoist in an alienated world'. It may be noted that this is, to a large extent, in keeping with Samoa's normative negotiation of the individual/collective relationship. However, given the intrinsic bias slightly in favour of the Samoan collective noted above, the Samoan collective needs to be relatively liberalised.

The pertinent considerations include the recognition of competing or conflicting interests in society, striking a more favourable balance between individual liberty and community interests, and a broad conception of the good society that rejects the determinism of community interests and provides a framework of rights and liberties within which people may pursue their interests either individually or collectively. Instead of forcing people to espouse and conform to a particular view of life, diverse world views are tolerated and social cooperation in the pursuit of diverse interests is more vigorously promoted. Even though the individual is invariably rooted in the community, nonetheless, she must always retain her liberty, including her right to criticise, revise or even change her view of what is good. Individuals must not be tied to the pursuit of a particular conception of the good but must be allowed to choose and live according to his own conception of the good life. The individual, for her part, must exercise her rights and liberties in a manner that is responsible, considerate, consistent with community values and objectives, and does not fracture or destroy human relationships.

There is a need to redefine the contours of the existing rights discourse as well. Instead of rights in the abstract, they need to be re-conceptualised as relative to the distinctive social structure and value system of a given community. Deconstructing the notion that rights have an unchanging, universal application, we must take seriously the fact that notions of rights do shift and change, depending on particular contexts.[11] And most certainly, we need to reconstitute the exceedingly isolationist, atomistic and individualistic conception of rights in the liberal-individual camp, and emphasise the notion of rights that affirms solidarity as well.[12]

As noted above, internationalisation and globalisation now significantly influence perceptions of the (post)modern self. Waldron (1995:100) is quite correct that we now 'live in a world formed by technology and trade; by economic, religious, and political imperialism and their offspring; by mass migration and the dispersion of cultural influences'. But hybridisation can be taken only so far. That is, the 'hybrid lifestyle' that Waldron seems to be promulgating, if taken too far, will ultimately produce utterly transcendental selves that are neither here nor there; they belong nowhere because they are everywhere. But most certainly, the celebrated citizen of the world must have originated from some particular place, some specific country, some distinctive culture that the so-called citizen of the world may legitimately call his own. Thus, Waldron's (1995:100) charge that immersing 'oneself in the traditional practices of, say, an aboriginal culture might be a fascinating anthropological experiment, but it involves an artificial dislocation from what actually is going on in the world' overlooks the point that the citizen of the world is ultimately a Fijian, a Samoan, a Tongan, a New Zealander, or an Australian.

Finally, the emancipation of the individual from collective determinism which liberalism heralds is always a refreshing antidote to the reduction of the individual to a mere cog in political or cultural systems. The legitimate caveat is this: liberalisation does not mean destruction. '[F]inding a way to liberalise a cultural community without destroying it is a task that liberals face in every country, once we recognise the importance of a secure cultural context of choice' (Kymlicka 1995:170).

Freedom of movement and residence versus banishment: the Samoan individual, the Samoan collective, and the dilemma for a courteous judiciary

This section uses the problem of reconciling the constitutional right to freedom of movement and residence with the Samoan custom of banishing people from a Samoan traditional village to ground the issues raised in this chapter. My point of departure is the Samoa Court of Appeal's approach to constitutional interpretation. Treating the Constitution of Samoa as *sui generis,* the court emphasised the particular history and distinctive social structure of Samoa as pertinent factors of constitutional interpretation. In the area of fundamental rights and liberties, the court counselled the avoidance of a mechanical legalism and a dogmatic, pedantic approach in favour of a careful balancing of individual rights and liberties with the custom and tradition of the Samoan people. The court's approach, in turn, raises a number of important issues to which the following discussion will advert in due course.

The right to freedom of movement and residence is guaranteed by article 13(1)(d) of the Constitution of Samoa 1960: 'All citizens of Western Samoa shall have the right to move freely throughout Western Samoa and to reside in any part thereof'. Clause 4 of article 13 imposes limits— 'reasonable restrictions...in the interests of national security, the economic well-being of Western Samoa, or public order, health or morals, for detaining persons of unsound mind, for preventing any offence, for the arrest and trial of persons charged with offences, or for punishing offenders'—on the right to freedom of movement and residence. Underlining the significance of article 13(1)(d), Professor Davidson in the Constitutional Convention 1960 affirmed this as an important right subject to 'the practical restriction that one should possess some land on which to live or to be living in someone else's house and on their land with their permission' (Constitutional Convention of Western Samoa 1960:Vol. I, 199–200). In substantive terms, this is a right of action which presupposes a person or subject (A) with a legal and/or moral warrant to have or do something (X), and that it is legally and/or morally wrong for other persons (B and C) affected by the exercise of that right to refuse to honour A's right.

The legality of banishment[13] was one of the issues in the Samoa Court of Appeal case of *Italia Taamale & Others* v *The Attorney-General* (CA. 2/95B) which, as Lord Cooke put it at 2, 'raises an issue of importance in Western Samoan society as to banishment from a village' and which at 32 was 'a test case which the appellants were justified in pursuing'. The issue was whether banishment violated article 13(1)(d). The facts included a petition by the council of *matais* of the village of Sapunaoa to have the appellants and their families banished from the village. The allegations included the appellants' insulting behaviour and refusal to comply with village obligations. Under section 75 of the Land and Titles Act 1981, Samoa's Land and Titles Court on 28 January 1994 granted a banishment order and ordered the appellants to leave the village. On 11 April 1994, the appellants filed an application for leave to appeal to the Appeal Division of the Land and Titles Court under section 79 of the Land and Titles Act 1981. The Appeal Division under section 89 of the Land and Titles Act 1981 suspended the banishment order.

On 9 September 1994, by way of case stated, the matter was reserved for the opinion of the Supreme Court on the issue whether the banishment order issued by the Land and Titles Court was violative of article 13(1)(d) and article 4 of the Constitution which vests power in the Supreme Court to enforce the rights in part II and to 'make all such orders as may be necessary and appropriate to secure' the enjoyments of those rights. On 23 January 1995, the case came before Sapolu CJ who held that the banishment order was not in breach of the Constitution and that the Land and Titles Court has jurisdiction to issue banishment orders.

On 10 February 1995, a notice of appeal to the Court of Appeal was filed and granted. And so it was that the case came before the Court of Appeal for hearing on 7 August 1995. Upholding the Chief Justice's decision, the Court of Appeal held at 31 that '[i]t is that history and social structure [of Samoa] and those references in the Constitution which lead us now to hold that, within the meaning of article 13(4), banishment from a village is, at the present time, a reasonable restriction imposed by existing law, in the interests of public order, on the exercise of the rights of freedom of movement and residence affirmed by Article 13(1)(d)'.

I confirm that the court's approach is the more reasonable and rational one. However, critical analysis of the central planks of the court's decision unravels important issues which illustrate the dilemma which confronted the court. *Italia Taamale* also brought to the fore the issue of liberty being divided along dichotomous lines and described as 'two types of freedom, the foreign and the local one' (Constitutional Convention of Western Samoa 1960:Vol. I, 206), a mindset which continually threatens to divide society on a single axis, producing a conflict with very serious implications. I note the following matters.

1   The court held that banishment from a Samoan traditional village is a custom long established in Samoa, relying on the *Report on Matai Titles, Customary Land, and the Land and Titles Court 1975* and the Chief Justice's findings which confirmed banishment as an important sanction vested by custom in the village council of *matais*. In upholding that custom, the court appropriately deferred to the custom and traditions of the community. That said, whether or not the Samoan judiciary had successfully performed its constitutional role of protecting the individual, the weak, the vulnerable, and the disadvantaged remains a moot point. The Court of Appeal did set out at 28 a number of 'principles and safeguards' which should limit the Land and Titles Court's exercise of the power to issue banishment orders. Accordingly, the court's jurisdiction is to be exercised only 'for truly strong reasons', including the preservation of public order and the stability of village life and organisation. In cases where the individual outrageously indulges in an idiosyncratic assertion and practice of his rights and liberties, banishment is perhaps appropriate. Even so, banishment remains an extreme measure of social control and an order to that effect must never be lightly made.

2   Extolling the virtues of banishment actually masked issues of justice and fairness which must have been nuanced and more forcefully addressed. Banishment, despite its proclaimed virtues, often (if not always) affects an entire family, 'innocent people such as children' as the Court of Appeal put it at 29. A timid reminder, perhaps, given the subjunctive tone in which

it was expressed. Nevertheless, a note of reservation had been struck. The highest court of the land had spoken with a note of caution, thus signalling (hopefully) the eventual dismantling of the fallacy that there is nothing wrong with banishment. Where innocent people are in fact affected, one wonders whether there is any credible legal and/or moral justification for the suffering of innocent victims, unless we resort to the suspect Hebrew view of God visiting the sins of the fathers on their children.

Moreover, as the Chief Justice correctly noted, in most cases the onus is on the banished person to seek reconciliation through a public display of remorse and appeasing the displeasure of the village council with a lavish presentation of foodstuffs and fine mats. This is in keeping with Samoa's traditional means of dispute resolution predicated on restorative justice. While acknowledging the need for reconciliation and applauding the banished individual for taking the initiative to end the estrangement with the collective, it is difficult to overlook how the banished person is made to suffer both the indignity of physical dislocation and the economic price for reconciliation. Both the social and economic costs, I might add, are separate penalties for the one and same offence. If this is not double jeopardy, then perhaps we need to rewrite our law books.

3   Whereas the Court of Appeal's approach of applying the Constitution with due regard to its Samoan setting is warranted, the issue is that people are being banished even for the most trivial of reasons, the right to freedom of movement and residence is still being violated, and the unresolved issue of the justification of banishment continues to haunt both the Samoan people and judiciary. The Supreme Court case of *Aloimaina Ulisese & Others* v *Lands and Titles Court Tuasivi & Others* (4 November 1998), decided after *Italia Taamale*, is cited as evidence. The case involved the banishment of the plaintiffs and their families from their village under a 1994 banishment order by the Land and Titles Court. The plaintiffs in June 1998 issued a Motion for Judicial Review of the court's 1994 decision, a Declaratory Order that the decision was wrong in law and fact, and a rehearing of the case. The plaintiffs alleged that the Land and Titles Court had acted

unreasonably and outside the law, and was negligent in exercising its jurisdiction. The grounds included (a) the banishment of a whole family, (b) that the court gave no reasons for the banishment of a whole family, and (c) that members of the family who were not parties nor served with the proceedings were in fact banished.

'It was accepted for the purpose of this case,' Young J noted at 8 'that the allegations mentioned above were true'. There was therefore a clear breach of article 9(1) on fair hearing. It was also a violation of clause 3, which guarantees that a person charged with an offence 'shall be presumed innocent until proved guilty according to law'. On the facts, the presumption of innocence was effectively ignored in their case; they were adjudged guilty (of an unknown offence) without proof. The failure to serve them with the proceedings was, in addition, an infringement of clause 4 which guarantees a person charged with an offence rights such as the right to be informed of the charge against him, the right to defend himself, and the right to examine witnesses both for and against him. On the facts, most of the plaintiffs were neither informed of the charges against them nor given the opportunity to defend themselves. Clearly, this was a blatant miscarriage of justice. Fundamental rights were violated by an institution of the state, raising issues of fairness and natural justice. Those rights violations question in a fundamental way the propriety and legality of banishment.

4   In Samoa, with its intrinsic bias slightly in favour of the collective, the court's decision becomes a rather questionable prescriptive solution to the issue of the increasingly problematic relationship between the Samoan individual and the Samoan collective. That is, the decision tends towards creating and perhaps reinforcing a claustrophobic society in which the individual has little autonomy.

As noted above, the problem is the predisposition to exalt and reify the collective, thereby ignoring the individual as 'an active being' and reducing him to a cultural dope who acts according to social determinants and the axiomatic laws of society, a mere 'tape recording of his culture', an actor playing out a predetermined role in a script provided by society in the manner of a puppet. The collective in this social structure is really a 'gigantic Alcatraz' or 'a forbidding prison' wherein the individual suffers from the determinism of an imperialistic collective. This does not condone the individual acting as a 'spoiled brat', making idiosyncratic assertions of his rights or liberties. Nor do I intend to disparage unnecessarily the importance of the collective and the institutional order acting as a shield against terror, a sheltering canopy: 'The walls of society are a Potemkin village erected in front of the abyss of being [and they] function to protect us from terror, to organise for us a cosmos of meaning within which our lives make sense' (Berger 1976:170). That notwithstanding, a collective with a lot of power over the individual is a threatening reality. It is not difficult to use a variety of gods—cultural, religious, economic, political —as a façade for abuses of power.

5   Central to the court's decision was the maintenance of public order. But public order is an amorphous term, and disruption of it can be anything from a simple act that interferes with quiet living to sedition and rioting. Sometimes, public order in Samoa carries a distinctive connotation: obeying the decrees of the village councils. Conversely, disobeying those decrees indiscriminately means public disorder. Whether or not the decrees are just is secondary, and the individual's reasons for disobeying them are seldom taken into account. The invocation of public order as justification for the punishment meted out cannot hide the suppression of the individual.

Underpinning the notion of public order is the functionalist axiom, the view that society has needs such as integration. In this theoretical framework, social procedures, practices and institutions have functions relative to the accomplishment of the needs of society. There may be problems with this functionalist explanation if it is taken too far. For instance, the functionalist axiom may be ontologically wrong in the sense that the notion of society with needs (engendered by the analogy on which it is based)[14] involves the error of reification, treating as an organism something that is not.

The axiom also creates a static view of society, a utopian society that is in a perpetual state of equilibrium and in which there are no conflicts or changes. Consequently, it ignores change and conflict as essential variables in society, and the precarious nature of the social order given the fact that every society undergoes changes and experiences conflicts everyday and at every turn. In fact, every society is threatened by attacks from external forces or by internal revolutions such as by a competing version of society. The subjective reality of society is similarly precarious built up as it were through the process of socialisation, which is never completely successful, and maintained by contact with others who are liable to change or disappear. And, while the symbolic universe may indeed be challenged by an alternative social order, most often it is the power struggle among those who inhabit the same social world, but who seek to transform it in different directions (that is, a contest between different versions of what the social order should be), which must be acknowledged, illuminated, and resolved.

The axiom entails a related unacceptable corollary: the aims, needs, interests, beliefs, fears and doubts of the individual members of society could be excluded from a functionalist explanation. Sometimes, it excludes what individuals think and feel, their aims, needs, interests, beliefs and doubts. It ignores the ability of people to make rational choices relative to the achievement of their aims and so forth. It creates humans who have no influence on the operation and direction of their society. This is because society is seen to be governed by latent or invisible axiomatic functional laws. Once this proposition is granted, it is a short step to the reductionist view that people are really cultural dopes, tape recordings, and mere actors playing out pre-determined roles on some panoramic stage. The main player in this theatrical drama is a reified society which confronts individuals as a fixed entity— overwhelming and overbearing; a kind of breathing reality with needs such as public order.

6   In order to make banishment a Samoan custom that has acquired the force of law, the court took into account statutory provisions and relevant case law.[15] In the final analysis, the court was bound by the doctrine of *stare decisis*, and its adherence to precedents constructed an 'idealised model of the legal process' (Kairys 1982:11–17, 11). As a critical mechanism of legal reasoning, *stare decisis* required the court to follow precedents faithfully. In principle, this is supposed

to produce not only correct results but certainty, stability and continuity in the legal system. As an essential feature of legal discourse, *stare decisis* gave the court's reasoning a formal face. In its operation, *stare decisis* is supposed to involve the court applying precedents in an objective, non-political, almost scientifically mechanical manner. In actual practice, however, some precedents are followed and others rejected simply by distinguishing them.

This issue also surfaced in *Italia Taamale*. I note, for instance, the practice direction issued by Sir Gaven Donne (then Chief Justice and President of the Land and Titles Court of Samoa) that 'no further banishment orders should be made as they were in violation of the Constitution', relying primarily on the inconsistency between banishment and articles 13(1)(d) and (2)(1) and (2). As expected, the Court of Appeal at 21 dismissed the direction on the ground that 'a practice direction cannot settle the law and is usually made without the benefit of hearing argument from counsel'. The court also rejected a press statement by St John CJ to the effect that banishment violated provisions of the Constitution and was therefore unconstitutional. In short, the court could logically decide the legality of banishment by adopting one possible interpretation of the issue and ignoring available alternatives. But the legality of banishment was, it may be argued, amenable to a different answer to the one the court came out with. In justifying banishment as a reasonable restriction in the interests of public order, the court expressed a clear vision of society. By focusing on public order, the court made a clear political preference in favour of the collective over the ethic of individual liberty, perhaps reflecting a suppressed intent to retain a particular order of values, typically the existing one.

This raises a plethora of questions concerning the practice of strict adherence to the doctrine of *stare decisis*. Despite its usefulness, the doctrine is most certainly not perfect; it makes the law 'introspective and backward-looking' (Thomas 1993). Sometimes *stare decisis* is such an open-ended doctrine that one can do almost anything with it. But, then again, the doctrine is necessary to create the picture of judges simply declaring and applying the law, faithfully following precedents. Yet, such a picture of judges could very well be a fairytale no longer tenable in the modern world. And we do not have to go along with the full panoply of the critical legal studies genre to support the view that sometimes the law can be really incoherent and contradictory.

7   Also critical to the Court of Appeal's decision was the construction of banishment as a reasonable restriction.[16] In *New Windsor Corporation* v *Mellor* [1975] 3 All ER 44, Lord Denning held that for a custom to be good, it must be both reasonable (that is, not contrary to reason, and what is contrary to reason cannot be consonant to law) and certain. As an illustration, Lord Denning referred to two different uses of land. In 1666, the owner of a parcel of land (Bachelor's Acre) complained that his fellow villagers were destroying his grass by dancing on it in line with a village custom of using that land for recreation purposes. Applying the two-limb test, the custom was deemed a good one since it was certain (that is, it was part of the village's history and way of life) and reasonable (that is, it was necessary for the villagers to have their recreation). But if the land in question was arable land being used for farming, then the owner had every right to stop horsemen from riding over the land and destroying his crops.

   Banishment, like villagers enjoying themselves in dance and other pastimes on Bachelor's Acre, is a custom that has been practised in Samoa for a long time. In this respect, banishment is certain, satisfying the second limb of Lord Denning's test. Unlike the villagers using Bachelor's Acre for recreation purposes, banishment means depriving people of the right to reside in their own homes and requiring them to depart from their land. In this respect, banishment is much more serious than horsemen riding over arable land and destroying the owner's crops. The first limb of Lord Denning's test, that a custom must be reasonable, is not satisfied. It may be argued that, since banishment is contrary to reason, it cannot be consonant with law.

   The notion of reasonableness is nevertheless hard to gauge. Lord Cooke in *Webster* v *Auckland Harbour Board* [1987] 2 NZLR 129 (a judicial review case) associated reasonableness at 131 with reason, and unreasonableness with something 'outside the limits of reason'. In another review case, Lord

Diplock in *CCSU* v *Minister for Civil Service* [1985] AC 374 at 410 associated unreasonableness with something 'so outrageous in its defiance of logic or moral standards that no sensible person who had applied his mind to the question to be decided could have arrived'. It seems clear from those authorities that reasonableness is a broad concept, with broad categories such as reason and morality providing pointers. It means different things to different people in different situations.

8   There is a causal nexus between banishment and Samoa's land tenure system. To some extent, the issue is the limited force of a private property right for the Samoan individual residing on customary land which, by law and in custom, belongs to the collective (the family and the village).[17]

There are two issues which need clarification here: (a) the correlation between banishment and the existing land tenure system in Samoa, and (b) the institution of communal ownership of customary land.

First , I offer the following observations in respect of the connection between banishment and the Samoan individual's limited property rights in customary land. Relevant for present purposes is the principle that 'a man's house is his castle'. The issue is the sanctity of the home predicated on the moral dignity of the man—whatever and whoever he is—who inhabits the home. Lord Cooke (1988:160), underlining this principle, enjoined that the 'sanctity of the home, subject to strictly limited exceptions, can be seen as an example of a right existing by natural law'.

The axiom is, furthermore, about a person's common law right to enjoy the security and privacy of his home, and to defend his home and property. The case of *Entick* v *Carrington* (1765) 19 State Trials 1030 involved officers of the English government who, pursuant to warrants issued by the Secretary of State, raided homes in search of materials connected with John Wilkes' pamphlets attacking government policies and the King himself. Entick, an associate of Wilkes, brought a civil action of trespass against the State agents for breaking and entering his house and seizing his papers under a bad warrant. Delivering the court's judgment, Lord Camden said at 314

> The great end, for which men entered into society, was to secure their property. That right is preserved sacred and incommunicable in all instances, where it has not been taken away or abridged by some public law for the good of the whole...By the laws of England, every invasion of private property, be it ever so

minute, is a trespass. No man can set his foot upon my ground without my licence, but he is liable to an action, though the damage be nothing; which is proved by every declaration in trespass, where the defendant is called upon to answer for bruising the grass and even treading upon the soil.

Holding that the Secretary of State had no jurisdiction to seize the defendant's papers, the court held that the warrant to seize Entick's papers was illegal and void. Critical to the court's decision was Entick's right of property in his land, home, and chattels protected by law. Underpinning Entick's right of property is the concept of legal ownership as a bundle of rights to possess, use, lend, gift, mortgage, alienate, use up, consume, and/or otherwise deal with that property (Honore 1984). Although Honore does not include the right to exclude, that appears explicitly as a constituent of the rights to possess and to security. Legal ownership thus entails the right to exclude others, even the King himself, from interfering with the quiet enjoyment of one's property. Associated with the right of exclusion is the right to protect one's property against all and sundry.

Unlike Entick, the property rights of a Samoan individual living on customary land are much less substantial and exclusive since customary land belongs to the group. At best, the individual has only the right to possess, use, and enjoy customary land; the family and village council retain an ultimate reversionary interest in that land since Samoa's land tenure system vests ownership of customary land in the collective. Collective ownership, of course, has its benefits such as the non-alienation of land and beneficial title. However, collective ownership should not be idealised; it is problematic.[18] For instance, collective ownership supports the banishment of people from their homes. Lacking an exclusionary right in the land on which the individual lives, it is not difficult at all to banish or even forcibly evict him from that land.

Important also is the justification of private ownership (Nozick 1974). Everyone has a natural right to own property, including the fruits of one's own labour in terms of the Lockean appropriation theory. The instrumental or utilitarian justification of private property is predicated on a number of grounds. Allowing the individual to enjoy the fruits of his labour is conducive to invention and industry. Ownership and control of private property also contribute to personality development; in a real sense, they make a person responsible and provide the incentive to work towards increasing the value of one's property.

Of equal significance as well is the connection between private property and liberty, that private property is 'necessary to liberty' (Dahl

1985:80). As Jennifer Nedelsky (1988:241) has noted, '[p]roperty set bounds between a protected sphere of individual freedom and the legitimate scope of governmental authority'. This was, to some extent, the issue in *Entick*. The court's decision affirmed Entick's liberty in his own home and in the ownership of his chattels. This proposition has been extended to embrace more than just property rights. 'It is certainly the case,' argues Nedelsky (1988:261) 'that property has traditionally been associated with the values of independence, privacy, autonomy and participation'. And '[t]he right to private space [in a person's home] is an essential privacy principle' (Longworth and McBride 1994:3).

Of course, private property in capitalist terms has its own defects.

> Property as an exclusive right of a natural or artificial person to use and dispose of material things...leads necessarily, in any kind of market society...to an inequality of wealth and power that denies a lot of people the possibility of a reasonably human life. The narrow institution of property is bound to result in such inequality, in any society short of a genetically engineered one that would have ironed out all differences in skill and energy (Macpherson 1977:73).[19]

Be that as it may, for present purposes, the issue is the relative ease with which people can be banished under customary property regimes due to their lack of exclusionary rights. Certainly, banishment will not cause a social revolution. Underlining the need to securely protect the individual's property and privacy rights, I quote verbatim what William Pitt said in the English Parliament in 1763: 'The poorest man may in his cottage bid defiance to all the force of the crown. It may be frail—its roof may shake—the wind may blow through it—the storm may enter, the rain may enter—but the King of England cannot enter—all his force dares not cross the threshold of the ruined tenement'.

Second, concerning the institution of communal ownership of customary land, I take the view that there is no philosophical, legal, or moral impediment to collective ownership of property, and that communal ownership of customary land constitutes an instance of group rights defined by a common interest that grounds a group right (on the 'collective' conception of group rights) and/or a clear identity as a group (on the 'corporate' conception of group rights).

Adopting a broad view of the moral standing of the group for right-holding purposes, it may be argued that such moral standing is based on the collective moral status of the individuals in the group (the collective conception) and/or the moral status of the group itself as a moral community in its own right (the corporate conception). In my view, there is no discrepancy between the two conceptions of the moral standing of the group. Hence both could be invoked to ground and explain the moral standing of the group for right-holding purposes. On either conception, however, there is always the gnawing issue of the proper relationship between the individual and the collective in cases of conflicting interests which disrupt 'a simple symmetry of interests amongst the holders of a collective right' (Jones 1999:370), on the one hand, and in cases where the 'group corporately may hold [or even exercise] rights against, or over, its members severally' (Jones 1999:372), on the other.

Finally, it may be noted that developing property rights into estates in fee simple is now a constant motif in the reform and development agendas in the Pacific (Toatu 2004; Gosarevski et al. 2004) And as Jim Fingleton (2004:97) has correctly reminded, contra misconceptions,

> [t]here is a great deal of misunderstanding about customary land tenures. One of the most common mistakes is to believe that customary tenure involves both the communal ownership and the communal use of land. In its extreme form, this view leads critics to see communal ownership as something like communism, whose fate it should share. On the contrary, communal ownership in countries like Papua New Guinea should be seen as a form of private property rights, albeit that the rights are owned by a group rather than by individuals.

Subject to the limitations of individual property noted above, my own position, as a Samoan, is that there needs to be a liberalisation of property rights in the sense of allowing customary land to be used for economic and commercial purposes (for example, through leasehold agreements) while, at the same time, ensuring that the rent money is equally divided amongst all the title-holders and that family land is not capable of alienation. This change, I emphasise, needs to be undertaken with caution, care, and a lot of sensitivity on the part of the donor agencies and international financial bodies pushing this agenda. Failing that, they run the risk of leading Pacific nations into wars over land and profits.

Conclusion

The Court of Appeal's promise to approach issues of rights and freedoms in a generous, unquibbling manner that avoids the austerity of a dogmatic legalism is most certainly the more reasonable and rational approach. Adopting a clinical approach, the court decided the case of *Italia Taamale* with courteous regard to the social structure and history of Samoa. Further constrained to circumscribe its interpretation of the law by reference to legal precedents and the judicial symbols of certainty and consistency, the Samoan judicial lion, it may be argued, could not help being less activist.

But, at least, we can understand the learned justices' dilemma: either reject banishment as a violation of the Constitution and thereby risk the wrath of the collective, or, justify banishment as a reasonable restriction imposed by law and suffer the moral pain of having to sacrifice the individual to indulge the collective. That said, it is perhaps the case that in a community of individuals who look up to the Court of Appeal as the most reliable guardian of their rights, any judicial activism by the courts would not be seen as a Machiavellian plot to overthrow the institutional order. Most certainly, it would not be dubbed judicial usurpation or idolatry.

Regarding the individual/collective dialectic, the appropriate approach, as hitherto argued, is not to promote a telescopic view of the issue, fortifying one type of rights over the other. Neither type, after all, provides a perfect solution to the problems of social life. Liberalism with its focus on individual rights may itself constitute a threat to society when it creates egoist individuals obsessed with nothing else but what they want. Improperly used, rights and freedoms become tutelary deities that sacralise and justify anti-social causes. Overused and exaggerated, the terms rights and freedoms lose meaning and value. As Lord Radcliffe (1961:viii) once warned, '[l]ike a cheap campaign button, they are pinned without discrimination upon this label and that...There is some danger that in western democracies the ideas of individual liberty and freedom will die of fatty degeneration of the muscles of the heart'. [20]

If liberalism has its pitfalls, communitarianism does not fare any better. A naïve preoccupation with the collective often manifests itself in the absurd reification and worship of the social order: society deified, 'god' as the deification of society, and religion as the sacralisation of society's requirements for human behaviour. In this worship, the individual is invariably condemned as a self-centred, amoral product of Darwin's selfish gene, and the reduction of the individual to a mere function of the system is publicly applauded as part of his education on the virtues and objectives of the collective.

In the final analysis, neither view adequately represents the real interests and needs of real people in the real world. Hutchinson (1988:93) aptly captures the need to take a middle-position between the two extremes as follows

[E]ach vision represents only a partial vision and incomplete depiction of social life and its possibilities. Neither is reliable or realisable as an exclusive basis for social organisation... [O]ne vision is the antithesis of the other. Yet there can be no synthesis for each is the consequence of the other and any attempt to expunge one serves ultimately to reinforce it: they are 'partners as well as antagonists'.

Notes

1   For an overview of human rights in the Pacific, see Bureau of Democracy, Human Rights, and Labor (2003).
2   On the need for a bill of rights for England, Lord Scarman (1992) has argued that '[n]o democracy can be considered safe whose freedoms are not encoded in a basic constitution'. In Australia, Justice Kirby (1997) opined that '[n]o-one says that a bill of rights alone will protect the rights of the people. But nor does majoritarian democracy in Parliament'.
3   See, for example, part II of the *Constitution of the Republic of Vanuatu*. The fundamental rights and liberties in part II are entrenched by articles 84 to 86; also Part I of the *Constitution of Tonga* which, by clause 79, entrenches fundamental rights and liberties given under part II.
4   For a vigorous defense of the individual-liberal position see, for example, Kukathas and Pettit (1990); and Kukathas (1995).
5   Compare Smith (1980:1), who states '[t]he dissolution of ethnicity. The transcendence of nationalism. The internationalisation of culture. These have been the dreams, and expectations, of liberals and rationalists in practically every country, and in practically every country they have been confounded and disappointed...Today the cosmopolitan ideals are in decline and rationalist expectations have withered. Today, liberals and socialists alike must work for, and with, the nation state and its increasingly ethnic culture, or remain voices in the wilderness'.
6   On communitarianism see, for example, Brett (1991) and Green (1991). For a Pacific view of collective rights, see Tomas (1998).
7   On the contingency of the self, see for example, Rorty (1989).
8   See, for example, Raz (1986); cf. Jones (1999). Jones distinguishes between what he calls the 'collective conception' of group rights and his own 'corporate conception' of group rights. Central to Jones' conception is the issue of the moral standing of the group for right-holding purposes. The following statement (1999:364) is instructive of Jones' view and the problems that it faces: 'Since, on my view, right-holding depends crucially upon moral standing, the conditions of moral standing will provide the conditions a group has to satisfy if it is to be a corporate right-holder. But since the prerequisites of moral standing are controversial (as is evident from disputes over whether any entity other than human persons can possess rights), that controversy must infect the question of which groups, if any, can possess corporate rights'.
9   To some extent, the word *matai* also carries the quasi-metaphysical connotation of being set apart or consecrated. Seen in this light, the bearer of a *matai* title is seen as in some sense divinely consecrated for a particular office, a kind of priest *ex officio*. See, for example, Meleisea (1987). While this may explain the special place which *matais* and the *matai* system hold in Samoa's cosmology, it tends to misrepresent the place of *matais* in the socio-cultural system. By structuring society on a vertical axis in accordance with a religious hierarchical ordering of the universe, this explanation runs the risk of elevating *matais* above the common fray and abstracting them from their *modus operandi* which actually gives them meaning, value and significance.

10   Gordon (1982:289) notes that '[the] process of allowing the structures we ourselves have built to mediate relations among us so as to make us see ourselves as performing abstract roles in a play that is produced by no human agency is what is usually called (following Marx and such modern writers as Sartre and Lukacs) reification. It is a way people have of manufacturing necessity: they build structures, then act as if (and genuinely come to believe that) the structures they have built are determined by history, human nature, and economic law'.

11   Thus MacIntyre (1984:220) notes 'we all approach our circumstances as bearers of a particular social identity. I am someone's son or daughter, someone else's cousin or uncle; I am a citizen of this or that city, a member of this or that guild or profession; I belong to this clan, that tribe, this nation...As such, I inherit from the past of my family, my city, my tribe, my nation, a variety of debts, inheritances, rightful expectations and obligations. These constitute the given of my life, my moral starting point. This is in part what gives my life its own moral particularity. This thought is likely to appear alien ... from the standpoint of modern individualism. From the standpoint of individualism I am what I myself choose to be. I can always, if I wish to, put in question what are taken to be the merely contingent social features of my existence'.

12   Rorty (1989:191) notes that '[o]ur sense of solidarity is strongest when those with whom solidarity is expressed are thought of as "one of us", where "us" means something smaller and more local than the human race'. Teasing out the moral and ethical dimensions of solidarity, Rorty (1989:192) grounds the basis of solidarity on 'the ability to see more and more traditional differences (of tribe, religion, race, customs, and the like) as unimportant when compared with similarities with respect to pain and humiliation—the ability to think of people wildly different from ourselves as included in the range of "us"'.

13   See also the Kiribati case of *Teitinnong* v *Ariong* [1987] LRC (Const) 517 and the Solomon Islands case of *Remisio Pusi* v *Leni and Others* (unreported) High Court, Solomon Islands, cc 218/95, 14 February 1997.

14   Pertinent to the functionalist axiom is the analogy between society and a biological organism, and the functions which the different organs of an organism perform for the good of the whole body in much the same way the different elements of society work together to maintain social order. See, for example, Giddens (1972).

15   The precedents included the *Samoan Offenders Ordinance 1922*, the *Samoa Amendment Act 1927*, and the case of *Tagaloa* v *Inspector of Police* [1927] NZLR 883.

16   Note the use of the amorphous term 'reasonable restrictions' in article 13(4). Cf. section 5 of the New Zealand *Bill of Rights Act 1990*, entitled 'Justified limitations'. The section provides that the rights and freedoms contained in the Bill of Rights may be subject only to such 'reasonable limits prescribed by law as can be demonstrably justified in a free and democratic society', with the burden of proof on those seeking to limit rights. Of some relevance also is clause 44(2) of the *Canadian Bill of Rights 1960* which provides: 'Every law of Canada shall, unless it is expressly declared by an Act of the Parliament of Canada that it shall operate notwithstanding the Canadian Bill of Rights, be so construed and applied as not to abrogate, abridge or infringe or to authorise the abrogation, abridgement or infringement of any rights or freedoms herein recognised and declared'.

17   Article 101 of the Constitution defines the types of land in Samoa: customary or native land, freehold land, and public land. In the case of customary land, the law makes the state the trustee of the beneficial owners of such land: *Western Samoa Trust Estates Corporation* v *Tuionoula* [1987] WSSC 1; [1987] SPLR 437 (19 January 1987). This is, of course, a debatable matter. Article 102 governs that

trusteeship by prohibiting the alienation of customary land or any interest therein by way of sale, mortgage, gift or otherwise. Nor shall customary land or any interest therein be used in the execution of loans and so forth. Parliament, however, may authorise through legislation (1) the grant of a lease or licence of customary land or of any interest therein, and (2) the taking of any customary land or interest therein for public purposes, subject to adequate compensation as required by article 14.

[18] Note, for example, Mill's (1970:795) criticism of the socialist ethic which allows collective ownership of property: 'It is the common error of Socialists to overlook the natural indolence of mankind; their tendency to be passive, to be slaves of habit, to persist indefinitely in a course once chosen. Let them once attain any state of existence which they consider tolerable, and the danger to be apprehended is that they will thenceforth stagnate; will not exert themselves to improve, and by letting their faculties rust, will lose even the energy required to preserve them from deterioration'. Whereas Mill's criticism is extreme and somewhat simplistic, there is a grain of truth to the claim that common ownership of land is not immediately conducive to economic development.

[19] Note also Barry (1986:86–7), who argues: 'As they [capitalists] accumulate more and more property, there is less and less for others. The relative positions of the parties with respect to property is not equal, for as one has gained the other has, of necessity, lost'. But, in a third world context like Samoa, we may need to initiate public policies to facilitate wide acquisition and ownership of property, while, at the same time, preempting the possibility of excessive concentration of property in a few to the detriment of the many. And, personally, I do not subscribe to or support the alienation of customary land.

[20] See also Glendon (1991) on the negative effects of rights claims such as eclipsing 'the moral, the long-term, and the social implications' of issues from political discourse.

5

The Pacific crisis of state legitimacy: courteous enemies, fragile alliances and uneasy bed-fellows

'A government is not legitimate merely because it exists', wrote Jeane J. Kirkpatrick, former United States Ambassador to the United Nations. This aptly expresses the crux of the issue: there is more to state legitimacy than mere empirical existence.

This chapter addresses the crisis of state legitimacy in Pacific nations, manifested in public disorder, coups, the collapse of law and order, corruption, state capture, violation of human rights, and so forth. A central part of the problem is that Pacific states are underpinned by modes of legitimacy (embodied in constitutions and statutes) that are, at times, mutually reinforcing and, at other times, violently at odds and mutually exclusive. When the latter case obtains, the issue of state legitimacy forces itself to the foreground and demands a serious hearing.[1] The characterisations failing state, collapsed state, and failed state—though intellectually nondescript—do say something about state legitimacy in the Pacific.

This analysis proceeds on the following premises. First, Pacific states exhibit a pluralist situation of multiform conflicts that either produce the impasse of irreconcilable contradictions or, more positively, negotiated (albeit uneasy) alliances amongst social institutions: legal liberalism, custom and traditions, modern politics, extra-legal cultural politics, religion, state institutions, civil society organisations, and so forth (Durutalo 2003). This institutional diversity reflects the increasing differentiation of interests, values and institutions in Pacific societies.

In a positive sense, pluralism means that a single centre of legitimate authority is replaced by several centres which have to achieve a minimum balance through continuous effort, and in relation to which individuals are required to define themselves and make their own decisions. The result is an extraordinary liberation resulting from the dispersion of interests, power, and control. The plurality of centres is, therefore, a kind of balancing mechanism which prevents a single centre from acquiring absolute power and control. However, pluralism sometimes breeds disorder and destroys unity. The state is but one expression of that unity: one state, one Constitution, one system of law, a common system of values tempering the (potentially) divisiveness of conflicting systems, one with a common modality shared by everyone. Part of the end-result of pluralism is that the state, with its promise of national unity under one government and one rule of law to which all citizens are equally subject, is often dismissed into the realm of lost illusions. When this happens, state legitimacy becomes an issue.

Second, the major principle for present purposes is that legitimacy presupposes, requires, and should mean government under the rule of law. In true constitutional democracies, the rule of law accords government formal, moral and practical legitimacy. When government is not government under the law, government rule becomes rule through arbitrary power and naked force. Whenever this happens, we find government operating on a trumped-up legitimacy that is carefully masked by the façade of democratic institutions.

The loss of legitimacy is due to a whole range of reasons, such as when lawmakers sit above the law and act outside the law. On this point, Windybank and Manning's (2003:1) assessment of the situation in Papua New Guinea warrants quoting in full

> Aid agencies talk about the need for 'good governance', 'institution strengthening' and 'capacity building', but PNG's dysfunctional institutions suffer from a lack of legitimacy as much as they do a lack of capacity or resources. The popular view is that there are two sets of laws—one for those with power and influence, who rort the formal system and get away with it, and another for the 'grassroots' or ordinary people. At issue is not the absence of laws or regulations, such as sanctions against the misappropriation of public funds, but a glaring lack of enforcement. Raskols mimic political leaders' corrupt behaviour at the street level, enriching themselves through theft. Law enforcement has not matched the escalation in crime so that gangs operate with relative impunity. When criminals and corrupt politicians go unpunished, people lose respect for state laws and the authority of central government collapses.

Whether or not this assessment is completely accurate is a matter of opinion. What it does show is that government legitimacy could be forfeited in any number of ways. The specific focus of this chapter is on tensions in Pacific legal systems engendered by competing assumptions about the law (its nature, quality, and function), tensions which often manifest themselves in uncertainty in the law and, in some cases, in the undermining of the authority and legitimacy of the rule of law itself. While seeking a resolution of those tensions, it must be emphasised that politics, religion, custom and traditions (and how those are differently represented) must ultimately yield to the demands of the rule of law as the overarching principle of legitimate governance.

Third, legitimation is an ongoing issue. Whenever the equilibrium of society is disturbed, the need for legitimation arises. And since 'no society is absolutely static or ever fully integrated, this equilibrium should be conceived of as dynamic or moving and always as only partial' (Chinoy 1968:186). This challenges the utopian view that society is (and should be) in a state of eternal equilibrium, a view spawned by the functionalist axiom predicated on the assumption that society is a persistent, stable, well-integrated structure of elements which contribute to the maintenance of society as an integrated system. Supposedly held together by an unbroken consensus, such a society is seen as always in a state of equilibrium and solidarity (Durkheim 1938; Merton 1957; Parsons 1951). Because of its focus on stability and equilibrium, functionalism is therefore uneasy about change, change that often results from conflicts and their resolution. We need, therefore, to take seriously tensions in the community, susceptible, as it should be, to multiform conflicts and their positive functions. For instance, conflict creates the need to define the identity of the community more clearly, strengthens the community's internal structures and organisation, and requires re-adjustment of the community's objectives and priorities (Simmel 1955; Coser 1956; Rex 1981).

Taken together, while functionalism appropriately focuses on integration, this should be counterbalanced by the conflict model's treatment of society as a conglomerate of diverse and competing interests. A one-sided focus on either integration or conflict produces a lopsided view of society as either a community without disagreements or a community in a perpetual state of warfare. Neither is a true reflection of the empirical situation.

Finally, in the Pacific, conflicts are cross-cutting in the sense that an ally in one conflict becomes an adversary in a different one. Sometimes religion huddles together with custom against legal liberalism; at other times, it is religion and legal liberalism against custom. In a positive sense, this prevents conflicts from falling along a single axis and unavoidably dividing society along dichotomous lines. Negatively, this makes legitimation—the aggregate of ways a particular social order is explained and justified to its members—a complex and difficult enterprise.

Ultimately, legitimation is about the construction and maintenance of a plausibility structure that is meaningful, relevant, authoritative and legitimate for the participants in a particular social world. Peter Berger (1967:45) defines a plausibility structure in the following terms,

> worlds are socially constructed and socially maintained. Their continuing reality, both objective (as common, taken-for-granted facticity) and subjective (as facticity imposing itself on individual consciousness), depends upon specific processes, namely, those processes that ongoingly reconstruct and maintain the particular worlds in question. Conversely, the interruption of these social processes threatens the (objective and subjective) reality of the worlds in question. Thus each world requires a social 'base' for its continuing existence as a world that is real to actual human beings. This 'base' may be called its 'plausibility structure'.

State legitimacy: sources, dimensions and manifestations

State legitimacy is variously conceptualised from different standpoints, with different interests, for different purposes, and with different results. It means different things to different people, depending on one's perspective, discipline, social context, needs, and interests.

Constitutionally, legitimacy lies in the consent of the governed and their acquiescence in the rule of a few, predicated on their acceptance of the justification (legal, constitutional, political, moral, ethical, and cultural) of the rule of a few over the many, something that no truly democratic government can do without. This is important in the respect that government rule is coercion, and such coercion must be publicly debated, defended, and comprehensively explained and justified. Normatively, legitimacy means state power is judged worthy of acceptance in accordance with a coherent set of standards such as justice and fairness. Normative legitimacy creates and underpins a normative relationship between the government and the governed. Procedurally, legitimacy means compliance with the requirements for certainty in, generality of, and equality under the law. These elements of positive law go to the issue of procedural justice in keeping with the democratic process of lawmaking which rather restrictively, for Jürgen Habermas (1996:448), 'forms the only... source of legitimacy' in the post-metaphysical age. Functionally, legitimacy is judged on the successful performance of those functions which government was instituted to serve—for example, the protection of citizens' rights, persons, property, peace and security. This performance-based legitimacy means that when government performs acts unrelated or even contrary to the functions it was instituted to serve, it loses the trust of the citizens and undermines or even loses its legitimacy.

In sum, legitimacy encompasses a whole range of interests: the source of government; normative principles; moral and practical acquiescence of the governed; citizens' trust in the governors; constitutional legitimacy based on the adherence to constitutional rules; and legal legitimacy when government is conducted according to the law. The diversity notwithstanding, it could be argued that the different facets of legitimacy ultimately converge at a single point, namely, government's authority to rule on behalf of the governed. This assumes the 'acceptance by the population at large of the place and the functions of established institutions' (Hughes 2003). That said, it must be noted that an *a priori* equation of acceptance with legitimacy may mask important issues (for example, injustice) which need to be exposed and addressed. We need, therefore, to question established assumptions and approaches, subjecting them to scrutiny and asking whether or not an established form of legitimacy actually masks the protection of the privileged status and interests of one segment of society at the expense of the rest of the body politic.

Relevant to the Pacific situation are Max Weber's theorems of legitimacy.

1   The dominant form and basis of legitimate authority in the modern world is rational-legal authority based on rational grounds and embodied in rules (constitutions, statutes, and regulations) that have been legally enacted and established.

2   Traditional authority, particularly in what Weber described as pre-modern societies, is based on the custom and traditions of a community, embodied in the people's way of life and transmitted through cultural traditions.

3   Charismatic authority is based on the personal charisma of a leader, manifested in ethical, heroic, or religious acts (Weber 1946).

Concerned primarily with modern Western societies, Weber's overriding interest was in the emergence of a goal-oriented rationality in virtually all spheres of life—political, economic, legal, aesthetic, and erotic. This new rationality, Weber claimed, has come to dominate social action formerly defined by tradition and religion.[2]

While confirming the fundamental significance of the law, Weber's theorisation holds interesting implications that need to be made explicit and explored. Weber's project was, in the first instance, an intellectualisation and rationalisation of all areas of life. But this has also condemned some important dimensions of life, somewhat arbitrarily perceived to be either totally irrational or not rational enough, to the realm of lost illusions. That is, they are no longer viable in the modern world.

Postulating an inevitable conflict between religion and the rational sphere of modern economics and the state, Weber (1946:357) wrote

> [i]n the midst of a culture that is rationally organised for a vocational workaday life, there is hardly any room for the cultivation of world-denying brotherliness. Under the technical and social conditions of rational culture, an imitation of the life of Buddha, Jesus, or Francis seems condemned to failure for purely external reasons.

Privileging economic rationalism, Weber dismissed the religious ethic of love of one's neighbour.

> The more the world of the modern capitalist economy follows its own immanent laws, the less accessible it is to any imaginable relationship with a religious ethic of brotherliness. The more rational, and thus impersonal, capitalism becomes, the more this is the case' (Weber 1946:331).

Postulating the incompatibility of religious ethics and political rationalism, Weber called for the elimination of ethics from the public arena of political reasoning. Since the state is based on power and serves the interest of power, any attempt to justify state coercion with ethical arguments generally and religious ethics in particular is hypocrisy as far as Weber was concerned. 'In the face of this,' he wrote 'the cleaner and only honest way may appear to be the complete elimination of ethics from political reasoning' (Weber 1946:334).

The incongruity of some of Weber's propositions with the self-understanding of Pacific societies will be noted where appropriate. Suffice to note at this juncture that Weber's theorems carry the danger of depersonalising human relationships in the worship of *laissez-faire* capitalism. It seems certain also that we can rationalise life from fundamentally different perspectives and in very different directions. Rationalism, after all, is a historical concept that covers a whole range of different things and assumptions, and our task is to find the pedigree of the intellectual child that we have adopted. 'What is this Reason that we use? What are its limits and what are its dangers?' (Foucault 1984:249).

Finally, a point often ignored is that Weber's theorems of legitimacy are really ideal types and that, in the real world, all three modes of authority legitimation may be adopted in a given empirical situation. To illustrate, Hitler's authority might have been due, to some extent, to charisma. But that was fortified by the rational-legal authority of German enacted laws and the emotion generated by the *Volksgeist*, a central tenet of the National Socialist Party ideology. Questioning the rationality of the holocaust that the Third Reich created, Jean-Francois Lyotard (1988:179) observes, 'Auschwitz refutes speculative doctrine. This crime at least, which is real, is not rational'. Sometimes rationality or reason is not really as liberating as Weber would have us believe.

Divine authorisation: the conservative alliance between religion, law and politics in the Pacific

The metaphysical, religious theory of legitimacy sources government in the will of God; government legitimacy accrues from divine authority. This is a fundamental refrain in the Pacific understanding of government and its legitimacy. We thus find in the preambles of Pacific constitutions declarations about the Christian God as the 'foundation' of a 'united and free Republic' (Vanuatu), 'the guiding hand' of the state (Solomon Islands), 'the Almighty Father in whom we put our trust' (Kiribati), the 'God who has always watched over [the Fiji Islands]', 'the Almighty and Everlasting Lord' (Tuvalu), 'the almighty and everlasting Lord and the giver of all good things' (Nauru), and 'the Almighty, the Ever Loving' and 'Omnipresent' God with 'sovereignty over the Universe' and whose commandments prescribe the limits within which state authority is to be exercised by the government on behalf of the people (Samoa). It seems obvious that religion is still a very strong (if not the strongest) legitimating force in the Pacific region. This is, of course, not novel, as Peter Berger (1967:32) has noted

> [R]eligion has been the historically most widespread and effective instrumentality of legitimation. All legitimation maintains socially defined reality. Religion legitimates so effectively because it relates the precarious reality constructions of empirical societies with ultimate reality…Religion legitimates social institutions by bestowing upon them an ultimately valid ontological status, that is, by locating them within a sacred and cosmic frame of reference.

Whereas the Enlightenment separated religion (private) from law and politics (public), and whereas the Enlightenment Project[3] invoked reason and science as the only ways of grounding legal theory and political vision, Pacific societies will not sever the umbilical chord between religion, law and politics, preferring to ground their states (in part) in religious belief and conviction. As the second guiding principle of the Constitution of Tuvalu 1978 has it, '[t]he right of the people of Tuvalu, both present and future, to a full, free and happy life, and to moral, spiritual, personal and material welfare, is affirmed as one given to them by God'.

This religious grounding challenges the epistemological view of the Enlightenment as the point of emancipation of humanity from superstition and tradition, an emancipation predicated on 'the notion of a scientific culture, in which everything was grounded in scientific doctrine or method, or committed to the flames as sophistry and illusion, as Hume put it' (Hollinger 1985:x). The problem is that rationality has not brought the world any closer to peace and justice. Weber's dismissal of ethics from the public arena is similarly arbitrary. Disputing Weber's dismissal of the ethic of brotherliness as misguided, Habermas (1984) notes that the ethic of human rights is itself derived from the ethic of brotherliness, but in a different form. Decrying the fracturing of human relationships that occurs when Weber's rational capitalism creates a rich élite and a poor mass, Habermas (1987:153–97) calls for the ethics of solidarity and social justice to mitigate the ruthlessness of profit seeking and power maximisation. Likewise, Weber's dismissal of salvation religion into the realm of lost illusions is flatly contradicted by the continuing validity of religion and the ongoing influence of religious ethics. Interestingly enough, the entire world of modernity has not been deserted by the gods; at least, the gods still live on in some quarters of the enlightened world.

Subject to qualifications and caveats set out below, religion remains a legitimate dimension of human existence and accords legitimacy to the politico-legal order, perhaps more so in the Pacific than in any other region of the (post)modern world. It needs to be noted, however, that the religious legitimation of power relations and patterns of authority raises important methodological and substantive issues which need to be addressed. Adopting Michel Foucault's (1982:231) skeptical approach, I dare say that '[m]y point is not that everything is bad, but that everything is dangerous'.

First, religious legitimation is partly a species of functionalism which, as a sociological approach, emerged in Europe in the nineteenth century mainly as a response to what was perceived as a crisis of social order precipitated by the emergence of a new industrialised society resulting in the loss of community. As a conservative type of sociology, functionalism focuses on the need for social order and integration. In this focus, religion is seen as a source of solidarity and integration. Whereas the importance of solidarity and integration should not be belittled, the issue, as noted in the previous chapter, is that a one-sided emphasis on the collective produces the worship of society: society deified, God as the deification of society, and religion as the sacralisation of society's requirements for human behaviour. The result, in many cases, is the suppression of the individual. This necessitates liberalisation of the collective to give the individual space to act, exercise her rights and liberties, and pursue her interests. This is an important challenge for most Pacific societies.

Second, reified belief systems sometimes function to construct, reproduce, maintain, reinforce, and legitimate systems of domination. That is, they mediate, moralise and divinise existing social relations, and even mystify the powerless into submission to the powerful. Married to the interests of the powerful in society, religion presents the social order as neutral, fair, and compassionate; it is not capricious or unjust. Injustices, inequalities, and vertical distances in the social order are carefully masked or explained away as being the will of God. That is, the existing pattern of power is divinely sanctioned as the normal order of things, not a human construction, and is therefore beyond questioning. The privileging of some individuals and groups, and the exploitation of others, is similarly not subject to debate. The arbitrary use of power by some to serve their own interests and to legitimate the domination of others are not amenable to discussion or criticism. It is the will of God (so it is claimed) that things are and should be the way they are. Behold, religion as opiate for the masses!

Interrogating the Pacific's religious heritage, I note the heinous manner in which religion has been used to justify unholy feats. The crusades, racism, patriarchy, and other social ills all claim religious legitimation, albeit a spurious one. We would do well therefore to heed the informed reminder that the Bible is not only about life, love and other noble virtues; the Bible 'of all books, is [also] the most dangerous one, the one that has been endowed with the power to kill' (Bal 1991:19).

We also need to change the basic terms of theological discourse in the Pacific to a positive affirmation of the individual, away from humanity as hopelessly depraved to a more positive affirmation of humans' ability to understand and plan their world. This requires a reinterpretation of, among other things, the Augustinian view of the fall as vitiation of both the moral and the intellectual capacities of humans. It could be argued (adopting the humanistic perspective of the Renaissance) that, morally, Adam fell down, but, intellectually, he fell up when he ate of the tree of knowledge and his eyes were opened to the wonders of the world of Copernicus and Newton. This positive view of humanity is itself rooted in a God who is not irrational, vindictive, or totalitarian. Rather, God is 'as beneficient as he is wise' (Cragg 1970:158). He created the world on a rational plan and has the foresight to endow humans with a spark of the divine reason which enables them to discover to their advantage the laws of nature and the purpose of human existence.

Third, religious legitimation inadvertently results in the exaltation, reification and deification of the state. This issue was discussed in chapter two and it does not require any labouring here. I need briefly note the following matters. There is, for example, something nationally sanctifying in viewing the state of Samoa as something divine, an eternally ordained metaphysical reality. Central to that metamorphosis of the state is Samoa's national motto, 'E fa'avae i le Atua Samoa' (Samoa is founded or based on God), which, for most people, is an article of democratic faith. From it, they distil the notion of the state as a divine reality with God as its source and foundation. In the popular mindset, the state of Samoa is (if anything) the unfolding of the divine purpose on earth and exists by divine decree.

In a positive sense, this sourcing of the state in divine authority gives state rule authority and legitimacy. Unfortunately, that construction— taken to the extreme—takes the state out of its earthly moorings, away from the people, and converts it into a supra-mundane entity imposed from above. But deifying the state has serious ramifications. Deified, the state becomes a government of angels (whose powers are wielded by an élite few), which Madison correctly opposed. Needing no external or internal controls, those wielding the power of the state rule as they please. Not only that, in this peculiar scheme, there is no need for the consent or the continuing concurrence of the governed as the proper basis of government. This is because (following the deification rationale of power) the state first came into being by divine authorisation; it rules by divine right, and its authority is sacrosanct. When this happens, the democratic state is not really different from the totalitarian German state which Hegel 'praise[d] as a god, and Marx ... curse[d] as a devil' (Kelsen 2000:172)—an omnipotent, all-embracing entity, 'an absolute end in itself' (Hegel 1952:80), deified as the 'march of God in the world [or even more aggressively as] this actual God' (Hegel 1952:141). Taken to its logical conclusion, a deified state, undergirded by the doctrine of the power state and the Nietzschean will-to-power, is defined by power and is justified in increasing power. Ultimately, the state becomes the embodied will to power.

The issue here is not freedom of belief. To see in the complex skein of historical causality the working out of some higher plan, and the emergence of the state of Samoa as the culmination of that plan, remains the responsible opinion of the believers. That notwithstanding, a deified state has very dangerous ramifications. There is, therefore, a need to disentangle the web of reinforcing factors (religious, cultural, philosophical, ideological, and historical) which created and continues to maintain the deification of the state.

Fourth, as noted in chapter one, most Pacific jurisdictions adopt a species of natural law (based on the law of God and Christian principles) in addition to legal positivism. For instance, the introduction and first recital of the preamble of the Constitution of Samoa 1960 affirm the sovereignty and omnipresence of God, and declare that the authority of the State of Samoa is limited by and subject to God's commandments, the divine law. Accordingly, God is the supreme lawmaker and his law is supreme; the law of God not only binds the state, it also governs and limits the state.

In theological discourse, the sovereignty of God and the supremacy of his law is not a problem; it is the apex of biblical truth. The problem is that in Samoa these declarations are much more than a declaration of the religious faith of the people, a theological declaration that has no legal force, as Professor Davidson was at pains to point out in the Constitutional Convention 1960 (Constitutional Convention of Western Samoa 1960:Vol. II, 886). Furthermore, in constitutional interpretation generally, constitutional preambles are usually treated as nothing more than a form of introduction, a constitutional ornament without legal force.

Whereas that might be true in a strictly positivist legal sense, it is not so for most Samoans who treat these constitutional affirmations as the most important and authoritative part of the Constitution.[4] This raises the issue of conflicting conceptions of the nature of the law. The internal actors in the social practice of law (lawyers, judges, and lawmakers) and outsiders (the citizens) understand and approach the law differently. The end-result is usually legal and moral confusion.

Positing the law of God as a permanent limit on state rule constitutes an appropriate check against the abuse of state power; the substance of state laws should be limited by normative principles. The 'indisputable truth that the command of an earthly superior which violated the law of God or Natural Reason,' enjoined Lord Radcliffe, 'not only owned title to no obedience but might even involve the positive duty of resistance' (Radcliffe 1961:6). Aquinas (1948:649) was just as blunt: 'an unjust law is not a genuine law'. In contrast to Austin's claim that the empirical existence of a legal rule is something independent from its merit or demerit, law—as the ordinary Samoan understands it—means just and fair promulgated laws that are compatible with the law of God. State lawmakers, on this view, do not have legal or moral authority to legislate the murder of blue-eyed babies, acts of blind hatred, the violation of rights, or some other unholy objective. Herein lies the major contribution of natural law: it generates the basic framework for the just state, organised in a way that respects justice, equity, and freedom. And as I categorically stated in chapter one, legitimate governance demands the rejection of legal positivism. As Allan (2001:218) has pointedly underlined,

> [T]he familiar distinctions between legal and moral authority and legal and moral obligation, though convenient for the purposes of descriptive legal theory, prove too crude for constitutional analysis. When rigidly applied, they confuse and distort practical reasoning, divorcing the interpretation of law too sharply from the requirements of justice and separating legal practice too stringently from the political ideals that underlie it...When the law demands obedience, it asserts that the relevant obligation is morally justified, consistent with the common good, and therefore entitled to the citizen's assent. Questions of legality and legitimacy cannot be separated: the identification of any measure as 'law', imposing genuine obligations, is always ultimately a matter of individual conscience. In making state demands subject to a moral test, the rule of law sanctions conscientious rejection—or radical interpretation—of rules whose (potential) injustice is sufficiently grave, notwithstanding that they meet formal conditions of validity.

In the final analysis, the citizens' moral assent is indispensable. For what use is the law if people do not obey it? And, clearly, it serves no useful purpose, relevant to the matter of practical governance, to attribute legal validity to a law that completely lacks any moral legitimacy and may, therefore, so far as possible, have to be resisted. Indeed, there is always the nagging danger that 'the natural tendency of such a doctrine [natural law] is to impel a man, by force of conscience, to rise up in arms against any law whatever that he happens not to like' (Bentham 1967:30). This danger could be averted, it may be argued, if the lawmakers themselves refrain from enacting laws that are morally and ethically repugnant according to the normal canons of right and justice. Citizens, too, should not abdicate their moral judgment to the lawmakers. Both sides of the equation are therefore indispensable and should be reciprocally regulating.

Advocating moral and ethical principles is, after all, not rationally naïve or objectively primitive, and, contrary to Weber's assertions, there is nothing rationally or objectively repugnant in being a 'Buddha, Jesus, or Francis'.

A number of theoretical and practical problems remain though. Theoretically, constitutionalism does not normally limit a secular sovereign (be it an individual or group of individuals) by imposing a super-sovereign on it. In principle, only God could rightfully claim that status and function. The problem is that humans are adept at appropriating God's sovereignty and exploiting it in the service of human interests, playing sovereign 'gods' to others. The secularisation of the notion of sovereignty was in fact spawned by the ignoble acts of Christians themselves. Enmity among Christians with rival claims to truth divided people and nations alike. Religious wars and persecution in God's name undermined the Christian principles of love and a common humanity. Consequently, since the eighteenth century, there has been an increasing secularisation of the doctrine of sovereignty. Furthermore, God, the super-sovereign in Pacific systems of government, is usually without a job. In the popular mindset, when God's commandments are flouted, the enforcement of his judgment is deferred until the culprit gets to heaven. On earth, our sovereign God is silent and idle, and his subjects can do whatever they want. And, in many cases, the refusal to be bound by state laws but only by the law of God is a convenient excuse for abdicating legal and moral obligations on earth. Anarchy is the result.

To avert such problems, constitutionalism to date privileges the secular concept of sovereignty—a sovereign bound by law; the lawmaker is himself bound by his rules. Ensuring every citizen's compliance with his legal and moral obligations on earth, including lawmakers, constitutionalism posits the equal subjection of all citizens to the rule of law. Preempting the exaltation of rulers or the state itself into some kind of deified entity, constitutionalism avoids the vertical structure of power and arranges power on a horizontal axis. In this non-hierarchical order, government powers are dispersed and divided into different functions which are distributed amongst the three branches of government. This structuring of government powers on a horizontal axis creates a system of careful coordination of specified powers and produces a web of mutual dependence amongst the three branches of government. Each subjects the others to continuing scrutiny in a self-regulating structure of separated powers, checked and balanced by a system of mutual jealousies.

It may be noted that, within this frame of qualifications and caveats, one of the negligent appropriations of God's sovereignty is the paradoxical violation of freedom of religion in the name of God, a biting issue in Samoa. In *Tariu Tuivaiti* v *Sila Faamalaga & Others* (1980–93) WSLR 17, St John CJ held that the plaintiff—banished from his village by the village council for not attending church on Sundays—was guaranteed freedom of thought, conscience and religion by article 11(1) of the Constitution, and that that right includes the right not to have any religion at all.[5] In *Mau Sefo & Others* v *The Land and Titles Court & Others* (SC, 1999), Wilson J held that the village council of Saipipi had no authority under the Constitution to prohibit the plaintiffs (members of a new denomination) from having bible classes or services in their own village. The village council's actions were, as Wilson J put it at 22, a form of 'religious intolerance', 'discrimination', 'religious persecution' and 'coercion' that was inconsistent with the spirit of the Constitution. Clearly, the problem was not God or religion *per se*, but misconstructions predicated on the misguided craving to have a monopoly on religious truth. The danger, oftentimes, is also the commercialisation of religion for personal interests and gain.

In defence of a very important freedom, I note the following matters. Underlining the fundamental significance of freedom of religion, Mason ACJ of the High Court of Australia in *Church of the New Faith* v *Commissioner of Pay-roll Tax (Victoria)* (1982–83) 154 CLR 120 affirmed at 130–1 that '[f]reedom of religion, the paradigm freedom of conscience, is of the essence of a free society'. Protection of this freedom is 'accorded to preserve the dignity and freedom of each man so that he may adhere to any religion of his choosing or to none'. Religion belongs to the conviction and conscience of every person. It is directed only by choice, never by coercion or violence. As Dickson J put it in *R* v *Big M Drug Mart Ltd* (1985) 18 DLR (4th) 321 at 354, '[i]f a person is compelled by the State or the will of another to a course of action or inaction which he would not otherwise have chosen, he is not acting of his own volition and he cannot be said to be truly free'.

For some people, the issue is religious truth. But whatever one's truth is, in law, we do not have any right to beat the drums of our religious rituals and the heads of our religious others. For others, the issue is the decision of the majority which, they argue, is both numerically and morally right. But Dickson J in *R v Big M Drug Ltd* (1985) has offered a trenchant reminder at 354, '[w]hat may appear good and true to a majoritarian religious group, or the State acting at their behest, may not, for religious reasons, be imposed upon citizens who take a contrary view'. To do so means indulging the tyranny of the religious majority.

Fortunately, the Samoan courts have taken a firm stand in protecting freedom of religion. Whenever they are asked to sanction the violation of this freedom, the response has been constant: this is the domain of liberty, in which the courts should not intervene other than to ensure that liberty is guaranteed and protected. This is in keeping with the legal principle enunciated by Murphy J in *Church of the New Faith v Commissioner of Pay-roll Tax (Victoria)* at 150, '[r]eligious discrimination by officials or by the courts is unacceptable in a free society...In the eyes of the law, religions are equal. There is no religious club with a monopoly of State privilege for its members'. In a sense, the courts are, in a challenging way, taking the initiative in erecting a wall of separation between state and church.

Indigenous custom and traditions: state legitimacy, the Pacific way

Rejecting Weber's dismissal of tradition as a viable mode of legitimacy in the enlightened world of modernity, I advocate the view that indigenous custom and traditions remain a viable source of legitimacy in some quarters of the enlightened world of modernity. The Pacific is a clear example.

In addition to what I said in chapter one, I believe that the recognition of custom is required for a number of reasons, for example, the sovereignty of the people, which demands that their practices and values are reflected in state laws and conduct of the state. A clear illustration is the recognition of community elders or chiefs as part of the apparatus of the state, as in Samoa's Head of State, Samoa's *matai-*only parliamentary candidacy, and the Great Council of Chiefs in Fiji. Grounding government in traditional values, the third, fourth and fifth guiding principles of the Constitution of Tuvalu 1978 mandate the adoption of Tuvaluan values in the conduct of government and public affairs. These include forms of community life; family life; 'agreement, courtesy, and the search for consensus, in accordance with traditional Tuvaluan procedures, rather than alien ideas of confrontation and divisiveness'; and mutual respect and cooperation.

The recognition of custom as a source of law also goes to the heart of a jurisprudence that is relevant to Pacific universes of meaning. It partly resolves the issue of the legal, moral, and practical justification for the peoples' acquiescence in the law as a manifestation of the state, a root question in jurisprudence. It is about constructing a jurisprudence of Pacific values. This is reminiscent of Montesquieu's enjoinder that the laws of a given state must be appropriate to the values, manners, and way of life of the people who stand to be affected by those laws.

In short, custom and traditions constitute a valid way of achieving state authority, validity, and legitimacy. Broadly understood, custom refers not only to a people's so-called habits of the heart, but also observable acts experienced as facts, intangible ideas that make up society's stock of knowledge, and moral precepts, values and objectives that guide community action. Dismissing it as having no relevance or force for lawmaking purposes is like turning an Eskimo's legal-social consciousness into that of an extra-terrestrial being in the Star Trek series.

My specific focus in this section is to highlight the issues arising out of the grounding of state legitimacy in custom and traditions.

Pacific legal systems share the common characteristic of legal pluralism—the problematic collision of legal liberalism and custom as sources of law. For instance, article 111(1) of the Constitution of Samoa defines law in the following terms

> Law means any law for the time being in force in Samoa; and includes this Constitution, any Act of Parliament and any proclamation, regulation, order, by-law or other act of authority made thereunder, the English common law and equity for the time being in so far as they are not excluded by any other law in force in Samoa, and any custom or usage which has acquired the force of law in Samoa or any part thereof under the provisions of any act or under a judgment of a court of competent jurisdiction.[6]

Much has been written on this topic. Part of the challenge is a definitive delineation of the substance, procedures, and structures of Pacific customary laws, systems of ethics which underpin those laws, and modes of governance which they employ. My own interest is in a socio-theoretical resolution of the two legal mindsets that is in keeping with the overall objective of this study: legitimate governance premised on the rule of law as its guiding and unifying principle.

Without slighting the seriousness of the clash between legal liberalism and customary laws, I take the view that too often (and not without good reason) conceptualisations disproportionately accentuate the notion of conflict. Accordingly, the relationship has been described as 'the inevitable conflict' (Davidson 1967:368; Stroupe 1996) between two 'competing legal systems' (Sapolu 1988:61). Jonathan Aleck aptly sums up the issue as follows: 'There is already a considerable scholarly literature built upon the assumption that the nature and dynamics of law and custom are so contraposed to one another as to be essentially incompatible' (Aleck 1995:3). Reducing Papua New Guinea's governance woes to a very simple formula, Windybank and Manning (2003:4) opine that 'the conflict between traditional tribal customs and the institutions of modern government lies at the heart of that nation's problems '.

On the conflict reading, the relationship, to use an analogy, is like that of out-marrying African tribes who, every morning, look over to their potential spouses in the neighbouring tribes and cry, they are our enemies, we marry them! True, the clash is much more than just a matter of mental disposition. From the point of view of custom, the struggle is against the hegemony of legal liberalism; from the perspective of legal liberalism, the struggle is against the imperialism of some customary rules which thwart the development of Pacific societies as modern democracies. Each order operates from an established infrastructure which defines its own norms; each propagates and defends a distinctive ideology which endows its respective order with meaning and purpose; each idealises its own value system, claiming to be an all-embracing order that leaves nothing outside its conceptual scope; and each prides itself on being self-sufficient and sustained by the power of its own logic. And, usually, one is bent on resisting or subjugating the other, on gaining dominance and control in the realm of social interaction. More often than not, this throws the social order into legal and moral confusion.

Be that as it may, the term conflict, while appropriate to some degree, presupposes an irreconcilable contradiction and invokes legitimating mechanisms that are exclusivist and nihilatory in the extreme since, on the conflict model, legal liberalism and custom confront each other as entities with greatly, even totally, different histories. To achieve a position of dominance in what is seen as an eternal power struggle, each must meet the other with 'the best possible reasons for [its] superiority' (Berger and Luckmann 1967:126) and dismiss the other as 'ignorant, mad or downright evil' (Berger and Luckmann 1967:125). But this is nihilation, the conceptual liquidation of the other, neutralising the other by reducing it to 'an inferior ontological status, and a not-to-be-taken-seriously cognitive status' (Berger and Luckmann 1967:132). Clearly, also, the conceptual cognates of the term conflict are violently uncompromising. Superiority engenders condescension, invites subordination, and justifies marginalisation. The term primitive is similarly perjorative; it smacks of (neo)colonial oppression.

This necessitates a reconceptualisation of the relationship not as a conflict between a good system and an evil one, but as competing conceptions of the good. If either mindset is allowed to exclude the other fully, important values will be lost as a result. It is imperative, therefore, to move legal discourse beyond the usual category of conflict, with its concomitant presupposition that one is intent on liquidating the other. We need to change the terms in which the relationship between the two legal mindsets is conceptualised.

There are practical problems as well. Legitimation requires and uses power; power means force; and force is applied by any number of means. Legitimation, according to Berger and Luckmann (1967:127), uses a stick, and 'he who has the bigger stick has the better chance of imposing his definitions of reality'. Accordingly, while some militantly privilege legal liberalism, others reactively privilege custom, and all use sticks to beat their legal definitions into the others' senses.[7] In Samoa, for example, the battle of sticks between legal liberalism and custom keeps occurring at critical points of the body politic—in parliament, the executive, the courts, villages, churches and families.

Attempting a legal fusion of the centre and the periphery, parliament enacted Samoa's Village Fono Act 1990 (the Act). The purpose of the Act is 'to validate and empower the exercise of power and authority by the Village Fono [council of matais] in accordance with the custom and usage of their villages and to confirm or grant certain powers; and to provide for incidental matters'. The Act may be praised for giving formal recognition to the authority of village councils, customary law, and traditional modes of governance. The Act also enables the delegation of powers and functions from central government to village councils for the administration and enforcement of law and order in accordance with customary law, and creates a cooperative venture between modern government institutions and customary structures.

Merits aside, the Act has created a range of issues. For instance, the extent and limits on the powers of village councils has been a continuing gnawing issue. Section 6 of the Act authorises councils to enforce village rules and impose punishment for non-compliance. But if the legislators thought that the councils would confine themselves to punishment such as monetary fines, fine mats, and foodstuffs, they were clearly wrong. Given formal statutory recognition, some village councils have punished as they wish, sometimes pursuant to the doctrine of implied powers. In popular opinion, the Act 'gave every village council the power to punish in whichever way it likes any person who refuses to obey its dictates' (*Samoa Observer*, February 1993). Abuse of the power to punish saw people being unnecessarily banished from villages. The case of *Italia Taamale* is a case in point. Perhaps the problem is not the Act itself but misconstructions of it. In any case, village councils' abuse of their statutory powers highlights thorny issues regarding the marriage of convenience between legal liberalism and custom in the Act. We thus find village councils using the law (the Act) to defeat the law (part II of the Constitution which guarantees and protects rights and liberties).

Giving village councils a role in the administration of justice is warranted for a whole range of reasons—for example, they can perform law and order functions in rural villages where there are no police officers to enforce state laws. But their incorporation into the formal structure of government has made every village council a into a kind of tribunal exercising quasi-judicial and executive functions. Arguably, this makes them subject to the rules and procedures of natural justice and brings them within the courts' review jurisdiction of administrative action. My misgiving is that a village council minded to abuse its statutory powers will always find the Act sufficient warrant to do that. It is no consolation either that the Act is subject to the provisions of the Constitution.

The problem is that for many *matais* the Act is now their political bible, a constitution in itself, one that overrides the provisions of the national Constitution. Hence the discrepancy between ideal (what the Act was intended to accomplish) and reality (what the Act has been made to accomplish) is not only marked but threatening. When a person is unnecessarily banished by order of the village council, the Act can always be cited as authority and justification—it is banishment according to the law. Quite frankly, whenever that happens, the Act is unavoidably unconstitutional.

Seeking a solution to our battle of sticks, I promulgate the view that we should abandon the partisan promulgation of two different types of law, the indigenous and the 'imported law' (Donne 1988:4), sometimes with ideological blindness. In keeping with the selective recognition of custom, the ultimate test is justice and fairness, whether or not a particular custom is contrary to the principles of justice and fairness relative to shared meanings. I cite in support of this proposition a statement of the Supreme Court of Papua New Guinea in *Public Prosecutor* v *Kerua* [1985] PNGLR 85. The issue was the legality of the native custom of murdering an adulteress. Kidu CJ, Bredmeyer J, and McDermott J held at 89,

> Custom can be taken into account in sentencing by virtue of the *Customs Recognition Act* (Ch 19), s 4 (e), but that section is subject to two important limitations. By s 3 of that Act customs cannot be recognised or enforced…if that is not in the public interest…The second limitation is in the Constitution. Schedule 2.1 provides that custom does not apply if it is repugnant to the general principles of humanity.

Outside extreme cases such as the above, custom may be taken into account in mitigation of sentence or as alternative means of dispute resolution. This would also shift the focus away from arbitration and the litigation neurosis which sometimes haunts Pacific courts, often resulting in the backlog of court cases.

Perhaps, also, the issue must not turn on the size of one's stick but on using the right stick in the right season and for the right reasons. Thus referring to the timely change from Samoa's *matai*-only suffrage (which deprived non-matais of the political right to vote for many years) to universal suffrage pursuant to the *Electoral Amendment Act 1990*, the Court of Appeal in *Le Tagaloa Pita & Others* v *Attorney General* (CA. 3/ 95) observed at 44, '[i]f we may borrow the imagery, the new generation, thinking hard and long about the matter and drawing on the wisdom and experience of earlier generations, has taken a fresh stick'. This underlines certain important matters. Democracy is a process; it is not a once-and-for-all event. Genuine democratic change can be very slow, but given time and grounded in the conviction of the people, change— if not unduly rushed or coercively imposed—will most certainly come. And change necessarily means liberalisation, not destruction.

In summary, the imagery of a perfect marriage between legal liberalism and custom—a 'unique amalgam' (Powles and Pulea 1988:xii)—is too nice. The marriage is an arranged one. As such, it is fraught with problems and challenges. Total exclusion of custom from the legal system would be disastrous; important values will be lost and it will always be counter-productive. Separating the systems and consigning one (usually custom) to a small corner of the legal universe is also problematic. The geometrical applications of laws, predicated on the notion of separated systems, will result in the institutionalisation of a divided legal order and the evil of fragmentation. It would also have adverse consequences for law and order. For example, for some people, the application of separate systems means the license to ignore one set of rules in favour of the other. Recasting the marriage metaphor, separation means the marriage is well on the way to dissolution. At the other end of the spectrum is the model of assimilation, which means, in effect, the absorption of custom into formal law. Custom, to put it bluntly, gets swallowed up. But this is just as untenable.

That leaves us with integration as the most viable option. The ideal is the creation of a porous national legal system that incorporates different legal mindsets and which does not exclude any. The emphasis here is on the interpenetration and intermeshing of the different legal mindsets, creating a porous legal system. Each mindset is taken on its merits. All mindsets are normative, with no one mindset being especially privileged. Furthermore, the differences between the legal mindsets, while sharp and sometimes very deep, are manageable and capable of resolution. The end result, hopefully, is a national legal system of discrete yet overlapping legal mindsets. The system must be fluid enough to adapt and self-adjust. It must be firm enough to ensure that fundamental values are not sacrificed or lost. And it must be robust enough to command from the people a broad consensus on its legitimacy.

I therefore urge a continuing search to find an optimal point where the different mindsets, in combination, achieve a result which best captures the aspirations of the Pacific peoples. Finding this elusive point is always a daunting task, and maintaining the line of compromise is likely to be subject to constant change. Perhaps this is warranted since the law must be responsive to the changing interests and needs of the people.

Dismantling the imagery of two fiercely opposed mindsets also requires a substantial revision of some of the main tenets of legal liberalism. Pursuing a genealogical questioning of the law and its foundational tenets, my purpose is to problematise the whole legal edifice by showing that things could be other than the way there are. Reiterating Foucault's skepticism, '[m]y point is not that everything is bad, but that everything is dangerous'.

A central feature of legal liberalism is rationality predicated on reason. For Aquinas, natural law is rooted in the divine will, discoverable through God-given reason: 'All law proceeds from the reason and will of the lawgiver; the divine and natural law from the reasonable will of God; the human law from the will of men, regulated by reason' (Henle 1993:63). In the Enlightenment philosophy of modernism, reason is seen as a universal faculty of humans which makes possible a rational life separated from contingent and distorting forces such as tradition, superstition, and emotion. For Immanuel Kant, '[r]eason proceeds by eternal and unalterable laws' (Kant 1965:9). Praising reason as a 'faculty of judgment...received from God', Rene Descartes (1979:35) confessed that, since God 'has not wished to deceive me, he certainly has not given me a faculty such that, when I use it properly, I could ever make a mistake'.

Allied to the dogmatic belief in reason is the Enlightenment belief in progress, that reason has emancipated humanity from superstition and traditions, and moves us toward an increasingly rational and just world. Thus Descartes (1931:5) spoke of reason as the 'method for finding out the truth...By method I mean certain and simple rules, such that if a man observes them accurately, he shall never assume what is false to be true, but will always gradually increase his knowledge and arrive at a true understanding of all that does not exceed his powers'.

Since the Enlightenment, reason has been consistently praised as the faculty with the power to liberate humanity from the bondage of misguided beliefs and practices based on superstition and blind tradition. In legal theory, the law is seen, even idealised, to be based on foundational, universal notions like reason and its intellectual offsprings of rationality and objectivity. Referring to the American legal fraternity, Roscoe Pound wrote, '[t]he American lawyer, as a rule, still believes that the principles of law are absolute, eternal, and of universal validity' (Frank 1970:59).

While taking those foundational notions as givens, it could be argued that the rationality of modern liberalism is often improperly contrasted with custom and traditions seen as subjective, emotionally-loaded and therefore (for some strange reason) irrational. Severing the umbilical chord between mind and heart, liberalism truncates the human self to a mere mental construct without feeling or affection, a mind without a body. This is in contrast to Pacific people's holistic world view, which understands the human self as a totality of ideas, emotions, flesh and blood, moral values, ethical convictions, and human associations, and also seeks to maintain the balance between mind and heart, subject to the dictates of one's conscience.

Then there are the painful facts of modern history: Auschwitz; ethnic cleansing; September 11 and the ongoing war in Afghanistan; the controversial war in Iraq with its socio-economic implications and the senseless killing of so many innocent people, including defenceless women and children; the scandals of Abu Ghraib prison and Guantanamo Bay; the ever-present danger of a nuclear war; global warming and the threat of a global environmental disaster; corporate fraud and the exploitation of workers in developing countries by multinational corporations; sexism, neurosis and other social ills. These and many other facts of history inevitably question in a fundamental way the proclaimed virtues of rationality, that is, reason's power and ability to bring about a just and fair world.

Condemning Auschwitz and disputing racism and fascism as rational solutions to political problems, Foucault (1982:210) notes, '[t]his was, of course, an irrationality, but an irrationality that was at the same time, after all, a certain type of rationality'. Thus, we must be suspicious of claims based on reason. Perhaps, the problem is the non-use of reason in public affairs, especially when individuals or groups take out their blind hatreds on innocent victims. But, in a real sense, the problem is also the misuse of reason, especially where the powerful exploit the powerless. As Foucault (1982:210) has noted, '[t]he relationship between rationalisation and excess political power is evident. And we should not need wait for the concentration camps to recognise the existence of such relations'.

Objectivity, another central feature of liberalism, is also amenable to serious questioning. That is to say, the notion of total objectivity cannot be tenable since it is impossible for anyone to approach facts, issues, conflicts and situations in a manner completely independent of one's perspective or with a mind free of bias. In fact, the questions one brings to an issue, and even the way questions are put, all presuppose a relativity of interest. Objectivity is therefore often a myth, necessary to construct and maintain an ideology.

Sometimes the avowed objectivity of reason is nothing more than a tranquiliser of the human senses, or just another word for indifference. This constitutes the Pacific epistemological challenge to the (sometimes) depersonalising objectivity of liberalism that treats people as if their minds are unconnected with their individual and corporate bodies within concrete social contexts.

Universality, too, needs to be tempered by contingency, by the customary laws and modes of governance that are rooted in a given community's normative universe of meaning, social practice, and discourse. This also applies to notions and practice of justice. Noting the embeddedness of justice, Michael Walzer (1983:312–3) explains, '[j]ustice is relative to social meanings...A given society is just if its substantive life is lived in a certain way—that is, in a way that is faithful to the shared understanding of its members'.

In Samoa's normative worldview, for instance, justice is primarily relational, rooted in personal relationships. Justice means, first and foremost, treating the other person with love and respect, affirming rather than dislocating him. It is governed by the ethic of respect and caring for one's human kin—parents, relatives, the elderly, those in authority, and neighbours. Justice, in Samoa's cosmology, also extends to the relationship between people and their physical environment. It means treating the earth as a kin worthy of respect and care. And there is God, the unseen partner in Samoan affairs, the author and final court of justice in Samoa's religious universe of meaning. Samoan justice thus moves on various planes at once. It is much more than a matter of procedure. Given the embeddedness of meanings, notions and practices, '[w]e must start from where we are', as Richard Rorty (1989:198) has urged.

My purpose has been to problematise some of the central notions of legal liberalism, not subvert or reject them. Rationality is of course essential, but narrowly construed as something of the intellect only, it becomes one-dimensional, masochistic, cold, and impersonal. Furthermore, rationality, if not subjected to critical analysis, can harbour irrational tendencies and promote inhuman objectives. And while reason's promise of bringing about a better and more just world remains a source of hope, the history of the modern world is a matter of concern. As Foucault (1984:85) has argued,

> Humanity does not gradually progress from combat to combat until it arrives at universal reciprocity, where the rule of law finally replaces warfare; humanity instills each of its violences in a system of rules and thus proceeds from domination to domination.

Questioning the proclaimed merits of the Enlightenment, Max Horkheimer and Theodor Adorno (1991:3, xi) wrote,

> [t]he Enlightenment has always aimed at liberating men from fear and establishing their sovereignty. Yet the fully enlightened earth radiates disasters triumphant...[M]ankind, instead of entering into a truly human condition, is sinking into a new kind of barbarism.

This raises the point that the good life really requires not only an enlightened intellect, but an educated heart governed and guided by moral and ethical principles. This is necessary not only in private life, but more especially in the public arena of law, politics, economics, governance, and development. Notably, in the Pacific, the private/ public distinction is not nearly as rigid as in modern liberalism's structuring of the social order. Moral imperatives and ethical values (religious or otherwise), predominantly confined to the private sphere in liberalism's world view, are just as public as clean air, public land, and other participatory goods in the Pacific.

A sociotheoretical resolution of the legitimacy problem

A potentially fruitful way of juxtaposing the different modes of state legitimacy in the Pacific, and conceptualising their relationship not as conflicts between good and evil but as competing yet mutually reinforcing conceptions of the common good, is the sociological category of the symbolic universe, employed as a heuristic construct. Within this sociological scheme, every institution has its place in a complex system of overlapping spheres of interest and influence.

More importantly, within the framework of the symbolic universe, the rule of law could be construed both as a tool for the construction and maintenance of a social world, and as the frame within which institutional contradictions are negotiated and resolved. In that sense, the rule of law provides the overarching legitimatory system of a social world, broadly understood in the sense of both the environment which a group of people inhabit and the world as they perceive it and to which they give form and significance through their special language and other meaningful actions.

Legitimation, according to Berger and Luckmann, refers in the widest sense to socially objectivated knowledge that serves to explain and justify a social order. At the level of objectivity, legitimation makes society's institutions (law, politics, religion, extended family, kinship, property rights, customary land, and so forth) objectively available to the members of society, as in the traditions instructing members about the nature and function of those institutions. At the level of subjectivity, legitimation makes those institutions subjectively plausible by telling the members of society why things are what they are and that they should act on this knowledge, here presented as right knowledge. It may be noted, in this connection, that legitimation's interrelated objective and subjective orientation problematises modernity's one-sided emphasis on objectivity, often to the detriment of what people accept as real and meaningful in their everyday subjective lives.

This is also in line with the operation of legitimation at multiple levels: from the initial use of meaningful vocabulary or a system of signs (*tama, teine, fa'afafine*) to explanatory theoretical statements (proverbs, maxims), explicit theories advanced and transmitted by experts, and, finally at the highest level, symbolic universes defined as 'bodies of theoretical tradition that integrate different provinces of meaning and encompass the institutional order in a symbolic totality' (Berger and Luckmann 1967:113). Knowledge, in Berger and Luckmann's view, includes both specialised intellectual systems and what people accept as real in their everyday pre-theoretical lives. The latter entails the certainty that phenomena are real, that we cannot wish them away, and that they possess certain characteristics. People take this ordinary world for granted and it is this knowledge that keeps them in society: 'It is precisely this "knowledge" that constitutes the fabric of meanings without which no society could exist' (Berger and Luckmann 1967:27). While knowledge, in the sense of intellectual systems and ideologies, is not rejected or its significance discounted, legitimation, properly understood and applied, must take into account this everyday, ordinary, pre-theoretical knowledge as a valid dimension of social reality. This challenges the legitimation systems of modernity predicated on complex rational systems of thought and practice to the exclusion of equally valid realities, seen as logically simplistic.

At all levels (including the pre-theoretical level epitomised by community myths), all forms of legitimation serve as machineries for the maintenance of the symbolic universe. The more clearly defined machineries include institutionalised, esoteric systems of philosophy, science, law, politics and theology managed by specialised elites. Legitimation thus has a very wide order of reference; it includes society's myths (stories, parables, allegories, and other cultural traditions) as well as specialised systems of knowledge (law, politics, philosophy). All are equally important means of legitimating and maintaining society's symbolic universe. Again, the recognition of custom and cultural traditions as valid means of legitimation and universe maintenance challenges modernity's rational systems of legitimation to the exclusion of other equally valid systems.

That brings me to certain functions of a symbolic universe and their significance for present purposes. First, the symbolic universe provides an integrating, all-embracing frame of reference; it encompasses the entire society and its diverse institutions, roles, processes and meanings. Whereas a high degree of integration of diverse social institutions may have been reached at the preceding level of explicit theories, it is only at the level of the symbolic universe that all sectors of society are integrated in an 'all-embracing frame of reference, which now constitutes a universe in the literal sense of the word, because all human experience can now be conceived of as taking place within it' (Berger and Luckmann 1967:113-4). At last, the entire society, notwithstanding its diverse institutional composition, now makes sense and 'a whole world is created' (Berger and Luckmann 1967:114).

In practical terms, custom and traditions, law, politics, religion, morality and ethics all have their legitimate places and functions in an inevitably (and understandably) strained relationship of coexistence within the framework of society's symbolic universe. Where and when two or more of them are in open conflict, and that conflict threatens to land the social order in anarchy, the challenge is not condemning one or all of them to oblivion, but renegotiating the balance of influence amongst them and thereby moving the social order to a new equilibrium. Thus, in this respect, the symbolic universe ultimately 'puts everything in its right place' (Berger and Luckmann 1967:116).

Second, the symbolic universe orders history. For the individual, the symbolic universe orders the different phases of his biography in a meaningful totality (including past, present and future) that transcends the individual's finite existence. For the institutional order, the symbolic universe orders its history by locating all collective events in a cohesive historical unity and engendering a sense of continuity by being linked with the past (the group's predecessors) and the future (its successors), a sense of belonging to a meaningful world that was there before they were born and will be there after they die.

This is important in a number of respects. We cannot screen out the past, at least not without becoming historically dislocated in the present. Institutions such as custom and traditions embody important memories of the past. These institutions cannot be discarded without destroying a people's identity, who they are and where they are going. The challenge, however, is not submersion in the past but allowing the past to inform the present while moving forward into the future. Where and when the past (interests, needs, practices, and objectives) becomes an unnecessary haunting concern in the present, it has to be reorganised and its irrelevant aspects discarded—that is, without destroying the past in its entirety.

Third, the ideal scenario is that, once the symbolic universe has been constructed and has satisfactorily explained and justified the institutional order, it will normally be inhabited—other things being equal—with a taken-for-granted attitude. The problem is that all things are seldom equal and that some members of society will always inhabit the symbolic universe with less conviction than others. For those particular members, the symbolic universe will be, to a greater or lesser extent, problematic. Cases such as these highlight the fact that every symbolic universe is 'incipiently problematic' (Berger and Luckmann 1967:123). It is threatened either by internal revolutions (for example, heretical versions of reality and social deviance) or by attacks from external forces (for example, a competing society with a greatly different history which 'views one's definitions of reality as ignorant, mad or downright evil'). Either way, the reality status of the symbolic universe is at stake, and this calls for legitimatory mechanisms that could be sophisticated and extreme.

Applying the foregoing propositions to the relationship between legal liberalism and Pacific custom, the problem is that some members of Pacific societies inhabit their legal (postcolonial, post-independent) universe, which combines legal liberalism and custom with less conviction than others. For those particular members, the legal universe will always be problematic. This requires, among other things, questioning why things are not equal as well as the continuing socialisation of those members into the procedures, practices and principles of the new legal order. This takes time and effort, but it must be done if all members of society were to be fully absorbed into the new legal order.

A more critical problem is (as already noted above) the disproportionate accentuation of the conflict and conceptualising the said conflict as one between a foreign system of law and an indigenous one. These premises inevitably set in motion a peculiar way of resolving the tension, namely, nihilation. This entails the use of theoretical arguments and forms of practice 'to liquidate conceptually' everything outside and therefore alien to one's universe of meaning (Berger and Luckmann 1967:132). This usually involves the denial of the reality status of external phenomena by giving them a negative, 'inferior ontological status, and thereby a not-to-be-taken-seriously cognitive status' (Berger and Luckmann 1967:132). In other words, the other is ontologically and cognitively liquidated.

My point is that what is often forgotten in the euphoric rush to polarise the issue is that the tensions between legal liberalism and custom occur within a single entity in the form of a national state wherein the architecture of governance, and the rules governing that architecture, are generally accepted. And central to that architecture of governance is the rule of law which, interestingly enough, includes among other things English common law and equity as well as custom and traditions as article 111(1) of Samoa's Constitution mandates. In light of that, it may be argued that a more appropriate way of conceptualising the tensions that the coexistence of different legal mindsets keeps coughing up is in terms of internal contradictions within the legal universe of meaning itself.

On this reading, the danger is not an external threat but an internal one, an internal problem in the form of legal deviance, the departure from established procedures and principles. Construed in this way, the appropriate response would be therapy, not nihilation. Therapy involves the application of theoretical resources and practices 'to ensure that actual or potential deviants stay within the institutionalised definitions of reality, or, in other words, to prevent the inhabitants of a given universe from emigrating' (Berger and Luckmann 1967:130). As a mechanism of dispute resolution, therapy develops a diagnosis of the deviation, how it could be resolved, and how deviants could thereby be re-socialised back into the reality status of the social order. This is a less radical way of conceptualising the relationship between legal liberalism and custom, and could also produce a more congenial relationship.

Indeed, deviance challenges the reality status of the community's plausibility structure and is no less dangerous. Nevertheless, deviance is, at best, not always a property inherent in some forms of behaviour but something conferred on such behaviour by a social audience and is, at worst, 'microsociological sabotage' (Berger 1976:151). Treated as a dimension of the continuing power struggle between competing versions seeking to transform the legal order in different directions, deviance should be accepted as the community's own problem, not someone else's. Owning the problem fosters a sense of responsibility in respect of solving that problem and avoids projectionist theories of blame.

Conceptualising the issue as an internal power struggle has other advantages. For one thing, it draws attention to the fact that the legal paradigm can and does change, shift, and self-adjust. For another, it exposes power as a legitimate consideration in any assessment of the construction of reality, including the construction of the legal order. Sometimes legal politics is reified, thus raising the issue of the legal majority pursuing their goals of actions to the exclusion of the interests of the legal minority. Finally, acknowledging the power struggle among competing versions of the legal order points up the ability of individuals or groups of individuals to change, transform, or even sabotage their legal world. Stated more positively, the issue is human agency or the 'ingenuity human beings are capable of in circumventing and subverting even the most elaborate control system' (Berger 1976:155), that is, the human capacity 'for innovation and [even] deviation' (Chinoy 1968:129). And, given the diversity of interests in any given society, the potential for internal power struggles is high.

While allowing for the plurality of interests, the Rawlsian 'fact of reasonable pluralism' (Rawls 1993:36–7), those diverse interests must ultimately yield to the procedural and normative dictates of the rule of law. Custom, traditions, legal liberalism, religion, politics (both traditional and modern) and every other social institution are all subject to the rule of law—publicly negotiated, consonant with the community's moral and ethical convictions, and democratically established. In the context of society's unity-in-diversity, the rule of law commands the equal compliance of all citizens with constitutional and legal rules, thus thwarting the decline of the social order into disorder and confusion spawned by pluralism. When sectional interests vie, or even destroy each other, for the control of the social order, the rule of law adjudicates on the basis of a single standard ('according to the law') equally applicable to all. In this respect, the rule of law functions to integrate society's diverse institutions and discrete processes, interests, and objectives. It negotiates and resolves contradictions, diffuses tensions and overcomes forms of aggression issuing from those tensions, on the basis of a single standard.

This is partly the critical role of the law which Habermas promotes for the resolution of class, economic, and political conflicts which, if not resolved, may lead to either a legitimation crisis and the consequent loss of citizens' faith in public institutions or a motivational crisis. Underlining the critical role of the law in the resolution of these conflicts Habermas (1996:429) explains,

[t]he lifeworld forms, as a whole, a network made of communicative actions. Under the aspect of action coordination, its society component consists of the totality of legitimately ordered interpersonal relationships. It also encompasses collectives, associations, and organisations specialised for specific functions. Some of these functionally specialised action systems become independent vis-à-vis socially integrated spheres of action, i.e. spheres integrated through values, norms and mutual understanding. Such systems develop their own codes—as the economy does with money and the administration with power. Through the legal institutionalisation of steering media, however, these systems remain anchored in the society component of the lifeworld. The language of law brings lifeworld communication from the public and private spheres and puts it into a form in which these messages can also be received by the special codes of self-steered action systems—and vice versa.

On this view, integration—'the typical purpose motivating the legitimators' (Berger and Luckmann 1967:110) and the ultimate objective of legitimation—takes the social system as a totality and gives each element of that totality—both public and private, central and peripheral, modern and traditional, objectives, acts and subjective meanings, personal values and shared norms—equal standing. It does not rule out of court individual intentions, plans, interests, and needs but rather affirms individuals as acting subjects. Nor does it ignore collectivities such as associations and organisations with their respective specialised functions. The law gives each of them 'legal institutionalisation' and thereby creates an integrated legal order.

Conclusion

I reiterate the basic proposition promulgated in this chapter: the rule of law accords government rule formal, substantive and practical legitimacy; all other modes of state legitimacy operate within the framework of the rule of law. Legitimacy entails the right to rule only within the framework of a normative relationship between government and governed based on shared norms and values, the observance of which is mandatory for both government and governed. The right to rule entails the authority to claim submission from the governed as well as the recognition that the right to rule could be justified, must be satisfied, and is in fact justified.

And so the rule of law is an essential human good, as this study has hopefully demonstrated. That said, I might add that it would be pretentious to entertain any extravagant notion that the rule of law embodies or guarantees all the essential requirements for a perfectly just society. In the ideal world, a common humanity, respect for the integrity of others, and the goodwill of all members of society will certainly render the need for rules superfluous in a world of spontaneous ordering. But as we all know, we do not live in an ideal world; we are not perfect and our neighbours are not perfect. We would love to have all the love, compassion, and goodwill the human heart can muster. But, perhaps, only the gods can achieve that, and we are not gods.

In the final analysis, we cannot help but resort to the governance of rules to ensure some hope for peace and some degree of protection for our persons and property, as well as the persons and property of our neighbours. And this is why the rule of law is indispensable, even in this postmodern twenty-first century and beyond. 'The better the society,' writes Grant Gilmore (1977:111) 'the less law there will be. In Heaven there will be no law, and the lion will lie down with the lamb…In Hell there will be nothing but law, and due process will be meticulously observed'.

Notes

[1]   This is reminiscent of the problem of legitimation crisis addressed by Habermas (1975).

[2]   In this new rationality, the individual takes centre stage. This compelling interest in the individual governs Weber's theory of social action in his *The Theory of Social Action and Economic Organization* (1947). Action, according to Weber (1947), may be rational in relation to a goal (*zweckrational* action) or rational in relation to a value (*wertrational* action). Both types of action start from the point of view of the actor as an intending, acting subject.

[3]   See Horkheimer and Adorno (1991).

[4]   Meleisea (1987:212), who states that '[t]he most publicised section of the Constitution [in 1962] was part of the preamble which declared that "Western Samoa should be an Independent State based on Christian principles and Samoan custom and traditions". For the Samoans who had not seen the Constitution or who were not fully aware of the contents and functions of a Constitution in a modern state—and this constituted the vast majority—the fact that Samoa was founded on God and their own customs and traditions gave them pride and was sufficient reason to celebrate'. I need add that this is still the case in 2005.

[5]   Article 11(2) imposes limits on the right to freedom of religion as reasonable restrictions 'in the interests of national security or of public order, health or morals, or for protecting the rights and freedom of others, including their rights and freedom to observe and practice their religion without the unsolicited interference of members of other religions'.

[6]   On the rules of recognition of custom in the different Pacific jurisdictions, see especially Ntumy (1993).

[7]   In favour of English common law over against custom see, for example, *Teitinnong v Ariong* [1987] LRC (Const) 517; also *Siemens v Continental Airlines* 2 FSM Intrm. (Pn. 1985). Cf. St John CJ in *Saipaia Olomalu* at 36: 'They [the constitutional framers] left Samoan culture where it had always been, on the land and in the family organisation, but they super-imposed on that culture a national government framework, selecting from many modern constitutions what they thought was the best available to satisfy the aspirations of nationhood and the preservation of such part of their culture compatible with nationhood'. A rather radical and arbitrary way of putting it.

References

Ackermann, B., 1991. *We the People: foundations*, Harvard University Press, Cambridge, Massachusetts.

Adelman, S. and Foster, K., 1992. 'Critical legal theory: the power of law', in I. Crigg-Spall and P. Ireland (eds), *The Critical Lawyers' Handbook*, Pluto Press, London:39–43.

Aleck, J., 1995. 'Introduction: custom *is* law in Papua New Guinea', in J. Aleck and J. Rannells (eds), *Custom at the Crossroads*, Faculty of Law, University of Papua New Guinea, Port Moresby:1–6.

Alexander, L. and Sherwin, E., 1994. 'The deceptive nature of rules', *University of Pennsylvania Law Review*, 142(4):1191–227.

Alfange, D. Jr., 1993. 'Marbury v Madison and original understandings of judicial review: in defense of traditional wisdom', *The Supreme Court Review*, 1993:329–446.

Alford, W. P., 2000. 'Exporting "the pursuit of happiness"', *Harvard Law Review*, 113(7):1677–82.

Allan, T.R.S., 2001. *Constitutional Justice: a liberal theory of the rule of law*, Oxford University Press, Oxford.

Althusser, L., 1971. 'Freud and Lacan', *Lenin and Philosophy*, trans. B. Brewster, Monthly Review Press, New York:218–9.

Anere, R., Crocombe, R., Horoi, R., Huffer, E., Tuimaleali'ifano, M., Van Trease, H. and Vurobaravu, N., 2001. *Security in Melanesia: Fiji, Papua New Guinea, Solomon Islands and Vanuatu*, Report for the Regional Security Committee (FRSC) Meeting, Suva, 25–26 June.

Aquinas, St Thomas, 1948. 'The essence of law', in A. Pegis (ed.), *Introduction to St Thomas Aquinas*, Random House, New York:609–50.

Aquinas, 1993. *The Treatise on Law*, R.J. Henle (ed.), University of Notre Dame Press, Notre Dame.

Arrow, K., 1972. 'Gifts and exchange', *Philosophy and Public Affairs*, 1(4):343–62.

AusAID, 2000. *Good Governance: guiding principles for implementation*, AusAID, Canberra.

Austin, J., 1955. *The Province of Jurisprudence Determined*, Weidenfeld and Nicolson, London.

Bailyn, B., 1990. *Faces of Revolution: personalities and themes in the struggle for American independence*, Alfred A. Knopf, New York.

Bal, M., 1991. *On Story-telling*, Polebridge Press, Sonoma.

Barber, B., 1983. *The Logic and Limits of Trust*, Rutgers University Press, Brunswick.

Barnes, A., 1977. *Interests and Growth of Knowledge*, Routledge and Kegan Paul, London.

Barry, V., 1986. *Moral Issues in Business*, Third edition, Wadsworth Publishing, Belmont.

Bartlett, R., 1995. A Fiduciary Obligation Respecting the Delivery of Services to Aboriginal Communities, paper presented at the Australian Law Teachers Association Conference, Cross Currents: internationalism, national identity and the law. Available online at http://www.austlii.edu.au/au/special/alta/alta95/bartlett.html.

Batley, P., 1996. 'The state's fiduciary duty to stolen children', *Australian Journal of Human Rights*, 2(2):177–94.

Bentham, J., 1948 [1776]. *A Fragment on Government*, Basil Blackwell, Oxford.

——, 1967 [1789]. *An Introduction to the Principles of Morals and Legislation*, ed. W. Harrison, Basil Blackwell, Oxford.

——, 1970 [1782]. *Of Laws in General*, ed. H.L.A. Hart, Athlone Press, London.

——, 1982 [1781]. *An Introduction to the Principles of Morals and Legislation*, ed. J.H. Burns and H.L.A. Hart, Methuen, London.

Berger, P.L., 1967. *The Sacred Canopy: elements of a sociological theory of religion*, Doubleday, Garden City.

——, 1976. *Invitation to Sociology: a humanistic perspective*, Penguin Books, London.

—— and Luckmann, T., 1967. *The Social Construction of Reality: a treatise in the sociology of knowledge*, Doubleday, New York.

Beyleveld, D. and Brownsword, R., 1986. *Law as a Moral Judgment*, Sweet and Maxwell, London.

Bickel, A., 1962. *The Least Dangerous Branch: the Supreme Court at the bar of politics*, Second edition, Yale University Press, New York.

Blackstone, W., 1966. *Commentaries on the Laws of England*, Oceana, New York.

Bowles, S. and Gintis, H., 1986. *Democracy and Capitalism: property, community, and the contradictions of modern social thought*, Routledge and Kegan Paul, London.

Braithwaite, V. and Levi, M. (eds), 1998. *Trust and Governance*, Russell Sage Foundation, New York.

Brett, N., 1991. 'Language laws and collective rights', *Canadian Journal of Law and Jurisprudence*, 4(2):347–60.

Burchell, G., Gordon, C. and Miller, P. (eds), 1991. *The Foucault Effect: studies in governmentality*, Chicago University Press, Chicago.

Bureau of Democracy, Human Rights, and Labor, 2003. *United States Country Reports on Human Rights 2002*, Bureau of Democracy, Human Rights, and Labor, US Department of State, Washington, DC.

Caldwell, J.L., 1984. 'Judicial sovereignty—a new view', *New Zealand Law Journal*, 11:357–59

Campbell, I.C., 2004. The quest for constitutional reform in Tonga, paper presented at Political Culture, Representation and Electoral Systems in the Pacific, Port Vila, 10–12 July.

Chanock, M., 1985. *Law, Custom and Social Order: the social experience in Malawi and Zambia*, Cambridge University Press, Cambridge.

Chinoy, E., 1968. *Sociological Perspective*, Random House, New York.

Cohen, M. (ed.), 1961. *The Philosophy of John Stuart Mill: ethical, political, and religious*, Random House, New York.

Coleman, J.L., 2001. *The Practice of Principle: in defence of a pragmatist approach to legal theory*, Oxford University Press, Oxford.

Commission on Security and Cooperation in Europe (CSCE), 1990. *Document of the Copenhagen Meeting of the Conference on Human Dimensions of the CSCE*, Commission on Security and Cooperation in Europe, Vienna.

Constitutional Convention of Western Samoa, 1960. Official Report of the Proceedings of the Constitutional Convention of Western Samoa, 2 volumes, Legislative Department, Mulinu'u.

Cooke, R., 1988. 'Fundamentals (Constitutional Law)', *New Zealand Law Journal*, 5:158–65.

Corwin, E.S.,1963. *The Doctrine of Judicial Review: its legal and historical basis and other essays*, Peter Smith, Gloucester.

Coser, L., 1956. *The Functions of Social Conflict*, Free Press, New York.

Cragg, G.R., 1970. *The Church and the Age of Reason 1648–1789*, Revised edition, Penguin Books, London.

Crocombe, R. (ed.), 1987. *Land Tenure in the Pacific*, University of the South Pacific, Suva.

—— and Jonassen, J.T., 2004. Political culture, representation and the electoral system in the Cook Islands, Paper presented at the Conference on Political Culture, Representation and Electoral Systems in the Pacific, Port Vila, 10–12 July.

Dahl, R., 1985. *A Preface to Economic Democracy*, University of California Press, Berkeley.

Dallmayr, F., 1990. 'Hermeneutics and the rule of law', *Cardozo Law Review*, 11(5–6):1449–69.

—— and McCarthy, T. (eds), 1977. *Understanding and Social Inquiry*, University of Notre Dame Press, Notre Dame.

Davidson, J.W., 1967. *Samoa Mo Samoa: the emergence of the independent state of Western Samoa*, Oxford University Press, Melbourne.

Denoon, D. (ed.), 1997. *The Cambridge History of the Pacific Islanders*, Cambridge University Press, Cambridge.

Descartes, R., 1931. *The Philosophical Works of Descartes—Volume 1: rules for the direction of mind*, ed. and trans. E. Haldane and G.R.T. Ross, Cambridge University Press, Cambridge.

——, 1979 [1641]. *Meditations on First Philosophy*, trans. D. Cress, Hackett, Indianapolis.

Devlin, P., 1965. *The Enforcement of Morals*, Oxford University Press, London.

Dicey, A. V., 1959 [1885]. *Introduction to the Study of the Law of the Constitution*, Tenth edition, MacMillan, London.

Donne, G., 1988. 'Introduction', in G. Powles and M. Pulea (eds), *Pacific Courts and Legal Systems*, Institute of Pacific Studies, University of the South Pacific, Suva:4–9.

Duncan, R., 2004. 'Review of *Swimming Against the Tide? An assessment of the private sector in the Pacific* by P. Holden, M. Bale and S. Holden', *Pacific Economic Bulletin*, 19(2):132–33.

Durkheim, E., 1938. *The Rules of Sociological Method*, Free Press, New York.

Durutalo, A.L., 2003. *Re-thinking the basis of 'legitimacy' in the context of South Pacific governments*, Research School of Pacific and Asian Studies, The Australian National University, Canberra, unpublished.

Dworkin, R.M., 1977. *Taking Rights Seriously*, Duckworth, London.

——, 1986a. *A Matter of Principle*, Clarendon Press, Oxford.

——, 1986b. *Law's Empire*, Fontana, London.

Dyzenhaus, D., 2000. 'Form and substance in the rule of law: a democratic justification for judicial review?' in C. Forsyth (ed.), *Judicial Review and the Constitution*, Oxford University Press, London:141–72.

Elster, J. and Slagstad, R. (eds), 1988. *Constitutionalism and Democracy*, Cambridge University Press, New York.

Eminent Persons' Group, 2004. *Pacific Cooperation: voices of the region*, The Eminent Persons' Group Review of the Pacific Islands Forum, Pacific Islands Forum, Suva. Available online at http://www.mfat.govt.nz/foreign/regions/pacific/pif03/pdf/PIF%20Report.pdf.

Evans, M., 1993. *Outline of Equity and Trusts*, Second edition, Butterworths, Sydney.

Field, M., 1984. *Mau: Samoa's struggle against New Zealand oppression*, A.H. & A.W. Reed, Wellington.

Fingleton, J., 2004. 'Is Papua New Guinea viable *without* customary groups?' *Pacific Economic Bulletin*, 19(2):96–103.

Finn, P.D., 1995. 'A sovereign people, a public trust', in P.D. Finn (ed.), *Essays on Law and Government—Volume 1: principles and values*, The Law Book Company, Sydney:1–32.

Finnis, J.M., 1980. *Natural Law and Natural Rights*, Clarendon Press, Oxford.

Flathman, R., 1976. *The Practice of Rights*, Cambridge University Press, Cambridge.

Foucault, M., 1980. *Power/Knowledge: selected interviews and other writings, 1972-77*, trans. and ed. C. Gordon et al., Pantheon, New York.

——, 1982. *Michel Foucault: beyond structuralism and hermeneutics*, ed. H. Dreyfus and P. Rabinow University of Chicago Press, Chicago.

———, 1984. *The Foucault Reader*, trans. C. Hubert, ed. P. Rabinow, Pantheon, New York.

———, 1991. 'Governmentality', in G. Burchell, C. Gordon, and P. Miller (eds), *The Foucault Effect: studies in governmentality*, Chicago University Press, Chicago:pp.

Frank, J., 1949. *Courts on Trial*, Princeton University Press, Princeton.

———, 1970. *Law and the Modern Mind*, Peter Smith, Gloucester.

Freeman, S., 1990. 'Constitutional democracy and the legitimacy of judicial review', *Law and Philosophy*, 9(4):353–370.

Fuller, L.L., 1940. *The Law in Quest of Itself: being a series of three lectures provided by the Julius Rosenthal Foundation for General Law, and delivered at the Law School of Northwestern University at Chicago in April 1940*, Foundation Press, Chicago.

———, 1969. *The Morality of Law*, Revised edition, Yale University Press, New Haven, Connecticut.

Giddens, A., 1972. *Emile Durkheim: selected writings*, Cambridge University Press, Cambridge.

Gilmore, G., 1977. *The Ages of American Law*, Yale University Press, New Haven.

Glanville, G., 1957 [1911]. *Salmond On Jurisprudence*, Eleventh edition, Sweet & Maxwell, London.

Glendon, M.A., 1991. *Rights Talk: the impoverishment of political discourse*, Free Press, New York.

Goldsmith, M.M., 1980. 'Hobbes' "Mortal God": is there a fallacy in Hobbes' theory of sovereignty?', *History of Political Thought*, 1(1):33–50.

Gordon, R., 1982. 'New developments in legal theory', in D. Kairys (ed.), *The Politics of Law: a progressive critique*, Pantheon Books, New York:281–93

Gosarevski, S., Hughes, H. and Windybank, S., 2004. 'Is Papua New Guinea viable?', *Pacific Economic Bulletin*, 19(1):134–48.

Gough, J.W., 1950. *John Locke's Political Philosophy*, Clarendon Press, Oxford.

Government of New Zealand, 1985. A Bill of Rights for New Zealand: a white paper. Government Printer, Wellington.

Gray, J., 1989. 'Mill's and other liberalisms', in J. Gray (ed.), *Liberalisms: essays in political philosophy*, Routledge, London:217–38.

Green, L., 1991. 'Two views of collective rights', *Canadian Journal of Law and Jurisprudence*, 4(2):315–27.

Habermas, J., 1975. *Legitimation Crisis*, Beacon Press, Boston.

—— 1984. *The Theory of Communicative Action*, Volume 1, trans. T. McCarthy, Beacon Press, Boston.

——, 1987. *The Theory of Communicative Action*, Volume 2, trans. T. McCarthy, Beacon Press, Boston.

——, 1996. *Between Facts and Norms: contributions to a discourse theory of law and democracy*, Cambridge University Press, Cambridge.

Hamilton, W.H., 1931. 'Constitutionalism', in E.R.A. Seligman and A. Johnson (ed.), *Encyclopedia of the Social Sciences*, Vol. 4, McMillan, New York:255–60.

Hampton, J., 1986. *Hobbes and the Social Contract Tradition*, Cambridge University Press, Cambridge.

Harris, B.V., 1985. 'Bill of Rights: redistribution of power', *New Zealand Law Journal*, 2:49–53

Hart, H.L.A., 1961. *The Concept of Law*, Clarendon Press, Oxford.

——, 1963. *Law, Liberty and Morality*, Oxford University Press, London.

Hayek, F.A., 1960. *The Constitution of Liberty*, Routledge, London.

——, 1973. *Law, Legislation and Liberty—Volume 1: rules and order*, Routledge, London

——, 1976. *Law, Legislation and Liberty—Volume 2: the mirage of social justice* Routledge, London

——, 1979. *Law, Legislation and Liberty— Volume 3: the political order of a free people*, Routledge, London.

Hegel, G.W.F., 1952 [1821]. *The Philosophy of Right*, trans. T.M. Knox, Oxford University Press, Oxford.

Henle, R.J., 1993. 'Introduction', in St Thomas Aquinas, *The Treatise on Law*, ed. R.J. Henle, University of Notre Dame Press, Notre Dame, Indiana.

Hobbes, T. 1960 [1651]. *Leviathan*, ed. M. Oakeshott, Oxford University Press, Oxford.

Hodge, W.C., 1995. 'Lions under the throne: the least dangerous branch', in B.D. Gray and R.B. McClintock (eds), *Courts and Policy: checking the balance*, Brooker's Ltd, Wellington:91–116.

Hogbin, H.I.P., 1972. *Law and Order in Polynesia*, Christophers, London.

Hollinger, R., 1985. *Introduction to Hermeneutics and Praxis*, ed. R. Hollinger, University of Notre Dame Press, Notre Dame, Indiana.

Honore, M., 1984 [1961]. 'Ownership', in A.G. Guest (ed.), *Oxford Essays in Jurisprudence*, Oxford University Press, Oxford: 107–47. Reprinted in L.C. Becker and K. Kipnis (eds), *Property: cases, concepts, critiques*, Prentice-Hall, Englewood, New Jersey:78–87.

Horkheimer, M. and Adorno, T., 1991. *Dialectic of Enlightenment*, trans. J. Cumming, Continuum, New York.

Hughes, R., 2003. 'Corruption', in A. Jowitt and T.N. Cain (eds), *Passage of Change: law, society and governance in the Pacific*, Pandanus, Canberra:35–49.

Hunt, A., 1987. 'The critique of law: what Is 'critical' about critical legal theory?', in A. Hunt and P. Fitzpatrick (eds), *Critical Legal Studies*, Basil Blackwell, Oxford:10–19.

——, 1992. 'Foucault's Expulsion of Law: towards a retrieval', *Law and Social Inquiry*, 17(1):7–38.

Hutchinson, A., 1988. *Dwelling on the Threshold: critical essays on modern legal thought*, Irwin Law, Toronto.

Hyden, G. and Olowu, D. (eds), 2000. *African Perspectives on Governance*, Africa World Press, Lawrenceville, New Jersey.

Ives, D., 2004. 'Public sector reform in Papua New Guinea: the saga continues', *Pacific Economic Bulletin*, 19(1):80–93.

James, K., 2004. 'The role of the nobles' representatives in Tongan political culture and parliamentary representation', Paper presented at the Conference on Political Culture, Representation and Electoral Systems in the Pacific Conference, University of the South Pacific, Port Vila, 12–14 July.

Jennings, W.I., 1972. *The Law and the Constitution*, Fifth edition; University of London Press, London.

Jones, P., 1999. 'Group rights and group oppression', *The Journal of Political Philosophy*, 7(4):353–77.

Kairys, D., 1982. 'Legal reasoning', in D. Kairys (ed.), *The Politics of Law*, Pantheon Books, New York:11–17.

Kant, I., 1964 [1785]. *Groundwork of the Metaphysics of Morals*, trans. H.J. Paton, Harper & Row, New York.

——, 1965 [1781]. *Critique of Pure Reason*, trans. N.K. Smith, St Martin's Press, New York.

Kay, R.S., 1998. 'American Constitutionalism', in L. Alexander (ed.), *Constitutionalism: philosophical foundations*, Cambridge University Press, Cambridge:16–63

Kelsen, H., 1934. 'The pure theory of law: its method and fundamental concepts' [trans. C.H. Wilson], *Law Quarterly Review*, 50(200):474–98. Reprinted in in 1960 and 1978 in *Pure Theory of Law*, trans. M. Knight, University of California Press, Berkeley.

——, 2000 [1957]. *What is Justice?*, Union, New Jersey.

Kelsey, J., 1993. *Rolling Back the State: privatisation of power in Aotearoa/ New Zealand*, Bridget William Books, Wellington.

Kennedy, D., 1990. 'Legal education as training for hierarchy', in D. Kairys (ed.), *The Politics of Law: a progressive critique*, Revised edition, Pantheon Books, New York:38–58.

Kenneth, B., 1999. 'Customary law in the Pacific: an endangered species?', *Journal of South Pacific Law*, 3:n.p.

Kirby, M., 1997. A Bill of Rights for Australia—but do we need it?, Law & Justice Foundation of New South Wales, Sydney, 14 December.

Koloamatangi, M., 2004. Elections, political culture and the Tongan mind, Paper presented at the conference on Political Culture, Representation and Electoral Systems in the Pacific, University of the South Pacific, Port Vila, 12–14 July.

Kress, K., 1989. 'Legal indeterminacy', *California Law Review*, 77(2):283–338.

Kukathas, C., 1995. 'Are there any cultural rights?', in W. Kymlicka (ed.), *The Rights of Minority Cultures*, Oxford University Press, Oxford:93–119.

—— and Pettit, P., 1990. *Rawls' A Theory of Justice and its Critics*, Polity Press, Oxford.

Kymlicka, W., 1989. *Liberalism, Community, and Culture*, Oxford University Press, Oxford.

——, 1995. *Multicultural Citizenship: a liberal theory of minority rights*, Clarendon Press, Oxford.

Larmour, P., 2004. 'Institutional transfer and aid delivery', *Pacific Economic Bulletin*, 19(2):104–12.

Lawson, S., 2004. Democracy, power and political culture in the Pacific, Paper presented at the Conference on Political Culture, Representation and Electoral Systems in the Pacific, University of the South Pacific, Port Vila, 12–14 July.

Lerner, M. (ed), 1943. *The Mind and Faith of Justice Holmes: his speeches, essays, letters, and judicial opinions*, Random House, New York.

Llewellyn, K.N., 1941. *My Philosophy of Law*, Boston Law Co., Boston, Massachusetts.

Lloyd, D., 1985. *Introduction to Jurisprudence*, Fifth edition, Stevens, London.

Locke, J., 1988 [1690]. *Two Treatises of Government*, ed. P. Laslett, Cambridge University Press, Cambridge.

Longworth, E. and McBride, T., 1994. *The Privacy Act: a guide*, GP Publications, Wellington.

Lyotard, J-F, 1988. *The Differend: phrases in dispute*, trans. G.V.D. Abbeele, University of Minnesota Press, Minneapolis.

MacIntyre, A., 1984. *After Virtue*, University of Notre Dame Press, Notre Dame, Indiana.

Macpherson, B., 1977. 'Human rights as property rights', *Dissent*, 24(1):72–77.

Madison, J., 1961 [1788]. 'No.51: Madison', in A. Hamilton, J. Madison and J. Jay, *The Federalist Papers*, ed. C. Rossiter, New American Library, New York:320–25.

Maitland, F.W., 1901. 'The Crown as Corporation', *Law Quarterly Review*, 17(2):131–46.

——, 1911a. *The Constitutional History of England*, Cambridge University Press, Cambridge.

——, 1911b. *The Collected Papers of Frederic William Maitland*, ed. H.A.L. Fisher, CUP, Cambridge.

Malifa, T., 1988. The Franchise in the Constitution of Western Samoa: towards a theory of the Constitution incomplete, unpublished LLM Thesis, Harvard Law School, Harvard University, Cambridge, Massachusetts.

Marshall, G., 1971. *Constitutional Theory*, Clarendon Press, Oxford and Oxford University Press, New York.

Marx, K., 1975. *Early Writings*, trans. R. Livingstone and G. Benton, Penguin, Harmondsworth.

Mason, A., 1993a. 'The place of equitable doctrines in the contemporary Common Law world', in D.W.M. Waters, *Equity, Fiduciaries and Trusts–1993*, Carswell, Toronto:3–11.

——, 1993b. The Role of the Judge at the Turn of the Century, Speech at The Fifth Annual AIJA Oration in Judicial Administration, Melbourne, 5 November.

——, 1994. "The place of equity and equitable remedies in the contemporary Common Law world', *Law Quarterly Review*, 110:238–46.

——, 1995. 'The rule of law', in P.D. Finn (ed.), *Essays on Law and Government—Volume I: principles and values*, The Law Book Company Limited, Sydney:114–43.

McCoubrey, H. and White, N.D., 1993. *Textbook on Jurisprudence*, Blackstone Press, London.

Meleisea, M., 1987. *The Making of Modern Samoa*, Institute of Pacific Studies, University of the South Pacific, Suva.

Mellor, C., 2004. 'The labour market in Tuvalu', *Pacific Economic Bulletin*, 19(2):87–95.

Merton, R.K., 1957. *Social Theory and Social Structure*, Free Press, Chicago.

Mill, J.S., 1970 [1848]. *The Principles of Political Economy*, ed. D. Winch, Penguin, Harmondsworth.

Mootz, F.J., 1993. 'Is the rule of law possible in a postmodern world?', *Washington Law Review*, 68(2):249–306.

Morgan, E.S., 1988. *Inventing the People: the rise of popular sovereignty in England and America*, W. W. Norton & Company, New York and London.

Mulgan, R., 1995. 'The Westminster system and the erosion of democratic legitimacy', in B.D. Gray and R.B. McClintock (eds), *Courts and Policy: checking the balance*, Brooker's Ltd, Wellington:265–82.

——, 1997. *Contracting Out and Accountability*, Graduate Public Policy Program Discussion Paper 51, The Australian National University, Canberra.

Narokobi, B., 1982. 'History and movement in law reform in Papua New Guinea', in D. Weisbrot, A. Paliwala and A. Sawyerr (eds), *Law and Social Change in Papua New Guinea*, Butterworths, Sydney:1–21.

Nedelsky, J., 1988. 'American constitutionalism and the paradox of private property', in J. Elster and R. Slagstad (eds), *Constitutionalism and Democracy*, Cambridge University Press, Cambridge:241–73.

Nozick, R., 1974. *Anarchy, State and Utopia*, Basil Blackwell, Oxford.

Ntumy, M.A. (ed.), 1993. *South Pacific Islands Legal Systems*, University of Hawaii Press, Honolulu.

Okole, H., 2004. Westminster Practices in Papua New Guinea: governance in a Melanesian state, Paper presented to the Conference on Political Culture, Representation and Electoral Systems in the Pacific, University of the South Pacific, Port Vila, 12–14 July.

Ombudsman of Western Samoa, 1991. *First Annual Report 1990–1991*, Ombudsman of Western Samoa, Apia.

Owen, N.J., 1996. The State as a Fiduciary, Paper presented to the Seminar on the Recent Developments in the Law of Fiduciary Obligations, Law Society of Western Australia (Inc), Perth, 7 March.

Paine, T., 1979 [1792]. *Rights of Man*, ed. H. Collins, Penguin, Harmondsworth.

Palmer, G., 1987. *Unbridled Power: an interpretation of New Zealand's Constitution & government*, Second edition, Oxford University Press, Auckland.

—— and Palmer, M., 1997. *Bridled Power: New Zealand government under MMP*, Oxford University Press, Auckland.

Pargellis, S., 1968. 'The theory of balanced government', in C. Read (ed.), *The Constitution Reconsidered*, Harper & Row, New York:37–49.

Parsons, T., 1951. *The Social System*, Free Press, New York.

Pashukanis, E.B., 1978. *Law and Marxism: a general theory*, trans. B. Einhorn, Ink Links, London.

Paterson, D., 1999. 'Constitutional law', in J.C. Care, T. Newton, and D. Paterson (eds), *Introduction to South Pacific Law*, Cavendish Publishing Ltd, London/Sydney:81–112.

Posner, R.A., 1998. *Economic Analysis of Law*, Fifth edition, Aspen Law and Business, New York.

Powles, G. and Pulea, M., 1988. *Pacific Courts and Justice*, Institute of Pacific Studies, University of the South Pacific, Suva, and Faculty of Law, Monash University, Melbourne.

Rabinow, P. (ed.), 1984. *The Foucault Reader*, trans. C. Hubert, Pantheon, New York.

Radcliffe, C.J., 1961. *The Law and its Compass*, Faber and Faber, London.

Radcliffe-Brown, A.R., 1952. *Structure and Function in Primitive Society: essays and addresses*, New York, The Free Press.

Rawls, J., 1973. *A Theory of Justice*, Oxford University Press, London.

——, 1993. *Political Liberalism*, Columbia University Press, New York.

Ray, B., 2003. *South Pacific Least Developing Countries: towards positive independence*, Progressive Publishers, Kolkata.

Raz, J., 1979. *The Authority of Law: essays on law and morality*, Clarendon Press, Oxford.

——, 1986. *The Morality of Freedom*, Clarendon Press, Oxford; and Oxford University Press, New York.

——, 1994. *Ethics in the Public Domain: essays in the morality of law and politics* Clarendon Press, Oxford; and Oxford University Press, New York.

Lord Reid, 1992. 'The judge as law maker', *Journal for the Society of Public Teachers of Law*, 12(1):22–29.

Reilly, B., 2004. Social Choice in the South Seas: electoral innovation and the Borda count in the Pacific island countries, Paper presented to the Conference on Political Culture, Representation and Electoral Systems in the Pacific, University of the South Pacific, Port Vila, 12–14 July.

Rex, J., 1981. *Social Conflict: a conceptual and theoretical analysis*, Longman, London.

Rishworth, P., 1998. 'Civil liberty and democracy', in R. Miller (ed.), *New Zealand Politics in Transition*, Oxford University Press, Auckland:125–34.

Rorty, R., 1987. 'Thugs and theorists: a reply to Bernstein', *Political Theory*, 15(4):564–80

——, 1989. *Contingency, Irony, and Solidarity*, Cambridge University Press, Cambridge.

Rossiter, C., (ed.), 1961. *The Federalist Papers*, No.51, New American Library, New York.

Roughan, J., 2004. Social Unrest and Electoral Institutions in the Solomon Islands, Paper presented to the Conference on Political Culture, Representation and Electoral Systems in the Pacific, University of the South Pacific, Port Vila, 12–14 July.

Rubenfeld, J., 1998. 'Legitimacy and interpretation', in L. Alexander (ed.), *Constitutionalism: philosophical foundations*, Cambridge University Press, Cambridge:194–234

Russell, J.S., 1986. 'The critical legal studies challenge to contemporary mainstream legal philosophy', *Ottawa Law Review*, 18(1):1–24.

Salamon, L. and Anheier, H.K. (eds), 1998. *The Nonprofit Sector in the Developing World: a comparative analysis*, Manchester University Press, Manchester.

Salevao, I., 2002. The Constitutional Democracy of Samoa: a conundrum of gods, angels, idols & a courteous lion, LLM (Hons) Thesis, University of Auckland, Auckland.

——, 2004. Samoa's electoral system: cultural propriety & constitutional anomalies, Paper presented to the Conference on Political Culture, Representation and Electoral Systems in the Pacific, University of the South Pacific, Port Vila, 12–14 July.

Salmond, J., 1957. *Jurisprudence*, Sweet & Maxwell, London.

Sapolu, F.M., 1988. 'Adjudicators in Western Samoa', in G. Powles and M. Pulea (eds), *Pacific Courts and Legal Systems*, Institute of Pacific Studies, University of the South Pacific, Suva:61–66

Sarup, M., 1989. *An Introductory Guide to Post-Structuralism and Post-Modernism*, University of Georgia Press, Athens.

Scarman, L.G., 1992. Why Britain needs a written constitution, Charter 88 Sovereignty Lecture, London, 20 July.

Schauer, F., 1991. 'Exceptions', *University of Chicago Law Review*, 58(3):871–900.

Schlag, P., 1991. 'The politics of form', *University of Pennsylvania Law Review*, 139(4):801–932.

Sharpe, R.J., 1989. *The Law of Habeas Corpus*, Second edition, Clarendon Press, Oxford.

Simmel, G., 1955. *Conflict and the Web of Group Affiliation*, trans. K.H. Wolff, Free Press, Glencoe, Illinois

Smith, A., 1980. *The Ethnic Revival*, Cambridge University Press, Cambridge.

So'o, A., 2000. 'Civil and political liberty: the case of Samoa', in E. Huffer and A. So'o (eds), *Governance in Samoa: Pulega I Samoa*, Asia Pacific Press, Canberra; and University of the South Pacific, Suva:133–50.

Standish, B., 2004. Papua New Guinea's Democracy, Paper presented at the Conference on Political Culture, Representation and Electoral Systems in the Pacific, University of the South Pacific, Port Vila, 12–14 July.

Stephen, L., 1907. Science of Ethics, Second edition, Smith Elder and Co., London.

Stockwell, R.F., 2004. AV or not AV? That is the question in Fiji, Paper presented at the Conference on Political Culture, Representation and Electoral Systems in the Pacific, University of the South Pacific, Port Vila, 12–14 July.

Stroupe, L., 1996. *Cultural Conflict: a study of the Western Samoan legal system*, unpublished LLB (Hons) Thesis, University of Auckland, Auckland.

Sweeney, D., 1995. 'Broken promises: Crown's fiduciary duty to Aboriginal peoples', *Aboriginal Law Bulletin*, 3(75):4–7

Taylor, C., 1978. *Hegel and Modern Society*, Cambridge University Press, Cambridge.

——, 1989. *Sources of the Self: the making of modern identity*, Harvard University Press, Cambridge, Massachusetts.

Taylor, C., 1990. 'Irreducibly social goods', in G. Brennan and C. Walsh (eds), *Rationality, Individualism and Public Policy*, The Australian National University, Canberra:45–63

Teuea, T., 2004. 'Getting the institutional environment right for investment and growth in the Pacific', *Pacific Economic Bulletin*, 19(2):75–86.

Thomas, J., 1993. 'A return to principle in judicial reasoning and an acclamation of judicial autonomy', Monograph 5, Victoria University of Wellington, Wellington.

Thompson, E.P., 1975. *Whigs and Hunters: the origin of the Black Act*, Allen Lane, London.

Toatu, T., 2004. 'Getting the institutional environment right for investment and growth in the Pacific', *Pacific Economic Bulletin*, 19(2):75–86.

Tomas, N. (ed.), 1998. *Collective Human Rights of Pacific Peoples*, International Research Unit for Maori and Indigenous Education, University of Auckland, Auckland.

Toulmin, S., 1972. *Human Understanding*, Clarendon Press, Oxford.

Tucker, R. (ed.), 1978. *The Marx–Engels Reader*, Norton, New York.

Tyler, T.R., 1990. *Why People Obey the Law*, Yale University Press, New Haven.

Unger, R.M., 1984. *Passion: an essay on personality*, Free Press, New York.

United Nations Development Programme, 1997. *Governance for Sustainable Human Development*, UNDP Policy Paper, United Nations Development Programme, New York.

United Nations General Assembly, 1960. *Official Records of the United Nations General Assembly*, Document A/C4/SR, Fourth Committee, Part 1, 15th Session, United Nations, New York.

United Nations Trusteeship Council, 1961. *Report by the United Nations Plebiscite Commissioner*, Document T/1564, United Nations Trusteeship Council, United Nations, New York, 23 June.

Vaai, S., 1999. *Samoa Faamatai and the Rule of Law*, The National University of Samoa, Apia, Samoa.

Vile, M.J.C., 1967. *Constitutionalism and the Separation of Powers*, Clarendon Press, Oxford.

Waldron, J., 1995. 'Minority cultures and the cosmopolitan alternative', in W. Kymlicka (ed.), *The Rights of Minority Cultures*, Oxford University Press, Oxford:93–119.

——, 1998. 'Precommitment and disagreement', in L. Alexander (ed.), *Constitutionalism: philosophical foundations*, Cambridge University Press, Cambridge:271–99.

Walker, G., 1988. *The Rule of Law: foundation of constitutional democracy*, Melbourne University Press, Melbourne.

——, 1995. 'Some democratic principles for constitutional reform in the 1990s', in B.D. Gray and R.B. McClintock (eds), *Courts and Policy: checking the balance*, Brooker's, Wellington:183–205.

Walzer, M., 1983. *Spheres of Justice*, Basic Books, New York.

Weber, M., 1946. *From Max Weber: essays in sociology*, trans. H.H Gerth and C.W. Mills, Oxford University Press, New York.

——, 1947. *The Theory of Social Action and Economic Organization*, trans. A.M. Henderson and T. Parsons, Oxford University Press, New York.

——, 1966. *Law in Economy and Society*, ed. Max Rheinstein, Simon and Schuster, New York.

Winch, P., 1958. *The Idea of a Social Science and Its Relation to Philosophy*, Routledge, London.

Windybank, S. and Manning, M., 2003. *Papua New Guinea on the Brink*, Issue Analysis 30, Centre for Independent Studies, Sydney:1–7.

Wolff, R.P., 1968. *The Poverty of Liberalism*, Beacon Press, Boston.

Woodhouse, O., 1979. *Government Under the Law*, The J.C. Beaglehole Memorial Lecture, Price Milburn for the New Zealand Council for Civil Liberties, Wellington.

Woolcock, M., 1999. *Managing Risk, Shocks, and Opportunity in Developing Economies: the role of social capital*, Development Research Group, World Bank, Washington DC.

* 9 780731 537211 *